Relational Practice in Meeting Discourse
in New Zealand and Japan

Hituzi Language Studies

No. 1 *Relational Practice in Meeting Discourse in New Zealand and Japan*
Kazuyo Murata

Hituzi Language Studies
No. 1

Kazuyo Murata

Relational Practice in Meeting Discourse in New Zealand and Japan

HITUZI
SYOBO

Copyright © Kazuyo Murata 2015
First published 2015

Author: KAZUYO MURATA

All rights reserved. Except for the quotation
of short passages for the purposes of criticism
and review, no part of this publication may be
reproduced, stored in a retrieval system,
or transmitted in any form or by any means,
electronic, mechanical, photocopying, recording
or otherwise, without the written prior
permission of the publisher.
 In case of photocopying and electronic
copying and retrieval from network personally,
permission will be given on receipts of payment
and making inquiries. For details please
contact us through e-mail. Our e-mail address is
given below.

Hituzi Syobo Publishing

Yamato bldg. 2f, 2-1-2 Sengoku
 Bunkyo-ku Tokyo, Japan 112-0011
Telephone: +81-3-5319-4916
Facsimile: +81-3-5319-4917
e-mail: toiawase@hituzi.co.jp
http://www.hituzi.co.jp/
postal transfer: 00120-8-142852

ISBN978-4-89476-739-3
Printed in Japan

For Tommy and Miya

Preface

This study explores Relational Practice in meetings in New Zealand and Japan, focussing in particular on small talk and humour which can be considered exemplary relational strategies. It examines these two areas of Relational Practice, firstly in terms of their manifestations in New Zealand and Japanese meetings, and secondly in terms of the ways they are perceived in the context of business meetings.

This research takes a qualitative approach to the data analysis and employs a neo-Politeness approach to the analysis, a modified version of standard Politeness Theory. The concepts of Relational Practice and community of practice also proved to be of fundamental value in the analysis. Two kinds of data were collected: firstly meeting data from 16 authentic business meetings recorded in business organisations in New Zealand and Japan (nine from a New Zealand company and seven from a Japanese company). Secondly, perception data was collected in Japan using extended focus group interviews with Japanese business people (a total of six groups from three business organisations).

The research involves a contrastive study using interactional sociolinguistic analytic techniques to examine manifestations of small talk and humour in meeting data collected in different contexts. The first phase of the study is cross-cultural, comparing meetings in New Zealand and Japan, and adopting a combined etic-emic approach. The second phase of the study analyses and compares the use of small talk and humour in different types of meetings, i.e. formal meetings (known as *kaigi* in Japanese) and informal meetings (known as *uchiawase/miitingu* in Japanese) in New Zealand and Japan. A further aim is to explore how Japanese business people perceive New Zealand meeting behaviours in relation to small talk and humour and to consider what might influence people's perceptions of these aspects of relational talk.

The analysis of the authentic meeting data indicates that the important role of Relational Practice at work is recognised in both New Zealand and Japanese meetings, although the data also highlights potentially important differences in manifestation according to the community of practice and the type of meetings. The data demonstrates that Relational Practice is constructed among meeting members discursively and dynamically across the communities of practice and the kinds of meetings.

The analysis of the perception data indicates that while Japanese business people do not have identical evaluations of the manifestation of any particular discourse strategy, their perceptions are mostly similar if they work in the same workplace. The data also demonstrates that the participants' international business experience influences their perceptions. Furthermore the analysis indicates that manifestations of small talk and humour in New Zealand meetings are not necessarily evaluated by the Japanese business people in the same or similar way as by New Zealand people.

Through both the analysis of the meeting and perception data, this study indicates that people's linguistic behaviours and perceptions regarding Relational Practice are influenced not only by underlying expectations of their community of practice but also by those of the wider society in which the community of practice is positioned.

Acknowledgements

My favourite words are from Walt Disney: "All our dreams can come true, if we have the courage to pursue them." My dream of completing this book, however, would not have come true without the following people's warm support and encouragement. I wish to express my deepest gratitude to them.

Janet Holmes and Meredith Marra gave me their constant care, encouragement, and whole-hearted involvement at every stage. Their guidance, wisdom, and enthusiasm supported me throughout this process. And Rebecca Adams offered her invaluable guidance in regards to the perception task in my research.

An anonymous business organisation in Japan allowed their meetings to be recorded, and three anonymous business organisations also in Japan cooperated with the perception task. This study would have been impossible without their kind support.

The New Zealand dataset and its transcription were from the Language in the Workplace Corpus. The members allowed me to analyse their valuable data. In particular, Bernadette Vine helped me to select the meeting data from the corpus, and Julia de Bres helped me to understand Kiwi humour. All the members' support was greatly appreciated.

There were the members of the School of Linguistics and Applied Language Studies (LALS) who helped me make the simulation video clips. Also thanks to the Ph.D. students at LALS who provided valuable feedback on early stages of this project at the Ph.D. meetings, and who welcomed me in Wellington.

Deborah Laurs read my drafts at early stage of this project and Frank Daulton meticulously proofread my English throughout. Without their help and encouragement, I would not have been able to write up the chapters. Also my colleagues at Ryukoku University in Kyoto gave me a lot of warm words, valuable advice, and cooperated with the pilot perception task. They also have allowed me to visit New Zealand many times during this research project.

Finally, I would like to show my deepest gratitude to my family, Tommy and Miya, and my parents, Shoichi and Takako, for their endless love and care, understanding, encouragement and patience over the years. Especailly without their patience, this research could not have been completed. My dearest daughter, Miya, drew a wonderful picture in Chapter 5 to encourage me. I would like to give millions of kisses and hugs to her.

This book is based on my unpublished Ph.D. dissertation submitted to Victoria University of Wellington in New Zealand, which I have revised and modified. The publication of this book was supported by the Ryukoku University Research Fund. I would thus like to dedicate this book to all the people who have supported and encouraged me in the course of this research and publishing of this book.

Kazuyo Murata
January, 2015
Kyoto, Japan

Contents

Preface	VII
Acknowledgements	IX
List of figures	XVI
List of tables	XVII

CHAPTER 1

Introduction

1.1	Rationale for the research	1
1.2	Purpose of the research	4
1.3	Structure of the book	5

CHAPTER 2

Literature review: politeness theory

2.1	Politeness theory overview	9
2.1.1	Traditional approach	10
2.1.2	Modified B&L approach	12
2.1.3	Post-modern approach	15
2.1.4	Neo-Politeness approach	20
2.2	Politeness in workplace discourse	22
2.2.1	Relational Practice	23
2.2.2	Communities of Practice	25
2.3	Politeness from Japanese perspectives	27
2.4	Cross-cultural considerations	30
2.4.1	Politeness and culture	30
2.4.2	Etic and emic dimensions in a cross-cultural study	32
2.5	Summary	34

CHAPTER 3
Methodology

3.1	Data collection in the field of workplace discourse	37
3.2	Methodological design of meeting data	39
3.3	Meeting data collection in New Zealand: the Language in the Workplace Project	39
3.4	Meeting data collection in Japan	40
3.4.1	Preparation	41
3.4.2	Collecting data	42
3.4.3	Coding and processing data	43
3.5	Summary of the meeting dataset	45
3.6	Methodological design and the collection of perception data	48
3.7	Ethical considerations	48
3.8	Summary	49

CHAPTER 4
Meetings

4.1	Meetings	52
4.2	Formal meetings (*kaigi*) and informal meetings (*uchiawase/miitingu*)	54
4.3	Meetings in Japanese	57
4.4	Meetings from a relational perspective	60
4.5	Structures	61
4.5.1	Macro structures	61
4.5.2	Micro structures (topic progressions)	63
4.6	Meetings in this study	64
4.6.1	Meetings at company N	64
4.6.2	Meetings at company J	65
4.7	Structural characteristics of formal/informal meetings	66
4.7.1	Formal meetings	66
4.7.2	Informal meetings	77
4.8	Summary	81

CHAPTER 5
Small talk

5.1	Approaches to small talk	85
5.1.1	Classic approach	86
5.1.2	Discursive approach	88
5.1.3	Negotiative approach	89
5.2	Small talk in workplace discourse	90
5.2.1	Definition	91
5.2.2	Distribution	92
5.2.3	Topics	92
5.2.4	Functions	93
5.3	Small talk from Asian perspectives	94
5.4	Small talk and silence	95
5.5	Analysis of small talk	96
5.5.1	Small talk in formal meetings	96
5.5.2	Small talk in informal meetings	110
5.5.3	Target participants' linguistic behaviours regarding small talk	119
5.6	Summary	119

CHAPTER 6
Humour

6.1	Humour	123
6.2	Workplace humour	124
6.2.1	Definition	125
6.2.2	Classification	126
6.2.3	Distribution	129
6.2.4	Function	129
6.2.5	Workplace humour and culture	130
6.3	Responses to humour and laughter	131
6.4	Analysis of humour	132
6.4.1	Humour in formal meetings	132
6.4.2	Humour in informal meetings	149
6.4.3	Discussion	159
6.5	Emic perspective	161
6.5.1	Target participants' linguistic behaviours regarding Relational Practice	161

6.5.2 Interpreting the results from an emic perspective 162
6.6 Summary 166

CHAPTER 7
Perception task

7.1 Classic method for assessing language attitude from hearers' perspectives 170
7.2 Assessing participants' perceptions in authentic interaction 171
7.3 Assessing third party's perception: extended focus group interviews 175
7.4 Perception task 176
7.4.1 Overview 176
7.4.2 Participants 177
7.4.3 Video-clips and target discourse features 178
7.4.4 Procedures 182
7.5 Analysis 184
7.5.1 Japanese business professionals' perceptions about Relational Practice in New Zealand business meetings 185
7.5.2 What influences participants' perceptions 192
7.6 Summary 201

CHAPTER 8
Conclusion

8.1 Major findings 205
8.1.1 Formal meetings vs. informal meetings 205
8.1.2 Manifestations of small talk and humour 206
8.1.3 Perceptions of small talk and humour 208
8.2 Research contribution 209
8.2.1 Contribution to research on meetings and on workplace interaction 209
8.2.2 Contribution to politeness research 210
8.2.3 Contribution to cross-cultural and inter-cultural research 212
8.3 Future research 213

Appendix	217
References	243
Index	259

List of figures

Figure 1.1: The contrastive study in this book
Figure 3.1: Equipment set-up for the recording for formal meetings
Figure 3.2: Organisational chart: company N
Figure 3.3: Organisational chart: company J
Figure 4.1: An illustration of the five sections of a meeting (from Chan 2005: 90)
Figure 5.1: Locating small talk on the continuum (from Holmes 2000a: 38)
Figure 5.2: Japanese meeting participants' waiting for other members
Figure 5.3: Topic flow of the first 12 minutes of an informal meeting

List of tables

Table 2.1: Components of rapport management (from Spencer-Oatey 2000c: 15)
Table 2.2: Summary of characteristics among four approaches to politeness
Table 3.1: Summary of dataset
Table 3.2: Target participants in company N
Table 3.3: Target participants in company J
Table 4.1: Useful dimensions for comparing meetings (from Holmes & Stubbe 2003: 60)
Table 4.2: Summary of definitions of formal meetings (*kaigi*) and informal meetings (*uchiawase/miitingu*)
Table 4.3: The meeting data in Yamada's series of research
Table 4.4: Summary of dataset (same as Table 3.1)
Table 4.5: Details of informal meetings at company N
Table 4.6: Details of informal meetings at company J
Table 5.1: Changes in approaches to small talk
Table 5.2: Topic flow of pre-meeting phase
Table 5.3: Features of small talk in formal/informal meetings at company N and company J
Table 6.1: Features of a collaborative, supportive type of humour and a non-collaboratively constructed competitive type of humour
Table 6.2: Features of humour in formal/informal meetings at company N and company J
Table 7.1: Characteristics of the three business organisations
Table 7.2: Order of showing the video clips
Table 7.3: The duration of each group discussion

CHAPTER 1

Introduction

1.1 Rationale for the research

In a time of increased globalisation and growing opportunities for international business negotiations, researchers have begun to pay attention to business interaction (Harris & Bargiela-Chiappini 1997). Research on workplace discourse which draws on authentic workplace interactions covers a variety of workplace situations and includes various topics, approaches and theories (e.g., Bargiela-Chiappini et al. 2007; Bargiela-Chiappini 2009). However, most of the research has been conducted in English-speaking societies and/or Western countries.

In particular, there has been very little investigation of Japanese workplace discourse based on authentic interaction. Primarily due to issues of confidentiality, it is difficult to find business organisations that allow their workplace interactions to be recorded. To date, there have been only a handful of studies on Japanese business interactions (e.g., Yamada 1990; Takano 2005). I was fortunate to find a business organisation that allowed me to record their business meetings. This study will undoubtedly fill a gap in the empirical research on Japanese business interaction.

My interest in undertaking a cross-cultural study in New Zealand and Japan derived originally from my personal background. I spent my sabbatical in Victoria University of Wellington in the 2006 academic year and worked alongside the Language in the Workplace Project.[1] I was allowed to analyse sections from the corpus of this research project, which currently contains over 2,000 authentic interactions collected at various workplaces mainly in New Zealand. Since I am from Japan and have a native intuition about Japanese, it was natural to choose to do a contrastive study between New Zealand workplace language data and that of Japan.

In addition, there is a strong relationship between New Zealand and Japan, for example, in business. According to the Ministry of Foreign Affairs of Japan,

Japan is New Zealand's fourth biggest trading partner after Australia, the United States, and China.[2] Given the strong trade relationship between New Zealand and Japan, there are many opportunities for business negotiations between these two countries. However, no contrastive study of business interaction between New Zealand and Japan has ever been done. Understanding the differences between the two styles of business discourse may allow us to identify areas of potential breakdown in intercultural communication.

The next step was to choose an appropriate setting among the many situations that exist in a given workplace. Meetings are common in many organisations and are one of the primary communicative means for organisations (Bargiela-Chiappini & Harris 1997a; Barretta-Herman 1990; Boden 1994; Mintzberg 1973; Tracy & Dimock 2004). Moreover, in the field of business interaction, meetings are one of the major research focuses, and there is much research on meetings from a linguistic perspective (Bargiela-Chiappini & Harris 1997a). Meetings therefore offer ideal discourse for a contrastive, cross-cultural study from a linguistic perspective.

Reviewing the previous literature on meetings, I identified a number of areas where more research would be valuable. The first is regarding types of meetings. Although previous researchers on meetings acknowledge that formality is a crucial dimension of meetings (Schwartzman 1989; Boden 1994; Bargiela-Chiappini & Harris 1997a; Holmes & Stubbe 2003; Chan 2005), most research has focussed only on formal meetings (Asmuß & Svennevig 2009). Moreover in Japan, although there are different terms to refer to formal and informal meetings respectively, no researcher has undertaken contrastive research on *kaigi* (formal meetings) and *uchiawase/miitingu* (informal meetings).

The second area for further research involves consideration of the important relational perspective of workplace interactions. The primary purpose of meetings is to accomplish goals for the organisations (e.g., Tracy & Dimock 2004) and meetings involve *transactional activities* such as making decisions, solving problems, and giving information. The transactional aspects of interaction thus play an important role in meetings. However, meetings also serve a *relational function*, namely that of maintaining and strengthening collegiality and rapport among meeting participants. Meetings have also been considered as sites for the manifestation of power and politeness (Holmes & Stubbe 2003). Nevertheless most of the previous research on meetings has focussed on transactional aspects alone.

Identifying these gaps in the research motivated me to explore formal and informal meetings from a relational perspective.

Both Bargiela-Chiappini and Harris (2006) and Asmuß and Svennevig (2009) note the importance of the extensive empirical research on meetings from a relational perspective which has been conducted by researchers from the Language in the Workplace Project. Their research is based on authentic meetings, and they have found that small talk and humour are two exemplary discursive strategies regarding *Relational Practice*[3] (e.g., Holmes & Marra 2004; Holmes & Schnurr 2005). This is supported by other researchers. Research on small talk in workplace discourse demonstrates that small talk serves as a useful politeness device, making interpersonal relationships smooth (e.g., Saunders 1986; Coupland & Ylanne-McEwen 2000; Holmes 2000a; Kuiper & Flindall 2000; McCarthy 2000). Workplace humour also plays an important role in contributing to good workplace relations (e.g., Brown & Keegan 1999; Holmes & Stubbe 2003; Schnurr 2005; Holmes 2006b). It can be used to manage power relationships among team members by de-emphasising power differences (e.g., Brown & Keegan 1999, Pizzini 1991; Holmes 2000c). In addition to what has been discussed previously, preliminary investigation suggested that small talk and humour were salient in the meeting data for this research; I selected these two discursive strategies as focuses of analysis for this study.

According to previous research, small talk and humour tend to occur around topic transition points as well as at the opening and closing phases of meetings (e.g., Brown & Keegan 1999; Holmes & Stubbe 2003; Chan 2005; Schnurr 2005). Thus analysing these discursive strategies in meetings requires paying attention to meeting structures not only at the macro level but also the micro level. This indicates that examining how formal and informal meetings are structured was necessary as a preliminary step before analysing small talk and humour in meetings.

As well as analysing manifestations of small talk and humour, it is important to explore hearers' perceptions in terms of politeness theory. Politeness is an intricate concept and there have been longstanding debates about what to consider when investigating values of politeness. It is, however, generally agreed that linguistic politeness is an affective aspect of interaction (Brown & Levinson 1987; Kasper 1990; Holmes 1995, forthcoming; Mills 2003; Watts 2003).

Politeness has been researched from the perspectives of the ideal speaker and hearer. Early researchers (e.g., Brown & Levinson, 1987) focussed on how speakers employ linguistic strategies to show their consideration towards hearers. However, recently researchers have taken a more interactional perspective and define politeness as "discursively strategic interaction: i.e. linguistic devices perceived as having been used in order to maintain harmonious relations and avoid conflict with others" (Holmes 2012: 208). In recent work, politeness researchers (e.g., Eelen 2001; Mills 2003; Spencer-Oatey 2008a) argue that no utterance is inherently polite or impolite, and further suggest that politeness is negotiated discursively and dynamically among interactants, and that researchers should take interactants' perceptions into consideration when exploring politeness. To date, there has been little empirical research on the hearer's perception (Bilbow 1997a, 1997b) or evaluation of interaction (Spencer-Oatey & Xing 2003).

Analysing hearers' perceptions, Bilbow (1997a, 1997b) and Spencer-Oatey and Xing (2003) point out that national cultural expectations influence people's evaluations. On the other hand, analysing authentic workplace interactions, Marra and Holmes (2007) and Schnurr and Chan (2009) point out that in workplace discourse, people's workplace cultures affect their linguistic behaviours. It is expected that perception or evaluation of workplace discourse would also be affected by workplace culture. This suggests that considering national culture alone is not enough.

Accordingly, I decided to conduct a perception task as an important addition to the discursive analysis of politeness in meetings, using focus-group interviews of various Japanese business people as a data source. It was necessary to design this perception task to examine not only how the participants perceive and evaluate New Zealanders' small talk and humour, but what influences their perceptions of these linguistic behaviours. The results of the perception task aim to illuminate people's perceptions regarding politeness.

On the basis of what has been discussed in this section, it became apparent there were gaps in the research on meetings and politeness. The current study was designed to fill these gaps. The aims of this study are explained in the next section.

1.2 Purpose of the research

This study explores Relational Practice in meetings in New Zealand and Japan, focussing in particular on small talk and humour which can be considered exemplary relational strategies. The study examines these two areas of Relational Practice, firstly in terms of their manifestations in New Zealand and Japanese meetings, and secondly in terms of the ways they are perceived in the context of business meetings.

The research involves a contrastive study using interactional sociolinguistic analytic techniques to examine manifestations of small talk and humour in meeting data collected in different contexts. The first phase of the study is cross-cultural,[4] comparing meetings in New Zealand and Japan, and analysing and comparing the manifestations of small talk and humour in different types of meetings, i.e. formal meetings (known as *kaigi* in Japanese) and informal meetings (known as *uchiawase/miitingu* in Japanese) in New Zealand and Japan.

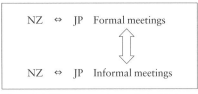

Figure 1.1: The contrastive study in this book

A second phase explores how Japanese business people perceive New Zealand meeting behaviours in relation to small talk and humour and to consider what might influence people's perceptions of these aspects of relational talk.

To achieve the above aims, two kinds of data were collected. The meeting data used for discourse analysis was from authentic business meetings recorded in two business organisations – one set from New Zealand (nine meetings: approx. 370 minutes) and the other from Japan (seven meetings: approx. 710 minutes). Four target people who were involved in most meetings were selected from each organisation as key participants whose discursive behaviour was compared in formal and informal meetings. For the perception data, extended focus group interviews (Berg 1998) with Japanese business people (six groups from three business organisations) were conducted in Japan. This study takes a qualitative approach to the analysis of both kinds of data.

To achieve the above objectives, the following research questions are addressed:

1. What are the structural characteristics that signal the organisation of formal and informal meetings in New Zealand and Japan?
2. What are the manifestations of small talk and humour in Japanese and New Zealand formal and informal meetings?
3. What perceptions do Japanese business professionals have about New Zealanders' use of small talk and humour in formal and informal meetings and what influences their perceptions?

1.3 Structure of the book

This book is organised into eight chapters. This chapter has offered justifications for the study, outlined the purposes of this study, and proposed three research questions. As described, the business meetings are analysed from a relational perspective, and politeness theory is taken as the theoretical framework. In Chapter 2, the research on politeness theory is reviewed, relevant issues are discussed, and the study's position on politeness theory is clarified along with key terms for analysing the meeting data from a relational perspective, such as

Relational Practice and community of practice.

In Chapter 3, the research methods adopted and the data collection methods used are described, introducing methodologies in the field of workplace discourse. In terms of the meeting data, I drew on recorded authentic business meetings in two business organisations – one in New Zealand and the other in Japan. With regard to the perception data, I selected a series of focus group interviews with Japanese business people conducted in Japan. The procedures and information about the participants are also described in this chapter.

In Chapter 4, the rationale for conducting contrastive analysis between formal and informal meetings is explained with reference to previous research on meetings. Then, after presenting a working definition of these two kinds of meetings, the structural characteristics of formal and informal meetings are summarised drawing on the previous literature. In the last half of this chapter, the meeting data for this study is introduced, along with selected results of the analysis in terms of meeting structures in formal and informal meetings as a preliminary step to facilitate the analysis of small talk and humour.

The results of the analysis regarding the manifestations of small talk and humour are presented in Chapters 5 and 6. In Chapter 5, where small talk is addressed, the first half of the chapter is devoted to a review of the relevant literature and the theoretical examination of small talk, and the last half to the analysis results of the meeting data. In Chapter 6, following a literature review, I discuss the characteristics of humour in the meeting data, describing distribution, instigators, types and categories, and functions. Then, I explore the target participants' linguistic behaviours regarding humour and reflect on the relationship of them to their linguistic behaviours regarding small talk. Finally, I propose an interpretation regarding the analysis results from an emic perspective.

The results of the analysis in terms of the perception of small talk and humour are presented in Chapter 7. The first part of this chapter is devoted to a review of the relevant literature and theoretical examination of how the hearers' perceptions are assessed with reference to previous research. After the procedures and methods of the perception task for this study are described, the results of the analysis are presented. In the last part of this chapter, the issue of what influences the participants' perceptions is discussed.

Finally, Chapter 8 summarises the findings and discusses the contribution of this research to various research fields and implications for further study.

I believe that this research will contribute to academic knowledge not only in regard to meetings but also workplace talk more generally, with implications for such fields as workplace discourse, cross-cultural research, and politeness research. I hope that this research will also foster better understanding and relationships between business professionals in New Zealand and Japan.

Before considering how the present study addresses the three research questions, it is necessary to review politeness theory, which is the framework of this study. This is the focus of Chapter 2.

Notes
1 See Chapter 3 for more detailed information.
2 http://www.mofa.go.jp/mofaj/area/nz/data.html
3 *Relational Practice* is referred to as politeness at work (Holmes & Marra 2004; Holmes & Schnurr 2005) and focuses on "other-oriented behavior at work" (Holmes & Schnurr 2005: 124). See Chapter 2 for a detailed discussion.
4 A *cross-cultural study* is defined as comparative research where data is collected from two different cultural groups, while an *intercultural study* focuses on interaction among people from different cultural groups (Gudykunst 2002; Bargiela-Chiappini & Nickerson 2003; Kecskes 2004; Spencer-Oatey 2000a, 2008a; Holmes 2012).

CHAPTER 2

Literature review: politeness theory

As described in Chapter 1, this study examines business meetings from a relational perspective with politeness theory as the main theoretical framework. The aim of this chapter is to introduce this theoretical framework, which is drawn on in the subsequent analysis.

In terms of politeness theory, while Brown and Levinson's (1987) approach is still widely accepted as providing the most comprehensive and influential framework, there have been dramatic developments of this theory in this century. For example, Spencer-Oatey (e.g., 2000b) takes a more culturally oriented-approach to politeness while Eelen (2001), Watts (2003), and Mills (2003) implement a radically new approach, incorporating social-theoretical insights, locating politeness in a theory of social practice. Politeness in workplace discourse has also started to draw attention and is being developed by researchers including Mullany (e.g., 2004) and Holmes (2006a).

The first part of this chapter reviews the research on politeness theory with reference to this diversifying trend, and the various issues this raises are discussed. Then this study's position on politeness theory is clarified along with key terms for analysing the meeting data from a relational perspective, such as Relational Practice and community of practice. The chapter closes by describing an emic-etic combined approach which is adopted for this cross-cultural study.

2.1 Politeness theory overview

Linguistic politeness is an intricate concept and there have been longstanding debates about what to consider when investigating politeness values. It is, however, generally agreed that politeness enacts affective aspects of interaction, or to be more precise, the interpersonal aspect of communication from a pragmatic point of view (e.g., Brown & Levinson 1987; Kasper 1990; Mills

2003; Watts 2003; Holmes 2012). Politeness was originally researched from the perspective of an ideal speaker and hearer. In seminal work by Brown and Levinson (hereafter B&L) (1987), they focussed on how speakers employ linguistic strategies to show their consideration towards hearers. While B&L's (1987) approach is still widely recognised as providing a seminal framework for investigating politeness, a new trend has also emerged.

Recent researchers take a more interactional perspective and define politeness as "discursively strategic interaction: i.e. linguistic devices perceived as having been used in order to maintain harmonious relations and avoid conflict with others" (Holmes 2012). These researchers also argue that no utterance is inherently polite or impolite and suggest that whether or not an utterance is heard as being (im)polite is dependent on interactants' perceptions and the interactional context in which it occurs.

Following Terkourafi (2005), this chapter categorises politeness theory trends into a *traditional approach* and *post-modern approach*, and adds several further categories namely a *modified B & L approach* and a *neo-Politeness approach*. In the next section, these trends are overviewed in chronological order.

2.1.1 Traditional approach

Researchers in the traditional approach include Lakoff (1973), Leech (1983), and B&L (1987). Each of their theories is inspired by Grice's (1975) Cooperative Principle (hereafter CP) (e.g., Terkourafi 2005; Bargiela-Chiappini & Harris 2006). Presupposing that human conversations are generally cooperative activities and communication is done effectively and logically, Grice (1975) proposed the CP which is expressed in terms of four conversational maxims, on the basis of which people convey and derive implicatures in order to communicate and interpret social meaning and content. The researchers applying a traditional approach attempted to account for deviations from the CP by considering them in terms of politeness phenomena. They regard a speech act as the basic unit of communication (e.g., Terkourafi 2005; Bargiela-Chiappini & Harris 2006), in which certain kinds of acts are performed such as greeting, describing, asking a question, making a request, giving an order, or making a promise.

It is generally agreed that Lakoff (1973) was the first to examine politeness from a pragmatic perspective (e.g., Eelen 2001; Usami 2002; Watts 2003). Connecting politeness with the CP, Lakoff (1973) suggests that politeness can be recognised as pragmatic rules, "dictating whether an utterance is pragmatically well-formed or not, and the extent to which it deviates if it does" (1973: 296). Though Grice's theory rests on the assumption of communication's rational efficiency, in normal conversation, the CP is almost never followed. In order to account for this apparent flouting of the CP, an ideal norm of communicative efficiency, Lakoff (1973: 298) proposes the following three politeness rules: (1) Don't impose; (2) Give options; and (3) Make the other person feel good, be friendly. Although Lakoff (1973) proposes a pragmatic approach to politeness, she does not account for the reasons and rationale for choosing these three rules in detail and her framework is not elaborated in this sense.

Leech's (1983) politeness theory also takes the CP as its point of departure and considers politeness as a deviation from the ideal norm of communication's rational efficiency. Leech (1983) takes the position that speakers always have the social goals of establishing and maintaining harmonious relationships with hearers, but these sometimes clash with communicative goals or illocutionary acts. In order to pursue this social goal, speakers often avoid conflict in interpersonal relationships by employing various linguistic strategies. For Leech (1983), politeness is a means for maintaining harmonious relationships or avoiding conflict, and he places it within a framework of interpersonal rhetoric. Leech (1983) locates the Politeness Principle along with the CP in order to account for deviations from the CP. The Politeness Principle is categorised into the following six subcategories: (1) Tact Maxim; (2) Generosity Maxim; (3) Approbation Maxim; (4) Modesty Maxim; (5) Agreement Maxim; and (6) Sympathy Maxim (Leech 1983: 132). Even though this comprises a more complex framework, it nevertheless seems possible to add many other maxims and sub-maxims.

Among politeness researchers, B&L's (1987) politeness theory remains seminal (e.g., Eelen 2001; Usami 2002; Terkourafi 2005). One of the reasons behind this is their attempt to provide a universal perspective on politeness.

One of the most important aspects of this theory is the concept of *face*, a concept introduced into academic discourse by Goffman (1967). In B&L's politeness theory, adapting the original concept, they define face as "the public self-image that every member wants to claim for himself" (1987: 61) and assume that "all competent adult members of a society have (and know each other to have)" it (1987: 61, parentheses in original). B&L employ face to refer to basic and universal human desires as they pertain to social interaction. Incorporating Durkheim's (1954) idea of positive and negative distinctions of descriptions of religious cults, B&L propose a dual concept of face. Face consists of two specific kinds of desires: the desire not to be imposed on and to have freedom of action (*negative face*); and the desire to be accepted, liked, and understood by others (*positive face*) (1987: 13). According to the approach, while the concept of face is universal, the kinds of acts that threaten face differ according to cultures.

B&L work on the assumption that certain kinds of speech acts, for example requests or disagreements, inherently threaten one's face and call them *face threatening acts* (FTAs) (1987: 60). In order to save face, speakers can choose different strategies from the five categorised in their theory. They are: (1) without redressive action, baldly; (2) positive politeness; (3) negative politeness; (4) off record; (5) don't do the FTA (1987: 69). According to B&L, the choice of politeness strategy depends on the weightiness of the FTA (Wx), which is determined by the value of the following three factors: the power (P) that a hearer has over a speaker, the social distance (D) between a speaker and a hearer, and the ranking of impositions (R) in a particular culture (1987: 76): Wx = D (S, H) + P (H, S) + Rx.

Though Lakoff's, Leech's, and B&L's approaches to politeness each have their own characteristics, the following are common features:

1. Their primary concern is how speakers produce particular linguistic strategies according to predetermined sets of principles.
2. They take prescriptive and normative perspectives on politeness.
3. Their focus is speech acts and their approach can be regarded as speaker-oriented.
4. The sets of principles are universal regardless of culture.

Among the researchers associated with a traditional approach, B&L's theory in particular has received much criticism. One of the main points of debate is that it fails to consider cultural aspects (e.g., Ide 1989; Matsumoto 1988, 1989; Spencer-Oatey 2000a). Other criticisms involve the focus on speech acts which lack discourse-level consideration (e.g., Spencer-Oatey 2000a; Usami 2002; Eelen 2001; Mills; 2003; Watts 2003) and the speaker-oriented approach rather than the hearer-oriented approach (e.g., Eelen 2001; Mills; 2003; Watts 2003). The research described in this book provides further support for these criticisms. Since this research is a cross-cultural study in New Zealand and Japan, culture-sensitivity is necessary for an appropriate framework. Meeting management is discursively and dynamically negotiated among meeting members and analysis at the discourse level is indispensable. Thus, a traditional approach to politeness is not appropriate for this research. In the next section, another approach is addressed.

2.1.2 Modified B&L approach

Criticising B&L's theory for lacking consideration of cultural aspects of face, Spencer-Oatey (2000b, 2000c, 2008b) suggests an expanded framework to account for the politeness phenomena in different cultures, adopting B&L's standpoint. Although her theory differs from B&L's claims in some respects, proposed revisions remain within the original maxim/rule-based paradigm and I describe it as a modified B&L approach. She employs *rapport management* rather than politeness to refer to "the use of language to promote, maintain or threaten harmonious social relationships in interaction" (2000b: 3). She also uses the term rapport management rather than face management "because the term 'face' seems to focus on concerns for self, whereas rapport management suggests more of a balance between self and other" (2000c: 12). Spencer-Oatey (e.g., 2000c) maintains that there are two motivations behind the management of relationships: face and sociality rights. Contending that "B&L's conceptualisation of positive face has been underspecified" (2000c: 13), she proposes two interrelated faces to explain people's basic desires for approval. That is, a desire for a positive evaluation in terms of personal qualities such as competence, abilities, etc. (quality face), and a desire for positive evaluation in terms of social or group roles, such as group leader or close friend (identity face).

Spencer-Oatey (e.g., 2000c) also argues that "the concerns [B&L] identify as negative face issues are not necessarily face concerns at all" (2000c: 13). She rejects the use of negative face, not regarding it as personal desire. Instead, she proposes a sociality right, defining it as "fundamental personal/social *entitlements* that individuals effectively claim for themselves in their interactions with others" (2000c: 14). Sociality rights also have two interrelated aspects: equity rights, referring to the personal entitlement to be treated as equals; and association rights referring to the social entitlement to have an appropriate association with others. The relationship between B&L's and Spencer-Oatey's ideas is shown in the following table.

	face management (personal/ social value)	sociality rights management (personal/ social value)
personal/independent perspective	quality face (cf. B&L's positive face)	equity rights (cf. B&L's negative face)
social/interdependent perspective	identity face	association rights

Table 2.1: Components of rapport management

(from Spencer-Oatey 2000c: 15)

As is indicated in the table, what B&L consider positive politeness includes quality face and identity face, the former associated with personal value and the latter with social value. By dividing face into two aspects and introducing the notion of sociality rights, Spencer-Oatey (e.g., 2000c) broadens the focus from individual to social issues. This extension of B&L's work is important in incorporating social aspects of individuals into the concept of face.

In addition, Spencer-Oatey (e.g., 2000c) argues that rapport is managed across five interrelated domains, in which a variety of strategies are realised: (1) *the illocutionary domain* (the performance of speech acts); (2) *the discourse domain* (the choice of discourse content, such as topic choice; and the management of the structure of an interchange, such as the organisation and sequencing of information); (3) *the participation domain* (the procedural aspects of an interchange such as turn-taking, inclusion/exclusion of people present, and the use/non-use of listener responses); (4) *the stylistic domain* (stylistic aspects, such as choice of tone, choice of genre-appropriate lexis and syntax, and the use of honorifics); and (5) *the non-verbal domain* (non-verbal aspects, such as gestures and other body movements, eye contact, and proxemics) (2000c: 20). By taking these five domains into consideration, the author extends the speech act basis approach into a wider view, in other words, the discourse level. She also points out that speakers' selections of strategy use in managing rapport are affected by: (1) people's rapport orientation; (2) contextual variables; and (3) pragmatic conventions. These factors play an important role in her theory. Notably, this indicates that the primary focus of Spencer-Oatey's theory may still remain with the speakers' side of politeness although she contends that "rapport management suggests more of a balance between self and other" (Spencer-Oatey 2000c: 12).

In Spencer-Oatey's theory, any utterance cannot be assessed as inherently polite or rude; rather politeness involves a social judgement. Politeness is "a question of appropriateness" (2000b: 3). This appropriateness depends on "cultural differences in ways of managing rapport" (2000c: 41). That is, culture plays an important role in determining appropriateness. She contends that "culture is operationalized primarily in terms of ethnolinguistic and/or national or regional political identity" (2000b: 4), for example, Chinese, Japanese, Americans, and so on. Taking cultural differences into consideration, her theory includes a range of principles, attempting to identify cultural patterns. Thus there are numerous research articles which contribute to the literature on intercultural or cross-cultural studies which follow Spencer-Oatey's theory. These include apologies in Japanese and English (Tanaka et al. 2008), negative assessments in interactions between Japanese-American colleagues (Miller 2000), intercultural meetings between British and Chinese (Spencer-Oatey and Xiang, 2000, 2008), and rapport negotiating in casual conversations between Germans and Chinese (Gunthner 2008). These studies support Spencer-Oatey's implicit view that all members of a cultural group are expected to behave the same or at least in a similar way.

In sum, in the modified B&L approach, Spencer-Oatey (2000b, 2000c, 2008b) adds the notion of *sociality rights* to that of face and moves the analysis from concentrating on individual concerns to social concerns. In addition, she maintains that rapport is managed across five interrelated domains including speech acts as one domain. By taking these domains into consideration, she extends a speech act approach to the level of discourse. However, her primary focus still lies on the speakers and the dynamic and discursive aspects of the construction of politeness are not much taken into consideration. Meeting discourse is dynamically constructed and a more dynamic approach to politeness is necessary. In the next section, a dynamic approach is introduced.

2.1.3 Post-modern approach

The post-modern approach to politeness (Eelen 2001; Watts 2003; Mills 2003) proposes a radically new framework, incorporating social-theoretical concepts, in particular applying the notion of *habitus*, a term originating in Bourdieu (1977, 1991), a French sociologist. Habitus is a social mechanism that "caters for regulated behaviour without the need for positing some external regulating force" (Eelen 2001: 222) and consists of "the set of dispositions to behave in a manner which is appropriate to the social structures objectified by an individual through her/his experience of social interaction" (Watts 2003: 274). In the post modern approach, habitus plays an important role in the assessment of politeness. The researchers in this approach place politeness within a theory of social practice, where "practice is observable in instances of ongoing social interaction amongst individuals, which most often involves language" (Watts 2003: 148), and they take a more dynamic approach to politeness than previous studies. While the traditional approach focussed on speakers' intentions for politeness strategy selections, the researchers in the post-modern approach give equal attention to listeners' interpretations conducted discursively and dynamically in on-going interaction.

Along with other researchers in the post-modern approach, Eelen (2001) views politeness as social practice, inspired by Bourdieu. According to Bourdieu (1977, 1991), *social* should be taken as "a reference to what goes on between human beings, between individuals, in the construction of social reality" (Eelen 2001: 246). Following this idea, focussing on the process of constructing of social reality, Eelen (2001) focusses on the evaluative aspects of politeness as "representations of reality" (2001: 247). For Eelen, concepts of politeness are "not simply the result of a passive learning process in which each individual internalizes 'the' societal/cultural politeness system, but are rather an active expression of that person's social positioning in relation to others and the social world in general" (2001: 224).

An important concept in Eelen's (2001) framework is habitus. He strongly rejects prescriptivism, saying that "the emphasis on variability and individual creativity even implies that prediction will no longer be possible" (2001: 247). However, he admits that there is a consensus in politeness, which he explains by using the notion habitus. People acquire habitus through their experience of social interactions. It is created by their previous interaction or their *history* in Bourdieu's (1991) terms, but at the same time the present interaction also constitutes and influences their own habitus. Eelen focusses on these dynamic and evolvable aspects. In addition, although a person's habitus shares commonalities with those of other people, it is unique to each individual, highlighting the variable aspect of habitus. For him, habitus is a part of the process of construction of social reality and its notable characteristics are variability and individual creativity.

Another characteristic of Eelen's (2001) framework is his categorisation of politeness. The author differentiates between *politeness1* and *politeness2*.[1] The former refers to "common sense notions of politeness" and the latter refers to "the scientific conceptualisation of politeness" (Eelen 2001: 30). According to Eelen (2001), the distinction between politeness1 and politeness2 corresponds to the distinction between *emic* and *etic*, both of which originated in anthropological linguistics and are applied to his politeness theory. Politeness1 (emic) can refer both to "the informants' conscious statements about his or her notion of politeness" and to "his or her spontaneous evaluations of politeness, (of his or her own or someone else's behaviour) made in the course of actual interaction" (2001: 77). Politeness2 (etic), on the other hand, can refer to "outsiders' accounts of insiders' behaviour, involving distinctions not relevant to those insiders" (2001: 78). That is, by politeness1, Eelen (2001) means a more everyday notion of politeness, while by politeness2, on the other hand, he means the more universal notion of politeness.

Eelen (2001: 246) criticises previous politeness theories for the following points: (1) being unable to explain impoliteness and politeness with the same theory; (2) overlooking the perspectives of hearers (the evaluative side of politeness); (3) stating a normative stance; (4) lacking details and outliers in analysing data; and (5) considering social reality as stable. In order to overcome these disadvantages, he proposes an alternative approach to politeness, suggesting a scientific politeness theory (politeness2) incorporating ideas from sociology. It should take ⋯

> ⋯ account of the hearer's position and the evaluative moment; [be] able to capture both politeness and impoliteness; provide a more dynamic, bi-directional view of the social-individual relationship; and thus acknowledge the individual (in terms of both variability and creativity) as well as evolution and change as intrinsic to the very nature of politeness (Eelen 2001: 247).

His overall purpose is to criticise previous politeness theories in detail and to make clear their disadvantages, incorporating social theoretical insights into politeness theory, and proposing conditions of an alternative scientific model of politeness (politeness2). However, the alternative model itself has not been elaborated sufficiently to be used as a realistic analytical tool.

Similarly criticising previous politeness theories for overlooking the ambiguities of the term politeness, Watts' (2003) adopted and developed Eelen's (2001) distinction of politeness, and distinguished *first-order politeness* (politeness 1) and *second-order politeness* (politeness 2). Watts (2003) also proposed a theory of politeness1 which is not prescriptive but descriptive, while Eelen (2001) argues that politeness2 is the appropriate focus for a theory of politeness,

Watts (2003) dismisses politeness2 as an unrealistic analytic tool, claiming that "there can be no idealised, universal scientific concept of (im)politeness (i.e. (im)politeness2) which can be applied to instances of social interaction across cultures, subcultures and languages" (Watts 2003: 23). For him, a theory of politeness should be a descriptive theory of politeness1 and be able "to offer a way of assessing how the members themselves may have evaluated that behaviour" (2003: 19).

Watts (2003) also contends that linguistic behaviour should not be seen as polite or impolite on a positive-negative continuum. According to his idea, specific strategies are neither inherently polite nor impolite but are open to interpretation because "it is impossible to evaluate (im)politeness behaviour out of the context of real, ongoing verbal interaction" and also "social interaction is negotiated on-line" (2003: 23). Thus it is impossible to know whether an utterance is (im)polite or not in advance and consequently to develop a predictive model of linguistic (im)politeness.

A unique aspect of Watts' (2003) theory is the distinction between *politic* and *polite* behaviour. Politic behaviour is "behaviour, linguistic and non-linguistic, which the participants construct as being appropriate to the ongoing social interaction" (2003: 21). On the other hand, polite behaviour is "behaviour beyond what is perceived to be appropriate to the ongoing social interaction" (2003: 21). Politeness theory should focus on politeness1, in particular linguistic (im)politeness, which is perceived to be beyond what is expectable (i.e. salient) behaviour. It should be able to "locate possible realisations of polite or impolite behaviour and offer a way of assessing how the members themselves may have evaluated that behaviour" (2003: 19-20). His notion of politic/polite behaviour is associated with Bourdieu's concept of habitus. What is construed as (im)polite by an individual is decided by his or her linguistic habitus and the available linguistic resources.

Both Eelen (2001) and Watts (2003) criticise the *Parsonian perspective*,[2] which is said to resemble the previous approach to politeness, for seeing individuals as powerless. "The Parsonian view of society consists of 'regularised' constraints on 'normal' or 'acceptable' social behaviour and sets of institutions" (Watts 2003: 147) and "these determine the structuring of social groups and the roles which individuals are 'expected' to play in those groups" (2003: 147-148). In this perspective, society determines human beings' behaviour, and culture and context are regarded as predetermined and static. Against this view, Eelen (2001) and Watts (2003) take Bourdieu's theory of social practice and argue that politeness is best considered as social practice and should be analysed in an ongoing process of interaction.

Watts' (2003) politeness theory is more realistic in that its focus is clearer than Eelen's (2001) theory. It is favourable for micro-level analysis of the data. However, it cannot be used for macro-level analysis of an entire discourse since it focusses only on detailed analysis of interaction and neglects tendencies in discourse at the macro level.

Along with Eelen (2001) and Watts (2003), Mills (2003) criticises previous approaches to politeness for drawing on an autonomous individual (model person) without taking him or her into consideration in relation to other people, for focussing on the speaker's side, and for analysing individual utterances without context, relying on only formal textual elements.

What distinguishes Mills (2003) from Eelen (2001) and Watts (2003) is the *community of practice* (hereafter CofP) framework in her alternative approach. Both Eelen (2001) and Watts (2003) contend that politeness is carried out within "arbitrary social organisations of space and time" and "individuals and groups are defined by their relative positions in them" (Watts 2003: 149), but neither of them define social groups. On the other hand, Mills (2003) answers the question and suggests that politeness is carried out within CofPs. The concept of CofP is based on the research of Lave and Wenger (1991) and Wenger (1998):

> A community of practice consists of a loosely defined group of people who are mutually engaged on a particular task and who have a shared repertoire of negotiable resources accumulated over time (Wenger 1998: 76).

Mills (2003) proposes that analysis should be conducted within a CofP framework. She contends that "politeness cannot be understood simply as a property of utterances, or even as a set of choices made only by individuals, but rather as a set of practices or strategies which communities of practice develop, affirm and contest" (2003: 9) and that "politeness and impoliteness play a key role in presenting and producing a particular type of identity, and negotiating a position in the community of practice" (2003: 9).

One of the important characteristics of a CofP is that it is not a static notion but an ongoing dynamic process. According to Mills (2003: 4), CofPs are "in a constant process of change, determined by the actions and assessments of individual members in relation to the group." They are not isolated from but affected by one another because people belong to many different communities and the shared practices of each group are different. Another important aspect of a CofP is that an individual is not seen as a stable and powerless entity but as playing a different role in each community, who "engages with others and is defined and changed by that engagement and contributes to the changes taking place within the community of practice" (2003: 30). Mills (2003) also integrates Bourdieu's notion of habitus into her theory. Drawing on the notion of habitus with the model of CofP, she states that what affects the assessment of appropriateness, which is closely related to politeness, is not only the individuals' habituses but also the CofP where they are involved. However appropriateness is not imposed but has to be determined by individuals' "assessing their own status in relation to other participants in the community of practice" (2003: 71).

Along with Eelen (2001) and Watts (2003), Mills (2003) maintains that politeness and impoliteness should not be considered as binary opposites but as a continuum and that analysis of (im)politeness can only be achieved through turning from the sentence level to the level of discourse. Criticising many linguists for assuming that interaction can be treated as if it were a text rather than a process, she takes the position that interaction should be viewed not as something which has been achieved but rather something which is still in the process of being worked out.

Mills (2003) also argues that researchers should analyse intentions and interpretations of linguistic acts discursively. Thus it is important for analysts to interview participants in order to investigate what is really going on in the interaction.

The notion of CofP provides Mills (2003) with an alternative framework and its crucial points are summarised in the following: (1) analysis should be conducted within a community of practice framework; (2) linguistic analysis should focus on discourse rather than sentences; and (3) participants should be consulted in order to come to an assessment of what was going on in an interaction. Her theory's key notion, CofP, made it more concrete in defining what kind of social group affects identifying politeness.

Although each of the researchers in the post-modern approach has distinctive features of their own, the following points are shared:

1. No linguistic expressions are inherently (im)polite. Politeness involves subjective, contextual assessment. What is evaluated as polite behaviour

is different according to the person and according to the local context.
2. Politeness and impoliteness should be seen as part of a continuum. A politeness theory should cover both impolite and polite phenomena within its framework.
3. Politeness is negotiated dynamically and discursively among interactants and thus should be captured at the discourse level, not at the speech act level. Moreover the perspectives of not only speakers but also hearers should be adequately taken into consideration in assessing (im)politeness.
4. Politeness theory should be descriptive, non-normative, and non-prescriptive.

One of these common characteristics raises a problem with the approach as an analytic tool. If post-modern views deny the possibility of predictions, that means they deny the possibility of theorising politeness. That is, their theory can describe micro aspects of interaction but could not explain a whole picture of politeness. Considering this research is cross-cultural and analyses meeting discourse, an appropriate framework is one which can cover all cultures as well as describe micro aspects of interaction, ideally focussing on workplace discourse. In the next section, another recent approach focussing on workplace interactions is described.

2.1.4 Neo-Politeness approach

The traditional approach and post-modern approach are the two contrasting mainstreams in analysing politeness among western researchers (Holmes 2012). Recent researchers (e.g., Holmes, Marra & Schnurr 2008; Mullany 2004, 2006, 2007) take a more flexible perspective on politeness based on their empirical study of politeness in authentic interaction. They have drawn on aspects of both these approaches, "incorporating the analytical categories of Brown and Levinson's approach, but rejecting post-modern claims which appear to lead down a pathway of infinite regress" (Holmes 2012: 212).

This combined approach does not rigidly apply B&L's notions of politeness (e.g., mitigation or avoidance of threatening other's positive/negative face) but interprets them more broadly. In this approach, researchers employ the most useful aspects of B&L's framework while also incorporating modifications which take account of its weaknesses. A neo-Politeness approach also draws on some aspects of the post-modern approach to politeness. Bargiela-Chiappini and Harris (2006) point out that the neo-Politeness theory and post-modern approaches to politeness, regardless of their considerable differences, both argue that politeness is most productively analysed "as a social practice which is both dynamic and interactive, with variability seen as a positive component that builds into human communication a capacity for social and cultural negotiation and change" (Bargiela-Chiappini & Harris 2006: 12).

In analysing workplace interaction, Mullany (e.g., 2006) combines the post-modern approach with some notions of B&L's framework. Basically adopting Mills's (2003) CofP based approach, she employs Goffman's (1967) notion of face along with B&L's FTA category. What distinguishes Mullany (e.g., 2006) from Mills (2003) is that Mullany places importance on the analyst's role. Mullany (2007) points out that Mills (2003) undervalues the analysts' role, against her contention that "only those who belong to the CofPs being studied are able to define whether a particular stretch of discourse can be analysed as (im)polite or not" (Mullany 2007: 78). The importance of the analysts' role is also supported by Holmes (2005) and Holmes, Marra, and Schnurr (2008). They contend that "identifying the linguistic devices used to express concepts such as politeness" is exactly what sociolinguists and discourse analysts can "contribute to understanding how language works" (Holmes, Marra, & Schnurr 2008: 195).

Researchers of the Language in the Workplace Project (e.g., Holmes & Marra 2004; Holmes & Schnurr 2005; Holmes 2006a) also take the neo-Politeness theory approach. They found the term *Relational Practice* appropriate to refer to what is meant by politeness in the workplace (see more details in the next section). Relational Practice under the neo-Politeness approach incorporates B&L's basic general terms, focussing on analysing authentic data at the discourse level while also utilising the concept of CofP.

What is common in the neo-Politeness approach can be briefly summarised:

1. Politeness is considered as social practice and negotiated in on-going interaction discursively and dynamically.
2. CofPs play an important role when analysing politeness in the workplace.
3. Analysts can contribute to interpreting politeness.

The characteristics of the traditional approach, the modified B&L approach, and the post modern approach of politeness discussed in this section are summarised in the following table.

Traditional approach	Modified B&L approach	Post-modern approach	Neo-Politeness approach
Lakoff (1973) Leech (1983) Brown & Levinson (1987)	Spencer-Oatey (2000)	Eelen (2001) Watts (2003) Mills (2003)	Holmes, Marra & Schnurr (2008) Mullany (2007)
Normative	(Moderately) normative	Non-normative	(Moderately) normative
Speech act based	Discourse based	Discourse based	Discourse based
Speaker-oriented	Mainly speaker-oriented, taking into consideration about hearer's assessment	Discursive negotiation between participants	Discursive negotiation between participants
Universal orientation	Culture sensitive	Context focussed	Both universal and culture sensitive

Table 2.2: Summary of characteristics among four approaches to politeness

Though each researcher's approach in the above table has distinctive features, the groupings suggest trends which have dominated the field. In the next section, since the data of the present study focusses on workplace discourse, relevant previous research in this field is addressed, and Relational Practice within the neo-Politeness approach is introduced and explained in detail. Following that, the specific approach to politeness taken in the present research is discussed.

2.2 Politeness in workplace discourse

The studies of politeness in business interaction, to which started to be drawn attention in the 1990s, include research on business meetings (e.g., Bargiela-Chiappini & Harris 1997a, 1997b; Locher 2004; Mullany 2007), leadership (e.g., Schnurr 2009a, 2009b), and various genres (e.g., Koester 2006) not only in mono-cultural settings but also cross- cultural and intercultural settings.

In a special issue of *Journal of Politeness* (2006) focussing on politeness in workplace discourse, Bargiela-Chiappini and Harris (2006) overview the field. In their article, they state that an important development in politeness research at work has been produced in the Language in the Workplace Project (hereafter LWP).[3] The LWP team has found from their vast amount of authentic workplace interaction that "most workplace interactions provide evidence of mutual respect and concern for the feeling or face needs of others, that is, of politeness" though, in the workplace discourse, transactional efficiency is required to achieve a task (Holmes & Stubbe 2003:5). In the next section, an important theory developed by the LWP researchers is introduced.

2.2.1 Relational Practice

Researchers from LWP (Holmes & Marra 2004; Holmes & Schnurr 2005; Holmes 2006a) explored the issue of what it means to be polite in workplace discourse and found that *Relational Practice*, which is derived from Fletcher's (1999) work, is a useful term for discussing politeness in the workplace. Fletcher (1999: 84) defines Relational Practice as "a way of working that reflects a relational logic of effectiveness and requires a number of relational skills such as empathy, mutuality, reciprocity, and sensitivity to emotional contexts." It covers a wide range of off-line, backstage, or collaborative work which is largely unrecognised in the workplace.

While Fletcher (1999) emphasises that Relational Practice is indexed as feminine behaviour and this results in its off-record and background status, the results of the analysis of various aspects of workplace interaction conducted by the LWP team have revealed that Relational Practice is employed not only by female workers but also male workers. In this sense, researchers from LWP extend Fletcher's concept of Relational Practice to a more general theory of politeness. Adopting the term Relational Practice, these researchers propose a new approach to politeness drawing on the neo-Politeness approach. It is the theory of Relational Practice. These authors emphasise the value of Relational Practice in analysing workplace interactions, interpreting B&L's (1987) notion of face more broadly, as indicated in the three criteria described below:

1. Relational Practice is oriented to the (positive and negative) face needs of others.
2. Relational Practice serves to advance the primary objectives of the workplace.
3. Relational Practice at work is regarded as dispensable, irrelevant, or peripheral.

(Holmes & Marra 2004:378; Holmes & Schnurr 2005:125)

Each component of Relational Practice is explained in the following way:

Relational Practice is oriented to the (positive and negative) face needs of others:
Relational Practice at work includes friendly, positive, or supportive verbal behaviour, which considers people's need to feel valued, as well as linguistic strategies and non-imposing distancing linguistic behaviours which show respect toward others. The former corresponds to positive politeness and the latter corresponds to negative politeness.

In the framework of Relational Practice, positive and negative politeness in B&L's (1987) terms is interpreted more flexibly, though the original target of analysis is confined to the speech-act level. However, while recognizing the limitations of B&L's (1987) approach to analyzing politeness, especially criticising their focus on individual utterances rather than more dynamic aspects of interaction, Holmes and Marra (2004) acknowledge that B&L's (1987) terms negative and positive politeness, especially if interpreted more broadly, continue to prove valuable in research in the workplace.

The LWP research, based on the analysis of a large amount of authentic data in workplace discourse, described negative and positive politeness, or face wants, incorporated within Relational Practice as appropriately "oriented to people's desire to be appreciated both for their special skills or distinctive expertise, and for their contribution as a team member" (Holmes 2006a: 75). In the Relational Practice framework, or neo-Politeness theory approach, face is interpreted in a way which makes the term applicable for analysing data at the discourse level. While the term is interpreted more flexibly and broadly, the interpretation is not arbitrary but is based on a large amount of empirical data.

I would like to emphasise that Relational Practice focusses on "other-oriented linguistic behaviour at work" (Holmes & Schnurr 2005: 124) and is "an expression of concern for the feelings of others" (Holmes 1995: 4). The current study thus takes the position that politeness involves a linguistic expression of consideration toward others rather than self interest.

Relational Practice serves to advance the primary objectives of the workplace:
In addition to its relational function, Relational Practice also serves more instrumental or transactional goals. In other words, Relational Practice is always relevant to the goal of furthering organisational objectives in addition to its interpersonal function. For example, while humour is identified as an exemplary Relational Practice strategy, such humour as subversive humour may strengthen solidarity between colleagues, but it may also be oriented to undermining rather than contributing to the organisation's objectives (Holmes & Marra 2004). Thus in this case, this kind of humour would not be counted as Relational Practice.

Relational Practice at work is regarded as dispensable, irrelevant, or peripheral:
Despite its relevance to workplace objectives, Relational Practice is typically regarded as dispensable, peripheral or distracting in the workplace. In other words, Relational Practice is frequently unrecognised, or considered irrelevant if not actually counterproductive. Thus, Relational Practice is found in particular phases of interaction. For example, exemplary Relational Practice strategies, small talk and humour, tend to occur around topic transitional points as

well as the opening and closing phases of meetings (Holmes & Marra 2002a, 2002b; Chan 2005). LWP's empirical study also illustrates that discourse markers such as *get back to the point*, *get back on track*, *enough digressing*, *enough (of that)*, provide clear evidence to support the claim that strategies used in the pursuit of Relational Practice are perceived as off-topic digressions that need to be kept under control (e.g., Holmes & Marra 2004).

Although the Relational Practice framework incorporates B&L's analytical categories in a broad sense, what distinguishes Relational Practice from the traditional framework is that it considers interaction to be dynamic and discursive, analysing authentic interaction at the discourse level.

2.2.2 Communities of Practice

In the Relational Practice framework, one of the key analytical concepts is *community of practice* (CofP). A CofP, which is also utilised in Mills (2003), is a concept which has been developed within a social constructionist framework following a theory of social practice (Holmes 2003). The social constructionist approach to the analysis of language emphasises the dynamic aspects of interaction. It makes use of detailed linguistic analysis of the ways in which individuals perform or create particular aspects of their social identities in specific situations and construct their memberships of certain groups through their language use. Thus this approach is appropriate for the microanalysis of interaction, regarding interaction dynamically and discursively.

Following Lave and Wenger (1991) and Wenger (1998), Eckert and McConnel-Ginet (1999: 186) define a CofP as "an aggregate of people who, united by a common enterprise, develop and share ways of doing things, ways of talking, beliefs, and values – in short, practice." The crucial dimensions of communities of practice are "mutual engagement" (i.e. ongoing regular interaction), "joint enterprise" (i.e. the shared objectives of the team or group), and a "shared repertoire" (i.e. a set of linguistic resources common and understood among group members) (Wenger 1998: 73). Applying these three dimensions to the workplace, not only a whole organisation but also a particular working team, for example, can form a CofP. A CofP approach focusses on the discourse which people use to construct their membership in a group.

Researchers from LWP adopt this frame, a CofP, in their analysis of each workplace or each particular working group. Their analyses have revealed that the manifestations of the verbal behaviours or linguistic strategies in terms of Relational Practice differ from one CofP to another, as well as in different specific workplace contexts and interactions within a CofP. In addition, the analysis within the CofP approach does not focus only on each CofP. It also allows for comparison across different CofPs.

So far, in this and the previous sections, standard politeness approaches and politeness in the workplace have been reviewed. I turn now to discuss what is the most appropriate approach and framework for the present research. Adopting politeness theory as a framework, the following requirements should be met.

1. Because meeting management is a dynamic process in which all participants play a part, a dynamic approach to politeness is required; politeness is regarded as discursive strategy in the ongoing process of interaction.
2. Given the present research is a contrastive study between New Zealand and Japan, it will involve not only microanalysis focussing on local management but also macroanalysis to present similarities and differences between New Zealand and Japan. The preferred framework is one which can account for analysis at both levels.
3. The data for the present research is workplace interaction and an appropriate approach is one which can take the workplace context into consideration.

With regard to the first requirement, among standard politeness approaches, the neo-Politeness approach is the most appropriate. It takes a dynamic view of interaction and regards politeness as a discursive strategy. It also requires detailed linguistic analysis. Considering the first condition only, the post-modern approach could be a possible candidate.

In terms of the second requirement, as discussed in this section, the analysis within the Relational Practice and CofP under the neo-Politeness approach can provide a means of linking micro-level linguistic processes with macro-level patterns. That is, the framework of Relational Practice and CofP can be used for a macro-level analysis as well as for a micro-level analysis and meets my second condition. By contrast, the post-modern approach cannot meet the second condition and is not an appropriate approach for the present study.

The third requirement is met with Relational Practice and CofP because this framework is based on workplace data like my own. The theory of Relational Practice has been developed to account for politeness at work, based on a wide range of authentic workplace interaction, and it is reasonable to analyse the data for the present research by employing this framework.

In addition to satisfying the three conditions, there are two more reasons why Relational Practice and CofP are appropriate frameworks for the present study. Holmes and Schnurr (2005) point out that small talk and humour, both of which are prominent in the New Zealand and Japanese data in the present study, are identified as exemplary discursive strategies of Relational Practice. All three dimensions of CofP are applicable both to the Japanese and New Zealand business meeting groups, which each constitute a CofP.[4] Thus I take Relational Practice and CofP within the neo-Politeness approach as the analytical frameworks for this research.

2.3 Politeness from Japanese perspectives

The previous sections have reviewed politeness theory among Western scholars. Since this research draws on Japanese data as well as English data, in this section, the issue of how politeness has been addressed from Japanese researchers is discussed, focussing on empirical research on politeness in Japanese.

It is generally agreed that Ide (e.g., 1989) offers the most influential paradigm among the approaches to Japanese politeness. Based on the analysis of one Japanese housewife's week of interactions and a quantitative analysis of a questionnaire on politeness between Japanese and Americans, Ide et al. (1992) emphasises that politeness from mainly English-speaking societies' perspectives has paid little attention to the discernment type of politeness, focussing instead on the volitional type, which is B&L's main concern. According to her, the volitional type of politeness is operated by speakers' active will, expressed by linguistic strategies, and employed in order to save face. The discernment type, on the other hand, is governed by speakers' *wakimae* or discernment, realised by linguistic forms, and employed as a response to society. *Wakimae* is defined as "the almost automatic observation of socially-agreed-upon rules and applies to both verbal and non-verbal behavior" (Hill et all. 1986: 348). In *wakimae*, "the participant is recognised as a member of society" rather than an independent individual (Ide 1992).

This conceptualisation of self is supported by Matsumoto (1988). She argues that "what is of paramount concern to a Japanese is not his/her own territory, but the position in relation to the others in the group and his/her acceptance by those others" (Matsumoto 1988: 405).

The choice of linguistic forms such as honorifics is thus governed by the socially obligatory norm. It systematically indexes speakers' sense of place or signals speakers' perception of social relationship with hearers or referents, and speakers' social identities. According to Ide (1989) and Matsumoto (1988), politeness in Japanese is motivated by considerations of sensitivities about one's place or position relative to others.

Ide (e.g., 1989) challenges B&L, asserting that their theory does not pay sufficient attention to the discernment type of politeness, which is governed by obligatory honorific principles rather than by one's volition. She claims that this type of politeness plays an important role in the Japanese politeness system. Ide (e.g., 2006) recently has extended her theory of *wakimae*, incorporating the theory of *ba*, or dual mode thinking, which was originally proposed by Shimizu (1996). In the extended theory, she takes a more dynamic approach to politeness and contends that one's sense of place is constructed dynamically and discursively. Her extended idea will be focussed on in Chapter 6.

Another Japanese politeness researcher is Usami (2002). She examined 72 Japanese dyadic conversations between unacquainted people, focussing on the effects of age and gender from a politeness perspective. The results of her qualitative and quantitative study indicate that the principles of honorifics cannot fully explain the manipulation of speech-level shifts, and that there are options for the voluntary use of strategic speech-level shifts in Japanese. That is, the shift in the appropriate use of speech-level from the polite or super-polite to the non-polite form serves as an indicator of positive politeness.

While Ide (1989) maintains that linguistic use related to honorifics is governed by discernment and that there is little room for strategic use, Usami (2002) claims that honorific use can be operated by one's volition and that some voluntary operation of honorifics serves positive politeness. Usami (2002) supports B&L's theory in that it accounts for discourse behaviour in Japanese. However she maintains that some weak elements remain in their theory, by pointing out that their focus is limited to politeness at the speech act level.

Usami (2002) defines discourse politeness as "the dynamic whole of functions of various elements in both linguistic forms and discourse-level phenomena that play a part within the pragmatic politeness of a discourse" (2002: 4). She contends that B&L's framework works at the dynamic level of discourse and would be applicable universally. She continues that such terms as face and positive/negative politeness in B&L's framework should be considered as postulated theoretical concepts in order to make the theory more explanatory. It can be argued that she advances B&L's theory, moving from the speech-act level to the discourse level.

Exploring how cultural notions of face could be conceptualised, Haugh (2005a) identified *kao, menboku, taimen,* and *mentsu* as terms for figurative senses of face in Japanese and noted that these terms cover "a complex network of inter-related meanings" (Haugh 2005a: 232). These concepts, or Japanese faces, correspond to "the multiple faces of an individual and/or group" and are "co-constructed through external, public evaluations of particular criteria by a certain audience" (Haugh 2005a: 232). Japanese faces can be "extended beyond individuals to encompass groups to which an individual belongs" (Haugh 2005a: 233) and are based on "the perceptions of 'what others (can) show they think of me/my group'" (Haugh 2005a: 232). Taking these culture-specific notions of face into consideration, Haugh (2005b, 2007) asserts that, based on the analysis of authentic interaction in Japanese, the notion of place plays an important role in Japanese politeness. According to Haugh (2005b, 2007), there are two aspects of place; one is *uchi*, the place one belongs (inclusion) and the other is *tachiba*, the place one stands (distinction). Thus, while people show intimacy, or belonging to the same group, they also show a distinction.

Haugh (2005b, 2007) analyses authentic Japanese conversations focussing on speech-level shift or use or non-use of honorifics. For example, speakers' use of speech-level down shift from a polite form to a plain form where honorifics are required is for showing *uchi*, or belonging to the same group. Another example shows that when refusing her senior, a speaker refuses in a humorous way employing honorifics. He points out from this example that the speaker shows intimacy or belonging to the same group at the same time showing distinction between the speaker and the hearer. He contends that the notion of place, which has two aspects, inclusion and distinction, can encompass volitional types of politeness as well as discernment types. His distinction between inclusion and distinction appears to be a promising direction for further research, but still needs development.

Another recent research on Japanese politeness based on authentic interaction is Geyer (2008). Taking a post-modern approach to politeness, Geyer (2008) analyses six faculty meetings at Japanese secondary schools. She explores how face-work is constructed and negotiated in several types of discursive practice including collaborative disagreement and talking about troubles. In her research, she takes Goffman's (1967) original concept of face, "the positive social value a person effectively claims for himself" (Goffman 1967: 5). She considers face not as a normative and uncontestable concept but as one constructed and negotiated discursively in interaction, following Eelen's (2001) conceptualisation of face. In analysing the data, she illustrates how speakers effectively claim their own positive self-image at the discourse level. Her approach to politeness in Japanese is unique.

The research on Japanese politeness overviewed so far identifies at least two issues in analysing Japanese from a politeness perspective: (1) whether politeness is normative or volitional; and (2) whether self is independent or group-oriented.

With regard to the first issue, recent politeness researchers of Japanese have started to extend their focus from the social rule governed, static honorific use to more dynamic, strategic, and action-oriented use and non-use of honorifics (Maynard 1993; Okamoto 1999; Cook 2008; Geyer 2008; Barke 2010). They have found that even social-index type politeness like honorifics can be used strategically, dynamically, and discursively. This point is interesting, and it suggests that there might not be a clear distinction between volitional type and discernment type, rather a continuum. Clearly then it is worth exploring whether and to what extent small talk and humour, which are the research focuses of the present study and considered as volitional types of politeness, could be governed by discernment, or norms.

With regard to the second issue, most researchers of Japanese politeness agree that Japanese "self" is group-oriented while English "self" is an independent individual. The present research is an empirical, cross-cultural study based not only on the analysis of authentic interaction but also on the analysis of Japanese business people's perceptions regarding politeness, and the rich data source should shed some light on this issue.

2.4 Cross-cultural considerations

In the previous sections, politeness has been addressed from various perspectives. Since the present research is a cross-cultural study and politeness and culture are associated with each other, in this section, politeness and culture are addressed. Following that, what is important in conducting a cross-cultural study is addressed.

2.4.1 Politeness and culture

Though there is a vast amount of research on culture and various definitions of it, in this section, I focus on culture in politeness research. It is evident from previous research that culture plays an important role in the assessment of politeness. However, among politeness researchers, what counts as culture had not been defined clearly before Spencer-Oatey (2000a). As noted in section 2.1.2, for Spencer-Oatey (2000a), politeness is "a question of appropriateness" (2000b: 3) and this appropriateness depends on "cultural differences in ways of managing rapport" (2000c: 41). While recognising its complexity, she defines culture in the following way:

> Culture is a fuzzy set of attitudes, beliefs, behavioural conventions, and basic assumptions and values that are shared by a group of people, and that influence each member's behaviour and his/her interpretations of the 'meaning' of other people's behaviour.   (2000b: 4)

In the previous section, I claimed the importance of analysing interaction dynamically and discursively. In order to do so, it is necessary to conceptualise culture as a dynamic notion that involves considerations of context. From this perspective, the following three weaknesses of Spencer-Oatey's (2000b) definition are indicated.

Members of a culture are regarded as powerless.

From Spencer-Oatey's (2000b) point of view, all members of a cultural group are expected to behave the same way or at least in a similar way, and the role of each member in a culture is not taken into consideration. Researchers from the post-modern approach point out this disadvantage. This is similar to Eelen (2001) and Watts's (2003) criticism of the Parosonian perspective, where society or cultural norms determine humans' behaviour.

As noted in section 2.1.3, Eelen (2001) and Watts (2003) take the theory of social practice and argue that individuals are not powerless but play roles in constructing culture. Using Foley's (1997) idea, Mills (2003) also claims that:

> Foley is attempting both to see the coercive or affirming force of certain cultural practices and to enable us to perceive a model for change at the level of the individual: in some ways, to reinscribe the agency without succumbing to the model of the atomistic individual who is in total control of their behaviour(Mills 2003: 31).

It is evident from the post modern approach's perspective that, in reality, each member plays an active role in constructing culture.

Culture is considered as predetermined.

The previous problem leads to yet another problem. From Spencer-Oatey's (2000b) point of view, each member of a culture is powerless and this suggests that culture is predetermined. This disadvantage can be overcome by the notion of habitus. In the post modern approach, habitus plays an important role in the assessment of politeness and politeness can be based on interactants' habitus. From Bourdieu's (1977, 1991) perspective, culture is a resource, or "capital" in his words, of habitus and habitus is not static but constantly being multiplied by capital. Habitus is considered as a set of dispositions shaping practices, perceptions, and attitudes that are considered regular (Watts 2003).

As individuals multiply their habituses, their resources are not fixed but variable and dynamic. That is, culture is not predetermined, but constantly constructed by its members.

The groups are associated with language groups.

Recognising a variety of social groups, as noted in section 2.1.2, Spencer-Oatey (2000b) states "culture is operationalised primarily in terms of ethnolinguistic and/or national or regional political identity" (2000b: 4), for example, Chinese, Japanese, Americans, and so on. In the cross-cultural and intercultural research reviewed in the previous section, cultural groups are also often associated with language groups.

Many language groups primarily consist of cultural groups, and play crucial roles in politeness assessment. However, people are not only members of language groups but also other social groups such as ethnic groups, their community groups, or workplaces, as relevant in my research. All these groups are able to construct culture. One possible solution is the notion of CofPs, and in Mills' (2003: 32) work she considers culture as "a set of assumptions made by the individual because of his/her involvement with groups where those values are affirmed and contested."

Applying such concepts as habitus, theory of social practice, and CofPs, in this study, I propose to use the following definition:

> *Culture* is a set of assumptions shared by most if not all group members and negotiated by them discursively, which affects assessment of (im)politeness. Culture is considered not as a static predetermined notion but as more dynamic and observable through people's communicative behaviour, especially their interaction.

Culture not only affect people's behaviour but also their perceptions, and plays an important role in (im)politeness. The participants in business meetings in the present study are not only members of an ethno-linguistic or national group — New Zealanders and Japanese — but also of a particular workplace or a CofP. It is worth exploring how culture influences their linguistic behaviours in terms of doing Relational Practice and also their perceptions about Relational Practice.

2.4.2 Etic and emic dimensions in a cross-cultural study

This section addresses what is important in conducting a cross-cultural study — comparative research where data is collected from two different cultural groups.

In conducting a cross-cultural study, there are two types of dimensions. They are etic dimensions and emic dimensions (e.g., Berry 1969, Triandis 1994; Trevor-Roberts et al. 2003).[5] *Etic dimensions* refer to universal or global constructs, and *emic dimensions* refer to local or culture-specific constructs. Researchers (e.g., Berry 1969, Triandis 1994; Trevor-Roberts et al. 2003) agree that "cross-cultural research needs to include both etic and emic constructs" (Triandis 1994: 74).

According to Trevor-Roberts et al. (2003), Berry's (1969) reason why etic and emic constructs are necessary for cross-cultural research is as follows:

> Berry (1969) ... argues that a phenomenon is rarely if ever purely etic or emic. In order to overcome this issue, Berry suggests that a combined 'etic-emic' approach should be used. Such a methodology is predicated on the idea that an etic phenomenon, such as leadership, may be manifested differently in different cultures. In effect, emic descriptions can modify the etic constructs to particular contexts
>
> (Trevor-Roberts et al. 2003: 518)

Regarding face and politeness, Bargiela-Chiappini and Harris (2006) agree with taking the combined etic and emic approach:

> Here relativistic and universalistic positions clash: the former emphasizes the uniqueness of phenomena and the context dependency of meaning and interpretation; the latter concentrates on what is common and can be compared. Rather than underscoring the contrast between these two perspectives, their complementarity could be exploited by identifying both emic (indigenous) and etic (universal) aspects of behaviour. Attention to "cultural commonality" as well as to "cultural difference" should be encouraged (Kagitcibasi and Poortinga 2000) in an attempt to capture phenomena that straddle the etic and the emic or have different manifestations in the two dimensions. Face and politeness are two such phenomena.
>
> (Bargiela-Chiappini & Harris 2006: 14)

In order to make the present cross-cultural research more explanatory, I take a combined etic-emic approach. Relational Practice is selected as an etic construct for the following two reasons: (1) Relational Practice is verified by analysing considerable amounts of authentic business interactions; and (2) the LWP data has been collected mostly from New Zealand workplaces, which "have become increasingly multicultural in recent years as a result of repeated waves of immigration from a wide range of countries" (Schnurr, et al 2007: 712). Moreover the LWP team have investigated how people do politeness not only in mainstream majority group workplaces (e.g., Holmes & Stubbe, 2003) but also in ethnic minority groups (e.g., Schnurr et al 2007; Holmes, Marra, & Vine 2011). Thus it is worth exploring whether it is applicable to the Japanese data.

Along with taking Relational Practice as an etic construct, I also consider the basic general terms such as face (want) and negative/positive politeness in the neo-Politeness approach as etic constructs. Not taking B&L's terms more rigidly or at the concrete level but interpreting them more broadly makes these basic concepts abstract enough to encompass the cultural specific underlying dimensions of politeness. In the present research, I consider positive politeness as being friendly and supportive to others and negative politeness as showing respect to others.

While etic dimensions address universal constructs, emic dimensions focus on revealing the implicit or underlying expectations which speakers bring into interactions (Haugh 2007). Peeters (2004a) calls them "communicative norms":

> *Intercultural (or cross-cultural) pragmatics* is the contrastive or comparative study of communicative norms; its aim is to reach a better understanding of the cultural value or values that underpin them, to detect new (i.e. previously undetected) cultural values, and/or to find supporting key words. In the absence of a contrastive or a comparative focus, this approach may be referred to as *cultural pragmatics*.
>
> (Peeters 2004a: 73, italics and parentheses in original)

To shed light on what emic constructs, or communicative norms are, the analysis of authentic interaction is necessary. In analysing the meeting data from a relational perspective in Chapter 5 and 6, the following questions will be explored: (1) whether Relational Practice (or the etic dimension) is applicable to the Japanese data; and (2) what the underlying expectations, or communicative norms are in the New Zealand and the Japanese meeting discourse respectively.

I consider that taking the combined etic-emic approach together with a cross-cultural research design will overcome the issues raised in analysing Japanese from a politeness perspective.

2.5 Summary

In this chapter, after reviewing standard politeness approaches, the theoretical frameworks developed for this research have been presented. Then politeness from Japanese perspectives has been reviewed and some issues on Japanese politeness have been raised. Finally, what stance to take in conducting cross-cultural study has been clarified. Keeping the frameworks for the present study in mind, in the next section, the methodology adopted in this research is described.

Notes

1 The politeness1 and politeness2 distinction originally derives from Watts, Ide, and Ehlich (1992). Eelen (2001) developed this further.
2 This originates in Talcott Parsons (e.g., 1966, 1967, in Eelen 2001: 188), an influential American sociologist whose ideas on the nature of society have spread to other fields of scientific thinking.
3 See Chapter 3, for more detail.
4 See Chapter 3 for more detail.
5 While Eelen (2001) limits emic and etic to evaluations or accounts of politeness, here these two dimensions are employed as more general concepts for cross-cultural study.

CHAPTER 3

Methodology

As described in Chapter 1, the current study has two objectives. The primary objective is to investigate manifestation of small talk and humour, analysing meeting data in New Zealand and Japan. A further aim is to explore how Japanese business people perceive New Zealand meeting behaviours regarding small talk and humour and what influences people's perceptions. In order to meet these two aims, two kinds of data are necessary: (1) meeting data collected from business people in New Zealand and Japan and (2) perception data collected from Japanese business people. The aim of this chapter is to describe the research methods and data collection procedures.

The first section of this chapter begins by briefly introducing the methodology used for data collection in the field of workplace discourse, and provides a rationale for the choice of the particular data collection method selected for this study. The second part of the chapter describes the methodological steps involved in collecting the meeting data. The next part of the chapter describes the meeting data that was collected in New Zealand and Japan, and introduces the meeting participants in each CofP and the target participants among them. The chapter closes by briefly outlining the perception data, which will be described in detail with its rationale in Chapter 7.

3.1 Data collection in the field of workplace discourse[1]

The focus in workplace discourse research has moved to more qualitative and micro-analytical approaches for the study of authentic workplace interaction. For example, Cooren (2007: xii) summarises the recent developments within the field of workplace discourse in the following way:

> Although the organizational communication field has historically been (and still is, in many respects) associated with quantitative analyses

relying on questionnaires and interviews, there is today a growing body of research that tends to seek access more directly to what actually happens in organizations.

In particular, since the 1990s researchers of workplace discourse have drawn attention to empirical research based on authentic workplace interaction, including a variety of workplace settings (e.g., Drew & Heritage 1992; Bargiela-Chiappini & & Harris 1997b). A number of researchers have proposed a combination of naturally occurring conversations and ethnographic observation, the latter used as a supplement to the former (e.g., Cicourel 1987; Koester 2006; Asmuß & Svennevig 2009). Koester (2006: 11) points out that one of the prominent features of workplace talk is that it is often difficult "for an outsider to understand what people are talking about" without the relevant background information. It can be argued that authentic workplace interaction and ethnographic observation, or background information obtained from participant interviews, are ideal data to analyse meetings, a major focus of workplace discourse.

Research on workplace discourse from a linguistic perspective takes a variety of methodological approaches such as: conversation analysis, corpus linguistics, genre analysis, rhetorical analysis, interactional sociolinguistics, communities of practice, and impression management (e.g., Bargiela-Chiappini & Nickerson 2002). Among them, conversation analysis is often employed to analyse workplace interaction, mainly focussing on turn design and the sequential structure of talk (e.g., Koester 2006; Asmuß & Svennevig 2009). However, in order to decide which approach to take, the analysis framework for the current study should be considered. As noted in Chapter 2, I take Relational Practice as the major framework for analysis. Relational Practice is manifested as discursive strategies negotiated among interactants, and emphasises the dynamic aspects of interactions (Holmes & Marra 2004; Holmes & Schnurr 2005). Analysing Relational Practice thus requires detailed linguistic analysis that considers the ongoing process of interaction, taking social relationships among participants into consideration. Interactional sociolinguistics is a type of discourse analysis whose focus is on discourse features which are used to negotiate meaning in interaction between participants. The main concern of interactional sociolinguistics is the interplay between "culture, society, and language" (cited in Asmuß & Svennevig 2009: 8; see also Schiffrin 1994). Compared to conversation analysis, interactional sociolinguistics is "more concerned with the larger societal context surrounding the interaction, such as the speakers' social identities in terms of gender, ethnicity, or (sub-)culture" (Asmuß & Svennevig 2009: 8). This approach is highly compatible with my analysis framework and I take this approach to analysing meeting discourse.

In sum, considering what has been discussed in this section, I employ naturally occurring meeting data, with supplementary ethnographic data and interviews with participants. I also take a qualitative approach to the data, using an interactional sociolinguistic approach.

3.2 Methodological design of meeting data

As described in Chapter 1, the current research involves a contrastive study to examine manifestations of small talk and humour in meeting discourse. The first component is cross-cultural, comparing meetings in New Zealand and Japan. The second component analyses and compares the use of small talk and humour in different types of meetings, i.e. formal meetings (known as *kaigi* in Japanese) and informal meetings (known as *uchiawase/miitingu* in Japanese) in New Zealand and Japan.[2]

In accordance with the above research design, the meeting data used for analysis has been drawn from authentic business meetings recorded in two business organisations – one set (including formal and informal meetings) from New Zealand and the other from Japan. In the following sections, I describe the process of data collection for the meeting data collected in New Zealand and then in Japan.

3.3 Meeting data collection in New Zealand: the Language in the Workplace Project

The New Zealand data is drawn from the Language in the Workplace Corpus. In developing the meeting data collection and its associated methodological design, I am greatly indebted to the Language in the Workplace Project (LWP).[3] The LWP began in 1996 to explore effective workplace communication under the direction of Professor Janet Holmes of Victoria University of Wellington. The aims of the project are to: (1) identify specific characteristics of workplace interaction in different workplaces from a sociolinguistic perspective; (2) investigate effective interpersonal communication strategies in a variety of workplaces; (3) explore the practical implications of the research findings in terms of workplace relationships, for providing useful input to human resource and professional development programmes; and (4) investigate cultural differences in workplace communication patterns.

The team has collected over 2,000 interactions, involving more than 500 people from various ethnic backgrounds. They include workers from government departments, commercial organisations, factories, and various small businesses. The majority of these recordings are 10-20 minutes in length, though some are as short as 20 seconds, and others are several hours long.

In terms of the data collection procedures, volunteers in each organisation typically record their own everyday work-related interactions, meetings and discussions. The LWP team has also collected telephone calls and social conversations, and videotaped a number of larger, more formal meetings from most workplaces. The basic methodological principles regarding data collection are as follow:

1. To give participants as much control as possible over the research process, and especially the data collection process.
2. To reduce the researchers' involvement in the physical collection of data to the absolute minimum.

(Holmes & Stubbe 2003:21, Marra 2003: 22)

The LWP team has researched many areas of workplace discourse (especially from a relational perspective) based on a large amount of authentic workplace interaction (e.g., Vine 2004; Holmes 2006a; Marra & Holmes 2007; Schnurr 2009b). It has been widely acknowledged as playing an important role in sociolinguistics and discourse study (Bargiela-Chiappini & Harris 2006; Asmuß & Svennevig 2009).

For the current study, nine New Zealand business meetings, totalling approximately 370 minutes of video and/or audio recordings, and their transcriptions were selected from the LWP corpus. The data was selected to match as closely as possible the potential Japanese data in terms of various meeting components such as size, purpose, frequency, and so on.

All the New Zealand meetings for the present study took place in a production company, pseudonymed company N, where the staff typically identify as Anglo/Pakeha and Pakeha norms prevail (Holmes, Marra, & Vine 2011). The meeting data was collected from November 2004 to April 2005. The dataset includes a total of nine meetings. Four target participants who were involved in most meetings were selected to observe whether the verbal behaviour of the same person differed in different kinds of meetings, i.e. formal and informal meetings. More details about the meetings, the target participants, and the participants' network addressed in this study are presented later in this chapter.

3.4 Meeting data collection in Japan

In this cross-cultural research of business meetings in Japan and New Zealand, the New Zealand data was drawn from recordings in the LWP data set as explained in the previous section. The Japanese data, on the other hand, was collected in Japan. The basic methodology for collecting the Japanese workplace data followed the standard process adopted by LWP researchers (e.g., Holmes & Stubbe 2003; Marra 2003; Chan 2005) to ensure comparability. The procedure includes the three stages described below (see also Chan 2005).

3.4.1 Preparation

As has been stated by the LWP researchers (e.g., Holmes & Stubbe 2003; Chan 2005; Schnurr 2005), personal networks play an important role in collecting authentic data in the workplace. Especially in Japan, business people are very reluctant to be video/audio-recorded and it was difficult to find potential companies to cooperate in this study.

In finding potential companies for this research project, I am greatly indebted to an acquaintance who has a large network in the business world in Japan. He asked a large number of companies to allow me to record their authentic meetings, but only one IT company, pseudonymed company J, agreed to their business meetings being video and audio recorded.

The acquaintance asked the company CEO to meet me and arranged the meeting opportunity. I met the CEO and talked about my research project, explaining it using a research information sheet for participants (shown in Appendix I). In this information sheet, a typical LWP initial proposal was translated into Japanese and revised to make it suitable for the Japanese context.

Once I received permission from the CEO, I asked him to allow me to meet the participants of those meetings that would be video-recorded. At the meeting, first, the CEO introduced me to the meeting participants and explained why he had decided to allow me to record the company's meetings. He said that because the company owed a lot to my acquaintance he had decided to cooperate in the data collection. In his speech, he employed the subject pronoun "*ware ware*", which refers to "we" or "our company", not he, himself, though the actual decision was his alone. Considering that the CEO started company J and is also an owner of this company, his decision would be absolute and he would hold this power.

After his speech, I distributed to each meeting participant: a research information sheet, a background information sheet, and a consent form (shown in Appendices I, II, and III).[4] The aims and methods of the research were outlined. Then I provided the participants with the opportunity for questions and comments, however everyone remained silent. The meeting participants were then asked to fill out a background information sheet and sign a consent form which they all did without comment.

3.4.2 Collecting data

Seven meetings were recorded in Japan, totalling approximately 710 minutes. As with the New Zealand meeting data collection, four target participants who were involved in most meetings were selected in order to observe whether the verbal behaviour of the same person differed in different kinds of meetings, i.e. formal and informal meetings. The meeting data was collected from April to July in 2007.

In recording formal meetings, I followed the LWP's methods of recording meeting data (e.g., Marra 2003; Chan 2005; Schnurr 2005). Two cameras, one wireless microphone, and an IC sound recorder were utilised. For good quality sound recordings and a large amount of HDD memory, the SONY DCR-SR60 was selected. A wireless Bluetooth microphone, Sony's ECM-HW1, was used since its effective range is up to 100 meters. An IC sound recorder, the Olympus Voice Treck V-50, was also employed because its sound file is WMA and compatible with my PC.

The two video cameras were set up on tripods in adjacent corners of the meeting room to capture all participants. The wireless microphone and IC sound recorder were laid on the table in the centre of the meeting room in

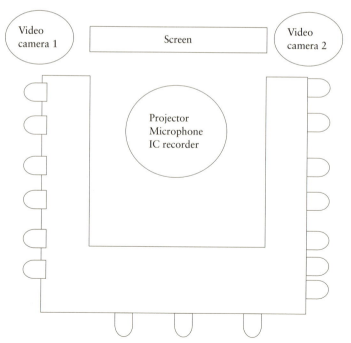

Figure 3.1: Equipment set-up for the recording for formal meetings

order to capture all participants' voices.

Following Marra (2003) and Chan (2005), I set up and turned on the recording equipment and left before any participants arrived and came back after the meeting room was empty. By doing so, the interactions which took place at the pre-meeting and post-meeting sections could be recorded. At one meeting, however, some participants conscientiously turned off the video recorders after the meeting finished and thus all the post-meeting phases were not video recorded on this occasion.

In addition to recording the whole meetings, the target participants were asked to audio-record the meetings. Each target participant was provided with an IC recorder (SONY ICD-U60 [512MB] or ICD-U70 [1GB]). They were asked to turn them on just after leaving their office for the meeting room or just after entering company J, and turn them off when coming back to their office or when leaving the company J building so that the interactions at the pre-meeting and post-meeting sections could be recorded. The target participants were also asked to record informal meetings involving the same participants as the formal meetings even if they were held outside the office.[5]

3.4.3 Coding and processing data

After the meeting data was collected, all video and audio recordings were copied onto three portable hard disks. Adapting the LWP system, the following labelling was employed: initial of the company; two letter-abbreviations of the kinds of meetings such as "FM" to represent formal meetings or "IF" to represent informal meetings; a two-digit number such as "01" to show the recorded meeting number; a two-digit number to represent the chapter or section number in the recording equipment; and the starting time of the example, as illustrated in the following:

JFM01_02, 15:30
JIF03_05, 18:05

In terms of the New Zealand data, these were renamed from their labels in the wider LWP dataset corresponding to the Japanese data. That is: initial of the company; two letter-abbreviations of kinds of meetings such as "FM" to represent formal meetings or "IF" to represent informal meetings; a two-digit number such as "01" to show the meeting number; a two- or four-digit number to represent the original LWP recorded meeting data number; and the starting time of the example, as illustrated in the following:

NFM01_02, 36:20

NIF06_0214, 11:50

The next step was transcribing all the data.[6] The transcription conventions were adopted from the LWP and some revisions unique to the Japanese data were added. They are outlined in detail in Appendix X. Throughout the book, all names have been replaced by pseudonyms to preserve confidentiality. As the following example shows, speakers were identified by their first names in the New Zealand data.

1   Jaeson: do you have the previous minutes Sharon?

When transcribing the Japanese data, the Hepburn style of Romanisation was employed, but long vowels were shown double vowels (e.g., *gokuroosama*, *miitingu*) in order to depict the actual pronunciation as closely as possible. In the Japanese data, speakers were identified by their family names because people are normally called by their family name in the workplace in Japan:

1   Komeda: それは何 地銀かなんか？
                     sore wa nani chigin ka nanka?
                     is this a local bank or something similar

Once all the data was transcribed, the next step was analysing the data in order to explore the structure of meetings and describe the characteristics of the Relational Practice strategies, small talk and humour. The final step was comparing the results of the analysis of the formal meetings and informal meetings and also the New Zealand and Japanese data.[7]

In analysing the Japanese data, follow-up interviews with the meeting participants were conducted when possible to clarify participants' reasons for their linguistic behaviour. I also asked about the company's background, and the social relationships among the meeting participants.

In analysing the New Zealand data, I consulted the LWP researchers who had conducted fieldwork at company N. In conducting cross-cultural study, Bargiela-Chiappini and Harris (1997a) refer to what is important as follows:

> Ideally, in order to conduct cross-cultural research then, it is necessary to proceed along two lines of inquiry: the *intra*-cultural and the *inter*-cultural, first taking advantage of native insights and then contrasting them with alternative non-native interpretations, for which teamwork is essential.   (Bargiela-Chiappini & Harris 1997a: 154)

In this project, I was fortunate to be supported by the LWP researchers in analysing the New Zealand meeting data. They provided me with useful interpretations and perspectives as native speakers of New Zealand English. Thus this research is not based only on my non-native interpretations.[8]

3.5 Summary of the meeting dataset

The meeting dataset analysed in this research consists of 16 meetings in total, nine from a New Zealand company and seven from a Japanese company. In order to compare formal meetings with informal meetings from a relational perspective, these were selected using the working definition introduced in Chapter 4. All the formal meetings are video- and audio- recorded data while all of the informal meetings are audio-recorded data.

The following table summarises the data collected from the two companies, company N in New Zealand and company J in Japan.

		Company N	Company J
Formal meetings	Number	3	3
	Participants	10-11	16
	Total recording time	275 min	479 min
Informal meetings	Number	6	4
	Participants	2 - 3	3 - 5
	Total recording time	97 min	229 min

Table 3.1: Summary of dataset

As noted earlier in this chapter, in both New Zealand and Japanese meetings, four target participants (who were involved in most meetings) were selected in order to compare the verbal behaviour of the same person in formal and informal meetings. The members of informal meetings were not fixed, and included all or some of the target participants, and sometimes other formal meeting members as well.

The following figures (3.2 and 3.3) provide an organisational chart indicating the relative hierarchy of the target participants and major members of the formal meetings in company N and company J respectively. Tables 3.2 and 3.3 summarise the target participants in each company.

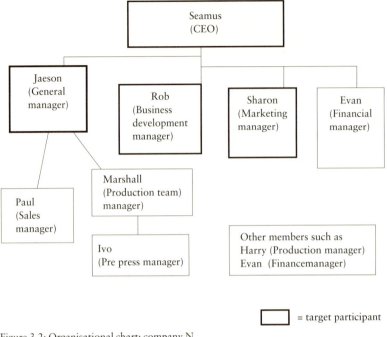

Figure 3.2: Organisational chart: company N

Name	Role
Seamus	CEO
Jaeson	General manager, chair of formal meetings
Rob	Business development manager
Sharon	Marketing manager

Table 3.2: Target participants in company N

As noted in Chapter 2, this study takes the CofP concept as an analysis framework. The crucial dimensions of a CofP are "mutual engagement" (i.e. ongoing regular interaction), "joint enterprise" (i.e. the shared objectives of the team or group), and "shared repertoire" (i.e. a set of linguistic resources common and understood among group members) (Wenger 1998: 73). While most formal meeting members of company N belong to different sections, all of them share the same building. They regularly meet (at least once a month at the formal meeting), share objectives such as promoting sales, and have a common a set of linguistic resources such as technical terms related to their company products. Thus all three CofP dimensions are applicable to the New Zealand business meeting groups and I consider them as constituting a CofP.

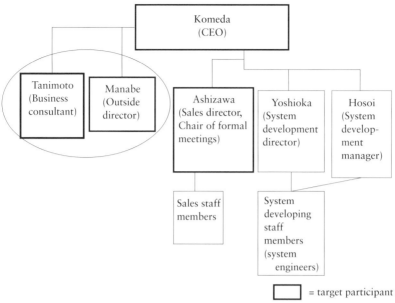

Figure 3.3: Organisational chart: company

Name	Role
Komeda	CEO
Ashizawa	Sales director, chair of formal meetings
Tanimoto	Business consultant
Manabe	Outside director

Table 3.3: Target participants in company J

Most participants of the formal meetings of company J work at the company's head office, but others work at one of the company's branches in another region. The dotted-line circle in figure 3.3 shows that Tanimoto and Manabe, who provide services to company J, are not employees of company J but work at the same consulting firm. Tanimoto is a business consultant and Manabe is an outside director of company J. Both are business partners of company J and have a strong relationship with the company.

Even though members of the formal meetings of company J do not work in the same office, they are in regular contact through e-mails and telephone, and meet more than once a month. They also share the same objectives such as promoting product sales, and they have a common set of linguistic resources such as technical terms related to their company products. Along with company N's formal meeting members, all three dimensions of a CofP are applicable to the

Japanese business meeting groups and I consider them to constitute a CofP as well.

In this section, the meeting data analysed in this study and detailed information about the meeting participants have been described. Details of the formal and informal meetings in New Zealand and Japan are given in Chapter 4.

3.6 Methodological design and the collection of perception data

For the perception data, an extended focus group interview (Berg 1998) with Japanese business people in Japan was selected as the most appropriate data collection method. It was designed to elicit a wide range of Japanese business people's perceptions of the Relational Practice strategies, small talk and humour, occurring in New Zealand business meetings.

As discussed in Chapter 2, recent politeness researchers (e.g., Eelen 2001; Mills 2003; Holmes & Marra 2004) argue that no utterance is inherently polite or impolite, but rather that politeness is constructed among interactants, i.e. both speakers and hearers. Thus when analysing Relational Practice, it is necessary to pay attention also to hearers' perceptions. Though it is ideal to explore the perceptions of interactants themselves, it was impossible to do so in this study because of its cross-cultural nature. Instead, it was more appropriate to explore third parties' perceptions since it is reasonable to assume that a third party could accurately indicate what participants bring to the interaction. Thus, a perception task to elicit Japanese business professional people's perceptions regarding relational talk in New Zealand business meetings was conducted.

For the task, nine scenes were selected, which highlight different manifestations of small talk and/or humour in the New Zealand and Japanese meeting data. Each scene lasted approximately 30 to 60 seconds. During the perception tasks, participants viewed each clip, responded to them according to a questionnaire, and then discussed their impressions in a group. The 16 participants were drawn from three business organisations: pseudonymed respectively Globe; Y&T; and Sakura. The details of the task procedures and rationales for the selected methodology will be discussed in Chapter 7.

3.7 Ethical considerations

All through the data collection (both the meeting and the perception data) in Japan, ethical concerns were seriously considered. The LWP team takes the position of "advocacy research" (Milroy & Gordon 2003: 84). That is, as argued by Cameron et al. (1992), the academic research should be *with* and *for* the community under investigation instead of *on* the participants (Marra 2008b; Holmes et al. forthcoming). Holmes and Meyerhoff (2003: 10) also underscore the importance of research being "directed by the needs and interests of the communities of speakers studied" not for "feeding academic appetite." I firmly endorse this research philosophy of LWP and follow it. As noted in Chapter 1, in Japan, it was very difficult to find participants to cooperate with the data collection partly because people are understandably quite reluctant to be recorded especially when working. For those who did agree to participate, I sent thank-you letters or e-mails after the recordings were finished and presented analysis summaries, which I tried to make useful and interesting for the participants.

3.8 Summary

In this chapter, the methodologies for the meeting data collection have been explained and those for the perception data collection have been briefly outlined. I make use of naturally occurring meetings in New Zealand and Japan. In analysing the meeting data, the main focus is interactional sociolinguistic analysis, supplemented by ethnographic information, for the purpose of interpreting authentic interaction. In analysing the perception data, the main focus is on the task participants' comments. All through the analysis, a qualitative approach to the data is applied.

Notes
1 There are various terms to refer to this research field such as *business communication* (Murphy 1998; Rogers 2001), *business discourse* (Bargiela-Chiappini & Nickerson 1999), *organisational communication* (Mumby & Stohl 1996), and so on. Among them, I employ the term, *workplace discourse* (Koester 2006) in this study because the term "workplace" corresponds to the Language in the Workplace project, which this study is indebted to for the data collection procedures and the New Zealand meeting data. Koester (2006: 1) considers that "naturally occurring talk in workplace environments" is within range of workplace discourse.
2 See Chapter 4 for a detailed discussion about the two types of meetings.
3 Details of LWP are also available at the following web site: http://www.victoria.ac.nz/lals/lwp/.
4 The LWP's usual documents were translated into Japanese and revised to make them applicable to the Japanese context.

5 One of the four target participants had problems using his IC recorder and could not record all formal and informal meetings.
6 I deeply appreciate the transcription support from the LWP researchers and research assistants for the New Zealand meeting data.
7 See Chapter 4 for the rationale for a contrastive study on formal and informal meetings.
8 The analysis of the meeting data is presented in Chapter 4, 5, and 6.

CHAPTER 4

Meetings

As outlined in Chapter 1, the first research question focusses on the structural characteristics that signal the organisation of formal and informal meetings. There are two motivations behind this question. First, this question is posed as a preliminary step to facilitate the analysis of small talk and humour. A consensus in the existing literature suggests that small talk and humour tend to occur around topic transitional phases as well as at the opening and closing phases of meetings (e.g., Holmes & Marra 2002a; Chan 2005). Analysing these Relational Practice strategies in meetings requires attention to both macro and micro level meeting structures. Thus, it is necessary to look at how formal and informal meetings are structured before analysing small talk and humour in meetings. Secondly, this question is posed to examine whether the types of meetings, formal and informal meetings, affect the structures of meetings. Even though previous researchers acknowledge that formality is a crucial dimension to characterise meetings (e.g., Schwartzman 1989; Boden 1994; Bargiela-Chiappini & Harris 1997a), most research has focussed on formal meetings (Asmuß & Svennevig 2009). In Japanese, although there are different terms to refer to formal and informal meetings respectively, no researchers have undertaken contrastive research on *kaigi* (formal meetings) and *uchiawase/miitingu* (informal meetings). This question has been formulated in order to guide research aimed at filling these gaps.

Following discussion of the relevant literature on meetings, I provide a more detailed rationale for conducting a contrastive analysis between formal and informal meetings. Then I propose a working definition of these two kinds of meetings, and summarise the structural characteristics of formal and informal meetings drawing on existing literature. In the last half of this chapter, the meeting data for this study is introduced, along with the results of the analysis in terms of meeting structures in formal and informal meetings.

4.1 Meetings

Meetings are common in many organisations and are typically the primary means of communication for organisations (Bargiela-Chiappini & Harris 1997a; Barretta-Herman 1990; Boden 1994; Mintzberg 1973; Tracy & Dimock 2004). Meetings are one of the major research focusses in workplace discourse (e.g., Chan 2005; Asmuß & Svennevig 2009). As discussed in Chapter 3, research on meetings from a linguistic perspective, as well as research on other business settings, takes a variety of methodological approaches such as conversation analysis (e.g., Kangasharju 2002; Ford 2010), corpus linguistics (e.g., Bilbow 2002), genre analysis (e.g., Bargiela-Chiappini & Harris 1997a; Antunes, Costa, & Pino 2006), communities of practice (e.g., Holmes 2006a), and impression management (Bilbow 1997a).

Though Cuff and Sharrock (1985: 158) assert that "researchers, like any other members of society, can commonsensically recognize a meeting when they see it", it is necessary to look at the working definitions which previous researchers have proposed before analysing the data.

Helen Schwartzman and Deidre Boden have written extensively about meetings. Schwartzman (1989:7) defines meetings as follows:

> [A] communicative event involving three or more people who agree to assemble for a purpose ostensibly related to the functioning of an organization or group, for example, to exchange ideas or options, to solve a problem, to make a decision or negotiate an agreement, to develop policy and procedures, to formulate recommendations, and so forth.

Boden (1994: 84) gives the following definition:

> [A] planned gathering, whether internal or external to an organization, in which the participants have some perceived (if not guaranteed) role, have some forewarning (either longstanding or quite improvisatorial) of the event, which has itself some purpose of "reason", a time, place, and, in some general sense, an organizational function.

Moreover, Marra (2003:13) uses the working definition of "a pre-organised gathering of at least 4 participants in a task-oriented group." She also adds such characteristics as agenda setting and having a chairperson. Bargiela-Chiappini and Harris (1997a:208) refer to meetings as "task-oriented and decision-making encounters" involving "the cooperative effort of two parties, the Chair and the Group".

Though the wording of each definition is different, these definitions identify common characteristics of meetings. They are purposeful, pre-organised, multi-participant gatherings which have a chairperson. While these definitions seem to consider meetings rather rigidly, there are other more loose definitions. For example, Holmes and Stubbe (2003: 59) identify meetings as "interactions which focus, whether indirectly or directly, on workplace business". This definition does not limit the gatherings to meetings which are pre-organised, multi-party, and have a chairperson.

Various definitions of meetings so far indicate that there are different types of meetings. Researchers of meeting discourse (e.g., Schwartzman 1989; Boden 1994; Bargiela-Chiappini & Harris 1997a; Holmes & Stubbe 2003; Chan 2005) agree that meetings are frequently distinguished along a dimension of formality and that there are distinctive features in formal and informal meetings.

Formal meetings tend to be larger, involve a predetermined chairperson, have pre-planned agendas, are likely to occur at pre-specified time, may be routinely held, and be recorded in the form of minutes after the meeting (e.g., Bargiela-Chiappini & Harris 1997a; Chan 2005). They also tend to have a specific venue and names such as "monthly meeting" and "staff meeting" (e.g., Schwartzman 1989). Formal meetings are relatively "information oriented" (Boden 1994: 84).

On the other hand, informal meetings tend to occur among smaller groups of people without an appointed chairperson or written agenda (Boden 1994; Bargiela-Chiappini & Harris 1997a). They are "more loosely planned and conducted" (Bargiela-Chiappini & Harris 1997a: 207). They seldom have a pre-designated chairperson, have no fixed membership or formal minutes, and are more "task and decision oriented" (Boden 1994: 86).

Holmes and Stubbe (2003: 60) illustrate variable features relating to the formality of meetings:

Large in size	Small in size (2-4)
Formal setting	Unplanned location
Starting time specified	Occurs by chance
Finishing time specified	Finishes "naturally"
Participants specified	Open to anyone
Formal procedures	Informal style
Explicit structured agenda	"Rolling" agenda
Tightly integrated group	Loosely connection
Mixed gender group	Same-gender group

Table 4.1: Useful dimensions for comparing meetings

(from Holmes & Stubbe 2003: 60)

According to Holmes and Stubbe (2003), these dimensions often influence the relative formality of a meeting. The dimensions on the left and right sides are likely to correspond to formal and informal meetings respectively. For example, formal meetings tend to concentrate at the more formal end of the scale in terms of interaction style, as well as on a number of other dimensions related to how tightly a meeting is structured.

While it is agreed that the formality is a crucial dimension and there are not only formal but also informal meetings, almost all previous research on meetings has focussed on formal meetings. This point is evident from the definitions of meetings discussed in this section. All the definitions except that by Holmes and Stubbe (2003) are concerned with formal meetings. This is also noted by Asmuß and Svennevig (2009). In the introduction to a special issue of *Journal of Business Communication* (2009) focussing on meetings, Birte Asmuß and Jan Svennevig criticise this and continue as follows:

> ... [I]nformal meetings seem to play an important role, too, because they are used for a significant amount of decision making in organizations and many social relationships are established ... We would like to point out that increased research in the field of informal meetings will shed significant light on the institutional accomplishments of formal meetings (Asmuß & Svennevig 2009: 10).

The authors claim that research on informal meetings has been missed and more and more research on informal meetings is expected.

4.2 Formal meetings (*kaigi*) and informal meetings (*uchiawase/miitingu*)

In the previous section, it was found that degree of formality is a crucial dimension which characterises different types of meetings, and that formal and informal meetings have distinctive characteristics respectively. In this section, I introduce the relevant Japanese terminology that distinguishes between formal informal meetings in the Japanese context.

While the English word *meeting* is employed to refer to both formal and informal meetings, in Japanese, there are two different terms. *Meeting* in English can be translated as *kaigi*, *uchiawase* or *miitingu* in Japanese.

Kaigi is translated into "meeting" in the *Shin Wa-ei Dai Jiten* (Japanese-English Dictionary, fifth edition, Kenkyusha, 2004) and as "to gather and discuss to decide something" in the *Kojien* (Japanese-Japanese dictionary, fifth edition, Iwanami Shoten, 2005, translated by the researcher).

Uchiawase is translated as "preliminary discussions, advance arrangements, and briefing session" in the *Shin Wa-ei Dai Jiten* (Japanese-English Dictionary, the fifth edition, Kenkyusha, 2004) and as "preliminary discussions" in the *Kojien* (Japanese-Japanese dictionary, the fifth edition, Iwanami Shoten, 2005, translated by the researcher). *Miitingu*, which is borrowed from the English word "meeting", is interchangeable with and is defined as "a relatively small gathering/meeting" in the *Daijisen* (Japanese-Japanese dictionary, Shogakukan, 2006, translated by the researcher).

While it is difficult to identify differences among *kaigi*, *uchiawase*, and *miitingu* from the definitions above, interviews with my colleagues and friends and my intuition suggest that, in everyday conversations, *kaigi* tends to be used to refer to a formal meeting, while *uchiawase* and *miitingu* tend to be used to refer to an informal meeting. This is also supported by the meeting data for the present research. Formal meetings which share common features with those of formal meetings discussed in the previous section are called *kaigi* by meeting participants. On the other hand, informal meetings which share common features with those of informal meetings discussed in the previous section are called *uchiawase* or *miitingu* as demonstrated in examples 4.1 and 4.2. In example 4.1, when Tanimoto is going into a room where an informal meeting is conducted, he calls the meeting "*miitingu*" (marked in bold by the researcher) as shown in line 4.

Example 4.1 [JIF03_05, 03:30]
1	Tanimoto:	ああ こんにちは
		aa konnichiwa
		hello
2		先日はどうもありがとうございました
		senjitsu wa doomo arigatoo gozaimashita
		thank you very much for the other day
3	Ashizawa:	今ちょっと
		ima chotto
		well
→ 4	Tanimoto:	ミーティング中なんですね
		miitingu chuu na n desu ne
		you are having an informal meeting aren't you?

Reference to the same informal meeting is also shown in example 4.2 below.

Example 4.2 [JFM03_01, 28:30]
1	Yoshioka:	まだ到着してない？
		mada toochaku shite nai?
		hasn't anyone come?

2　Baba:　まだ誰も来てない
　　　　　　mada dare mo kite nai
　　　　　　nobody has come yet
→ 3　　　　社長のところの打ち合わせが
　　　　　　shachoo no tokoro no uchiawase ga
　　　　　　an informal meeting with CEO
4　Yoshioka:　あっちで？
　　　　　　atchi de?
　　　　　　over there?
5　Baba:　はい
　　　　　　hai
　　　　　　yes

In example 4.2, when Baba is waiting for other formal meeting members to arrive, another member, Yoshioka, is already present. They are talking about the same informal meeting as in example 4.1. Baba refers to this informal meeting as "*uchiawase*" in line 3 (marked in bold by the researcher). The examples suggest that *uchiawase* and *miitingu* are interchangeable. This reflects linguistic reality. In other words, what was found in the authentic interactions in terms of relative formality is matched by the use of different terms, *kaigi* (formal meetings) and *uchiawase* or *miitingu* (informal meetings), to refer to the different concepts.

In this research, adapting characteristics of the definitions in the previous literature, I propose the following working definitions of formal meetings and informal meetings. A formal meeting is defined as one that has a specific name, a formal chairperson, an agenda, a pre-arranged starting time, a specific venue, and also that is routinely held, larger in number, and translated into *kaigi* in Japanese. On the other hand, an informal meeting is defined as one that does not have a specific name, a chairperson, a pre-arranged starting time, nor a

	Formal meeting *kaigi*	Informal meeting *uchiawase/miitingu*
Name	specific name	no specific name
Chairperson	formal chairperson	no formal chairperson
Agenda	agenda	no agenda
Venue	specific venue	no specific venue
Regularity	routinely held	not routinely held
Numbers	larger in number	smaller in number

Table 4.2: Summary of definitions of formal meetings (*kaigi*) and informal meetings (*uchiawase/miitingu*)

specific venue, and also that is not routinely held, and is translated as *uchiawase* or *miitingu* in Japanese. These working definitions are shown in the following table:

I acknowledge that not all formal and informal meetings conform to the above characteristics, and also that these two types are not always binary oppositions (e.g., Bargiela-Chiappini & Harris 1997a; Holmes & Stubbe 2003). However, it is reasonable to assume that formal meetings and informal meetings have different characteristics and functions especially as they are described by different terms in Japanese. How has previous research on Japanese meetings addressed this? In the next section, this question is considered.

4.3 Meetings in Japanese

To date, to the best of my knowledge, there is only a handful of research which focusses on meetings in Japanese. These include Kondo (e.g., 2005) and Geyer (2008) both of which focus on Japanese meetings, and Yamada (e.g., 1997) which analysed meetings in Japanese and English. In this section, these studies are introduced to examine if they make a distinction between *kaigi* (formal meeting) and *uchiawase/miitingu* (informal meetings).

Kondo (2005) undertook qualitative research focussing on a Japanese business meeting in terms of topic structure. Drawing on a 30-minute recording of a business meeting involving five participants from two different companies in Japan, she points out its characteristics. The most prominent feature is that the flow of the discussion is circular or spiral. Following Murakami and Kumatoridani (1995), the author categorises topics in a meeting into the following three types: new topics, derived (related to the previous topic), and recycled topics (related to the topics mentioned before in the meeting). The analysis results revealed 33 new topics (out of 73 topics), the remaining being derivation or recycled topics. The author points out that many occurrences of recycled topics resulted in a longer meeting. She also points out that there were no explicit topic transitional markers. To conclude, Kondo (2005) supports Yamada (1990, 1992) in that topic structure in Japanese meetings is spiral and topic shift is often used to avoid conflict with other participants. In her research, however, the author analysed only one meeting and her results cannot necessarily be generalised and applied to other Japanese meetings. She does not categorise the meeting into *kaigi* or *uchiawase/miitingu* nor mention this distinction.

Geyer (2008) analysed six faculty meetings involving six to seven people at Japanese secondary schools. She focusses on such discursive practices as collaborative disagreement, teasing, talking about troubles, and event description, to explore how interlocutors construct, display, and manage their discursive face in Japanese institutional talk. Though Geyer's (2008) data consists of authentic meetings, she does not conduct any literature review on meetings in her research. She does not categorise the meeting into *kaigi* or *uchiawase/miitingu* nor mention these two kinds of meetings.

A series of research of Yamada (1990, 1992, 1994, 1997a, 1997b) analysed meetings both in Japanese and English. The author conducted cross-cultural analysis between Americans and Japanese by analysing intra- and inter-cultural meetings. Her data can be summarised in the following table:

		Number of members	Nationality	Duration
1	Account executives' meeting	3	American	27 min
2	Section heads' meeting (*Kachookai*)	3	Japanese	20 min
3	Personnel meeting	2	American Japanese	28 min
4	Corporate banking meeting	4	2 American 2 Japanese	46 min

Table 4.3: The meeting data in Yamada's series of research[1]

Her primary data is the first two intra-meetings (No. 1 and No. 2 in table 4.3), both of which are bank officers' meetings conducted in English (No. 1) and in Japanese (No. 2) at different banks in the U.S. As backup data, two inter-cultural meetings (No. 3 and No. 4 in table 4.3) are presented. Both of them were conducted in English between Japanese and Americans held at the same bank where the Japanese meeting was recorded.

Yamada (1990, 1992) examined differences between American and Japanese topic-opening strategies and differences in topic shifts. Her data shows that the American business people tend to be more direct and straightforward in topic management than their Japanese counterparts. That is, the Americans are likely to raise a topic and conclude it verbally, while the Japanese tend to co-create topics and leave them open. Yamada (1990, 1992) contends that these differences reflect the underlying expectations for interaction in each country, within-group independence for Americans, and non-confrontation, or harmony for Japanese. As a result, the Japanese meeting appears to have a more casual, personal style than the American meeting.

Yamada (1997b) acknowledges *uchiawase* as a special type of meeting in the following:

[F]or the Japanese, personal conversation is often at the core of each interaction. *Uchiawase*, for example, are meetings in which managers

sound out the views and positions of the employees on a variety of eclectic topics. Because these meetings are informal, they are thought to produce more honest opinions about business proposals in circulation, and decision based on employee endorsement is thought to be more successful.
(Yamada 1997b: 122)

Yamada (1997b) classifies a small meeting among three Japanese managers in her data as *uchiawase* and contrasts it with another small meeting among three American managers in English. The author calls the former a relationship-driven meeting and the latter a task-driven meeting. Though these two meetings are similar in size, whether other components that constitute the meetings are similar or not is not mentioned except for the agenda, which is present in the American meeting but absent in the Japanese meeting. Considering what has been discussed so far in this chapter, it is reasonable to think this difference — whether there is an agenda or not — would be likely to affect meeting structure.

Though Yamada's series of research found interesting differences between Americans and Japanese communicative behaviours, the following three problems could be identified in her contentions. First, it is not reasonable to generalise what she found and apply her findings to all Japanese business meetings since she analysed only a limited amount of data, especially focussing on small meetings. Next, as discussed in the previous sections, meetings play an important role from a relational perspective. It is not reasonable to label Japanese meetings as relational-driven but American meetings as task-driven because the American meetings also inevitably have relational aspects. Moreover though she introduces *uchiawase* in her analysis, her classification is only based on size (the number of participants) and does not take account of other dimensions related to the classification according to the formality discussed in this chapter.

The discussion so far has provided a rationale for conducting contrastive analysis between formal and informal meetings. Though there are different terms to refer to formal meetings and informal meetings respectively in Japanese, no researchers have undertaken contrastive research on *kaigi* (formal meetings) and *uchiawase/miitingu* (informal meetings). It is evident that this is an important distinction that has not been recognised before in research on Japanese meetings. Moreover, as discussed in the previous chapters, the present research is the only empirical cross-cultural study regarding meetings in New Zealand and Japan. Thus it is worthwhile to conduct this contrastive research, i.e. (1) meetings in New Zealand and Japan, and (2) formal and informal meetings.

4.4 Meetings from a relational perspective

The primary purpose of meetings is to accomplish goals for the organisations (e.g., Bargiela-Chiappini & Harris 1997a; Holmes & Stubbe 2003; Tracy & Dimock 2004). Meetings undoubtedly involve transactional activities such as making decisions, solving problems, and giving information. The transactional aspects of interaction play important roles in meetings. Thus most of the previous research on meetings has focussed on transactional aspects, including a variety of topics. They include decision making (Yeung 2000; Huisman 2001; Marra 2003); negotiating (Dannerer 2001; Bennington et al. 2003), common agreement (Barnes 2007), questions in meetings (Ford 2010), topic management (Bargiela-Chiappini 1997a; Hanak 1998; Du-Babcock 1999), management of meetings (Linde 1991), and turn-taking (Boden 1994, Kjaerbeck 1998; Larrue & Trognan 1993; Silva 1994). However, in addition to the transactional goals, meetings also serve a relational function. Meetings are the sites for the manifestation of power and politeness (Holmes & Stubbe 2003).

As pointed in Bargiela-Chiappini and Harris (2006) and Asmuß and Svennevig (2009) and noted earlier, a large amount of extensive empirical research on meetings from a relational perspective has been conducted by researchers from the LWP.[2] Holmes and Stubbe (2003: 64) contend that meetings typically have "less obvious, frequently unacknowledged and relatively unconscious politeness functions and social objectives." These include maintaining and strengthening collegiality and rapport, serving to create team spirit. As discussed in Chapter 2, small talk and humour, both of which are the present study's focuses, are two exemplary Relational Practice strategies to which the LWP researchers have given extensive attention in their analysis of meetings (e.g., Holmes & Marra 2002a, 2002b; Chan 2005). They found that Relational Practice practices are manifested in particular phases of the meeting structure. They tend to occur around topic transitional points as well as at the opening and closing phases of meetings. Their research findings indicate that analysing Relational Practice strategies in meetings requires paying attention to meeting structures not only at the macro level but also the micro level. Thus, as a preliminary step, it is important to look at how formal and informal meetings are structured before analysing small talk and humour in meetings.

4.5 Structures

4.5.1 Macro structures

In the empirical studies on meetings, researchers agree on the identification of the three phases of meetings (Mintzberg 1973; Fisher 1982; Boden 1994; Solitt-Morris 1996; Bargiela-Chiappini & Harris 1997a; Marra 1998; Holmes & Stubbe 2003). They are: (1) opening, (2) main discussion, and (3) closing – though the authors may label these phases with slightly different terms.

The opening phases are often ritualised and conventionalised (Chan 2005; Schnurr, Marra & Holmes 2007). The opening sequences of meetings can be generalised from Boden (1994), Sollitt-Morris (1996), Marra (1998, 2008a) and Chan (2005) in the following way:

> A pause → Transitional marker → An indication of meeting start → An introduction to the first topic

The discourse markers for topic transition include *okay, um, so, alright, anyway*, and so on (Sollitt-Morris 1996; Marra 1998, 2008a; Chan 2005). The opening phases are generally initiated by the chairperson or another meeting participant with relevant authority (Bargiela-Chiappini & Harris 1997a; Chan 2005). This means that they are "invested with the unconditional power" (Bargiela-Chiappini & Harris 1997a: 209). At the same time, Chan's (2005) empirical research demonstrated that the meeting opening and closing are also collaboratively produced with participants' cooperation.

The next phase is the main discussion section "where the issues are more fully developed in an open-ended way" (Holmes & Stubbe 2003: 66). Thus this phase is typically the longest and the most complex in meetings. While the chair is in charge in the opening phases, other participants are allowed to initiate interaction in this phase (Bargiela-Chiappini & Harris 1997a).

The last section is the closing phase, which also comprises routinised sequences (Chan 2005; Bargiela-Chiappini & Harris 1997a). As in the opening phases, the chair initiates the closing section (Bargiela-Chiappini & Harris 1997a). At this stage, the issue is usually resolved at least temporarily or a consensus is reached or decision is made (Marra 1998; Holmes & Stubbe 2003). The closing sequences of meetings can be generalised from Boden (1994), Marra (1998, 2008a) and Chan (2005) in the following way:

> End of the last topic → A noticeable pause → Pre-closing (request for other business) → An indication of meeting closing

While these three phases are generalised in meetings, Chan (2005) adds two more phases to the three sections mentioned so far. She identifies "the pre-meeting section" as the period that "begins with the arrival of the first participant at the meeting rooms and lasts until the initiation of meeting opening" (2005: 99), and "the post-meeting section" as the period that "begins with the closing of the meeting and extends to the departure of the last participant from the meeting room" (2005: 99). Chan's (2005) categorisation of meeting structure is shown in the following way:

Figure 4.1: An illustration of the five sections of a meeting

(from Chan 2005: 90)

As pointed out by Mintzberg (1973), Boden (1994), and Asmuß and Svennevig (2009), meeting participants usually engage in informal conversation before meetings start and immediately after meetings close. Taking into consideration that this research focusses on small talk and humour, which are considered as typical Relational Practice strategies (Holmes & Marra 2004), the three sections (the opening, the main discussion, the closing) are not enough and this study follows Chan's (2005) five sections including pre-meeting and post-meeting.

In terms of the macro-structure of informal meetings, there is little detailed mention except Boden (1994) and Bargiela-Chiappini and Harris (1997a). Boden (1994) classifies meetings into formal and informal, and indicates that a structural characteristic of informal meeting openings and closings is that they can be unmarked and unclear. However, in her analysis, she does not divide the meeting data into formal and informal categories but the analysis results are shown according to the kinds of organisations such as a hospital or travel agency, or the kinds of meetings such as staff meeting, council, or research sales meeting.

Bargiela-Chiappini and Harris (1997a) state that the chair and the meeting participants cooperate in the openings and closings of informal meetings. The authors also found that the chair tended to exert little control over the interaction in the main discussion phase in informal meetings. However, their analysis focus is only one informal meeting and it is difficult to generalise their analysis to the structure of informal meetings.

4.5.2 Micro structures (topic progressions)

In the previous section, I have described how previous research on meetings has identified the structures of formal and informal meetings at the macro level. In this section, meeting structures at the micro level, i.e. topic structures, are addressed.

In analysing authentic meetings in the LWP corpus, Holmes and Stubbe (2003) identified two general types of topical structures: a linear pattern and a spiral pattern. They also found that both formal and informal meetings can have both aspects of these two topic structural types within them. According to Holmes and Stubbe (2003), in the linear topic organisation, topics are arranged according to an agenda, and reporting back or information gathering meetings are likely take this structure. There are also cases where off-topic talk is tolerated by the chair and/or the participants with a basic linear topic progression still identified. In the spiral topic organisation, on the other hand, the same point is often repeated several times, "each time receiving a little more discussion and taking the argument a little further" (Holmes & Stubbe 2003: 69). Planning meetings and brainstorming meetings tend to follow this pattern.

Holmes and Stubbe (2003) also point out a correlation between the goals or functions of a meeting, the relationship among meeting participants, and the characteristic structural pattern. According to them, for example, with regard to problem-solved or task-focussed meetings, the linear structural pattern is likely to occur when a problem requires logical consideration. If the problem seeks more creative thinking and new solutions, a spiral structure is favoured as brain-storming would be required.

Regardless of the types of meetings, the chair and/or another person with authority has the greatest influence on managing interaction or controlling its development in meetings, though the degree depends on the meeting type (Holmes & Stubbe 2003; Bargiela-Chiappini & Harris 1997a; Asmuß & Svennevig 2009). They employ such strategies as introducing topics on the agenda, closing topics by summarising discussions, and keeping the discussion on track (Bargiela-Chiappini & Harris 1997a; Holmes & Stubbe 2003; Asmuß & Svennevig 2009).

Asmuß and Svennevig (2009) give an interesting comment on topic orientation. In contrast to informal conversation, where every new contribution is locally relevant to the prior contribution (Schegloff & Sacks 1973), in meetings the participants may connect their utterances not to the previous speaker but to the agenda topic under discussion or to a contribution by another participant earlier in the discussion. Asmuß and Svennevig (2009: 169) state that, "Topic organization in meetings is not merely a local phenomenon but also a matter of orienting to the 'global' topic represented by the agenda."

In this section, research regarding meeting structures both at the macro and at the micro level has been reviewed. Since the distributions of small talk and humour are strongly related to meeting structures, the data set will be explored in relation to formal and informal meetings at company N and company J later in this chapter (see section 4.7). However, before examining the meeting structures, the meetings in the data set are described in the following section.

4.6 Meetings in this study

As introduced in Chapter 3, the meeting dataset for this study consists of a total of 16 meetings, nine from company N in New Zealand and seven from company J in Japan. Using the working definition of formal and informal meeting discussed in section 4.2, both kinds of meetings have been selected. From company N, there are three formal meetings and six informal meetings. Meetings from company J consist of three formal meetings and four informal meetings. The summary of the meeting data set is shown again below:

		Company N	Company J
Formal meetings	Number	3	3
	Participants	10-11	16
	Total recording time	275 min	479 min
Informal meetings	Number	6	4
	Participants	2 - 3	3 - 5
	Total recording time	97 min	229 min

Table 4.4: Summary of dataset (same as Table 3.1)

In the following section, meetings at each company are compared and contrasted according to the two types outlined in this chapter – formal and informal.

4.6.1 Meetings at company N[3]

Formal meetings at company N, a production company, were called management meetings and held once a month in a specific meeting room. The participants included the CEO and general managers from various sections such as production, sales, marketing and finance. The role of chair was assigned to Jaeson, the general manager. In the meetings, each manager reported to the group as a "catch up" for meeting members. The meetings can be categorised as a reporting type meeting. Each meeting lasted approximately one hour to two hours.

Informal meetings at company N, on the other hand, have contrasting components from those of formal meetings. For example, they did not have a specific name, a pre-determined chair, and were not routinely held. They did not have a specific venue but were held in the company office. The participants were not fixed and varied each time, but all of them involved the target participants as a selection criterion. The informal meetings include catch-up, brain-storming, and briefing meetings. They were much shorter than the formal meetings in my data. Details of informal meetings at company N are summarised in the following table:

Data No.	Participants	Duration
NIF01_05	3 (Jaeson, Seamus, Rob)	24 min.
NIF02_07	2 (Jaeson, Rob)	15 min.
NIF03_10	2 (Jaeson, Sharon)	12 min.
NIF04_13	3 (Jaeson, Sharon, Anna)	13 min.
NIF05_14	2 (Jaeson, Rob)	16 min.
NIF06_0214	2 (Jaeson, Paul)	17 min.

Table 4.5: Details of informal meetings at company N
(Target participants are shown in bold.)

4.6.2 Meetings at company J[4]

Formal meetings at company J had very similar characteristics to those of company N. They were called "sales strategy meetings," *hanbai senryaku kaigi* in Japanese, whose name included *kaigi* – formal meeting. These formal meetings were also held regularly, once a month in a specific meeting room. The participants included the CEO, sales director, system development director, business consultant, outside director, sales staff, and system development staff. The role of chairperson was assigned to Ashizawa, the sales director. In the meetings, each sales staff member reported to the group like company N. The only difference from formal meetings at company N is duration. The formal meetings at company J were longer than those at company N. Each formal meeting at company J lasted from two hours to more than three hours.

The informal meetings at company J also had very similar characteristics to those of company N. They had characteristics which contrasted with formal meetings. For example, they did not have a pre-determined chairperson, and were not routinely held. Though they did not have specific names, all informal meetings were referred to as *uchiawase* or *miitingu*. The participants were not fixed and varied each time but all involved the target participants. The difference in the Japanese informal meetings is the venue. Some informal meetings were held at company J's office, while others were held outside. One was held at a restaurant and another at the consulting firm where Tanimoto and Manabe work. Details of informal meetings at company J are summarised in the following table:

Data No.	Participants	Duration
JIF01_01	3 (Ashizawa, Tanimoto, Nio)	63 min.
JIF02_02	5 (Ashizawa, Tanimoto, Manabe, Yoshioka, Fukawa)	65 min
JIF03_05	5 (Ashizawa, Tanimoto, Manabe, Komeda, Hosoi)	36min
JIF04_22	6 (Ashizawa, Tanimoto, Manabe, Hosoi, Wada, Sumiyoshi)	65min

Table 4.6: Details of informal meetings at company J
(Target participants are shown in bold.)

In summary, while formal and informal meetings contrast with each other, each type has very similar characteristics at company N and company J.

4.7 Structural characteristics of formal/informal meetings

In this section, the structural characteristics of formal and informal meetings at both companies are analysed. As discussed in sections 4.4 and 4.5, identifying the structural characteristics of the meetings for this research is an important prerequisite to analysing small talk and humour.

4.7.1 Formal meetings

The formal meeting data is all video-recorded and is all of a reporting type. First impressions suggested a clear contrast between the quieter (surface) manners of meetings at company J and the louder (surface) manners at company N. In all of the meetings at company N, the interactions were louder and the pace was also faster than in the Japanese meetings. Overlapping also occurred much more often at company N's meetings than those at company J.

Despite this first impression, the structure of formal meetings at both CoPs is generally similar. Overall, the structures of formal meetings at both company N and company J correspond with the five sections proposed by Chan (2005). That is, the meetings consist of pre-meeting, opening, main discussion, closing, and post-meeting. The structural characteristics of formal meetings are illustrated following these five sections and contrasted.

Pre-meeting

In the pre-meeting sections, there are occurrences of small talk in both formal meetings at company N and company J, which is consistent with Chan's (2005) formal meeting data from New Zealand and Hong Kong.[5]

Opening

As shown in section 4.5.1, a synthesis of the literature suggests that meeting opening sections consist of the following three components: (1) a pause, (2) transitional marker, and (3) an indication of the meeting start. The opening sections of the formal meeting data at both companies generally consist of these three components. The following is an example of an opening section of company N's formal meeting.

Example 4.3 [NFM02_04, 08:30]   (Cf. Example 6.1)

1	Seamus:	is that now who are we waiting for
2	Jaeson:	just Harry
3	Veronica:	Harry
4	XM:	/Rob\
5	XM:	/Harry\ /Rob\
6	Jaeson:	/Rob's\ coming [drawls]: in:
7	Veronica:	is Rob coming
8	Jaeson:	bit later
9	XM:	what about [name] +
10	Jaeson:	he'll join us in a bit
11	Seamus:	can't wait forever
→ 12	Jaeson:	+okay ++ get into it + okay
13		thanks everyone for coming along
14		just like to welcome our newest member
15		to the management team + Darryl
16		+ who's now serving as the er pre press manager
17		and um we have a new i s manager
18		⋯ [*about 2 minutes deleted*]

→ 19 Jaeson: okay just going back over the previous minutes
  20   um I there's nothing really
  21   to cover off there was just one question
  22   I had that came up last time …

In line 12, Jaeson, the chair, starts the meeting. Following a pause and a transitional marker "okay", he starts with "get into it", which explicitly shows the meeting start. These three components are also found in the other formal meetings at company N. "Okay" and "alright" are typical transitional markers in the opening sections (see also Marra 2003). In addition to these components, other characteristics are common among the three formal meetings. From lines 1 to 10, an attendance check is carried out. The attendance check is also typical of opening sections (Boden 1994; Chan 2005). This kind of verbal head counting of participants including apologies by absent people is found before the meetings starts in all three meetings at company N.

Another common feature among the formal meetings at company N is that checking the previous meeting's minutes is the first item on the agenda. In example 4.3, after starting the meeting in line 12, Jaeson introduces new staff members in lines 13-17. Following these lines, in the section of transcript omitted (in line 18, see example 6.1 in Chapter 6) members are talking about introducing new staff in a humorous tone. Then, Jaeson stops the digression and returns to the meeting topic, checking the previous minutes in line 19. In the two remaining formal meetings, too, the first item on the agenda is checking the previous meeting's minutes. Consistent with the previous literature (e.g., Chan 2005), the opening section is routinised and the chair is in charge of progress. Attendance checking, however, is carried out by the chair and members cooperatively.

An interesting point in example 4.3 is that Seamus, the CEO, plays an influential role. While overall Jaeson, the chair, is in charge of progressing the interaction, precisely when to start the meeting is decided by the CEO's utterance in line 11. When Jaeson is wondering if they should wait for a member who has not come yet, Seamus, the CEO, proposes not to wait anymore. Following this remark, Jaeson declares the meeting open in line 12.

The formal meetings at company J have similar characteristics to those of company N. The following is an example of an opening section of company N's formal meeting.

Example 4.4 [JFM02_01,18:30]
  1   Ashizawa: はい (見渡して) 細井さん？
                 hai [looking around] Hosoi san?
                 well [looking around] Mr.Hosoi?

2	Komeda:	うん？
		un?
		well?
3	Ashizawa:	まだですね
		mada desu ne
		hasn't yet come
4		(10.0)
5		どこ行きはったんやろ？
		doko iki hatta n yaro?
		where is he now?
6	Komeda:	もう来るやろう
		mo kuru yaroo
		he will be coming soon
7		始めたら？
		hajimetara?
		how about starting?
8		(4.0)
9	Ashizawa:	いいですか？
		ii desu ka?
		all right?
→ 10		++ じゃあ はい あのー 販売戦略会議 えー始めます
		++ *jaa hai anoo Hanbaisenryaku kaigi ee hajimemasu*
		++ okay well let's start the sales strategy meeting now
11		じゃあ あのー 私の方からですね いきます
		jaa anoo watashi no hoo kara desu ne ikimasu
		okay well it's my turn I'll start
12		えー [会社名] ですね…
		ee [company name] desu ne…
		well I'll talk about [company name] …

In line 10, Ashizawa, the chair, starts the meeting. Following a pause and a combination of transitional markers, *jaa hai* 'okay then',[6] he starts with *hajimemasu* 'let's start', which explicitly expresses the meeting opening. These three components are also found in the other formal meetings at company N. *Hai* 'okay/yes' and *jaa* 'then' are typical transitional markers found at the opening sections. As seen line 1 to line 6 in example 4.4, the attendance check is also found in this formal meeting.

An interesting point in the Japanese example is that Komeda, the CEO, plays an influential role similar to that found in the New Zealand data (cf. also Chan 2005). While overall Ashizawa, the chair, is in charge of interaction progress, the CEO's utterances make explicit when the meeting should start. When

Ashizawa is wondering where meeting member Hosoi is, Komeda, the CEO, proposes to start in line 7. Following this remark, Ashizawa declares the meeting start in line 10.

There are two differences between company N's and company J's formal meetings. The first difference is that the chair explicitly announces the meeting name when the meeting starts. In example 4.4, Ashizawa, the chair, labels *hanbai senryaku kaigi* 'sales strategy meeting' when starting the meeting. In the other two meetings, too, he starts with introducing the meeting name at the opening. It could be argued that meeting opening is expressed explicitly and formally in the Japanese formal meeting data.[7] The other difference is that the previous meeting's minutes are not mentioned during the opening section.[8]

To summarise, the opening phases across the CofPs consist of the similar three components. The words in these phases tend to be formulaic in each CofP and, especially at company J, the openings sound formal. While the chair takes an initiative role through the phases, attendance checking is co-constructed together with the meeting members and the CEO plays an influential role across the CofPs.

Main discussion

Following the opening section, in both meetings, the reports start. The formal meetings of the two CofPs are report-type meetings. In the formal meetings at company N, each manager reports their section's situation or issues to the other members and these are discussed. In the formal meetings at company J, each member of sales staff reports about how their sales are progressing, including clients' situations, to other participants, who discuss them. In both meetings, question and answer sessions and discussion sessions are sometimes found during a report. These digressions are found more often in the meetings at company N.

In the formal meetings at company J, a report follows soon after the opening section. In the formal meetings at company N, on the other hand, humourous sequences accompanied by laughter occur around the first agenda item, checking the previous minutes, before the reports begin.[9]

In the formal meetings both at company N and at company J, topic transitions, or change of those reporting, are easy to find. This is because transitional markers explicitly indicate the transition points. In the formal meetings at company N, Jaeson, the chair, manages topic shifts. The order of reports seems to be fixed roughly in advance, but Jaeson often explicitly states who should speak ne   xt as shown in the following example:

Example 4.5 [NFM01_02, 55:20]
 1   Seamus: ⋯ Paul's team's gonna be encouraged

2		to pick it up to five hundred runs
3		and the stuff that we've traditionally called
4		nuisance value
5	XM:	mm
→ 6		(6.0)
→ 7	Jaeson:	okay [sighs] (5.0) Rob
8		we'll go back to health and safety after/wards\
9	Rob:	/[clears throat]\ [clears throat] + um thank you +++
10		um + we start to er + get to actually to to doing
11		things now [name]'s started full time on Tuesday···

In example 4.5, at the beginning, meetings members are talking about a manager's report. In line 6, the silence indicates the topic termination. Then, in lines 7 and 8, Jaeson changes the order of the next reports. The report about health and safety should be next, but he points to Rob, the business development manager. Then, Rob expresses appreciation for moving his report to an earlier position than expected. Among typical transition markers are "okay" and "alright", the same as found in the opening section. Silence also serves as a typical transitional marker as shown in example 4.5, as does thanking as shown in the following example.

Example 4.6 [NFM01_02, 86:2]

1	Rob:	···you know I'm quite confident I'm gonna enjoy
2		working with him on it +++
→ 3	Jaeson:	[tut] thank you Rob (um) Veronica
4		do you wanna give us a touch on health and safe/ty\
5	Veronica:	/oh well\ there's not really very much at all
6		since December we just got three injuries of sprain

In example 4.6, Rob, the business development manager, is talking about a potential franchiser to sell their company's products. After a short pause, Jaeson expresses his gratitude to Rob in line 3, which also serves as transitional marker.

Topic transitions are indicated mainly by the chair, but sometimes reports express these shifts. There are cases where they finish their reports explicitly as shown in the following example.

Example 4.7 [NFM02_04, 22:10]

1	Evan:	okay that's pretty much it unless anyone's got
→ 2		any questions about the accounts
3		(4.0)

→ 4   Jaeson   okay Paul

In example 4.7, Evan finishes his report explicitly in line 2 by asking meeting members whether they have questions about his report. Following silence in line 3, Jaeson employs "okay", a typical transition marker adding here, and points to the next speaker, Paul in line 4. Here, a reporter and the chair cooperatively make a smooth topic shift.

At the formal meetings at company J, since the order of reports tends to be fixed in advance, the reporters voluntarily initiate and/or finish their turns by themselves unless digressions such as question/answer or discussion sessions occur. The following is an example of topic transition.

Example 4.8 [JFM01_01, 12:30]
1	Wada:	そこらへんも含めて定期的にはやっています
		sokorahen mo fukumete teikitki ni wa yatteimasu
		including those I regularly provide [with *the necessary information*]
→ 2		はい 以上です
		hai ijoo desu
		okay that's it
3		(2.0)
4	Chida:	えーと じゃあ 私の担当分で
		eeto jaa watashi no tantoo bun de
		well then regarding my client
5		[会社名] さんが 開発の方は 今 [苗字] 課長を中心で進めて て…
		[company name] *san ga kaihatsu no hoo wa ima* [name] *kachoo o chuushin de susumetete*
		as for [company name] in system development now [name] manager is in charge and we are progressing

In example 4.8, Wada finishes his report in line 2 by saying *hai ijoo desu* 'okay, that's it'. Then following silence in line 3, Chida begins his report in line 4. In the formal meetings at company J, reporters tend to finish their reports by saying *ijoo desu* 'that's it' and/or employing a topic transtional marker *hai* 'yes/okay'. Following that, the initiation of the report is indicated by such transitional markers as *hai* 'yes/okay', *etto* 'well', and *jaa* 'then'. In this way, at this CofP, topic transitions are cooperatively and smoothly constructed between reporters.

On the other hand, when digressions or discussions occur around transitional phases, Ashizawa, the chair, returns to the agenda as shown in the following example.

Example 4.9 [JFM01_04, 27:40]

1	Kanda:	…あのー 経理の取締役とも話をしたことがあるということで
		…anoo keiri no torishimariyaku to mo hanashi o shita koto ga aru to iu koto de
		…well I have talked with accounting director
2		あのー [製品名] につないでいきたいと思います
		anoo[product name] ni tsunai de ikitai to omoimasu
		well I would like to promote [prodoct name]
→ 3		私からは以上です
		watashi kara wa ijoo desu
		that's it
4	Hosoi:	[会社名] って黒字が出ているうちに両方売っちゃった方がいいんじゃない？ [笑]
		[company name]tte kuroji ga deteiru uchi ni ryoohoo utchatta hoo ga ii n ja nai? [laughs]
		while [company name] is in good economical condition it would be better to sell both [of our products] wouldn't it?
5		[笑いがおこる]
		[laughter]
6		… [about 2 minutes deleted]
7		Ashizawa: 金が出えへんから支援はしませんよ という話はしたけど [笑]
		kane ga deehen kara shien wa shimasen yo to iu hanashi wa shita kedo[laughs]
		I said that since they didn't pay we would not support them [laughs]
8		[笑いがおこる]
		[laughter]
→ 9	Ashizawa:	はい
		hai
		okay
10		Sumiyoshi: はい えー 私からですが
		hai ee watashi kara desu ga
		okay well then, from me
11		[会社名] さん 前回お話しした人材派遣の会社です…
		[company name]san zenkai ohanashi shita jinzai haken no kaisha desu
		[company name] it is a staff service company which I also

mentioned last time

In example 4.9, after Kanda's report finishes in line 3, members start to talk about his client in a humorous way. This digression lasts about two minutes (in line 6), and then Ashizawa ends the digression by employing a transitional marker *hai* 'yes/okay' in line 9.

Regarding transitional markers, one difference is that thanking does not serve as a transitional marker at company J. There is no occurrence of expressing gratitude from the chair to any reporter after they finish their reports. Another prominent feature at company J is that each participant starts their reports with their client's name following a transitional marker as found in line 5 in example 4.8 and in line 11 in example 4.9. It is interesting to find that this corresponds with "name one's own deal" (Yamada 1997: 123) categorised as a conspicuous characteristic of "the task driven American meeting" (Yamada 1997: 122).

In sum, not only transitional markers but also silence signals topic transitions across the CofPs. At company N, the chair mainly manages the flow of the discussion phases, while at company J, reporters manage it themselves probably because the order of reports tends to be fixed. However, in the case of digressions, the chair returns the discussion to meeting talk. The examples in this section have demonstrated that smooth topic transitions are co-constructed between the chair and the meeting members and also among meeting members with the assistance of topic transitional markers.

Closing

The previous literature agrees that the closing sequences of meetings consist of: (1) end of the last topic, (2) a noticeable pause, (3) preclosing (request for other business), and (4) an indication of the meeting closing. The closing sections of the formal meetings at both company N and company J generally conform to this pattern although they do not correspond to them completely. The following is an example of a closing section of a formal meeting at company N.

Example 4.10 [NFM02_04, 67:00]
```
    1   Jaeson:     okay any general business
    2               (  )point people want to bring up
    3               ···[about 6 minutes deleted]
    4   Paul:       ···then it's a three month project
→   5               it really is knowing what we know now so
    6               (11.0)
    7   Jaeson:     okay + thanks everybody
```

In line 1, Jaeson, the chair, asks members whether there is other business. Subsequently, members talk about other business related matters and the discussion continues for about six minutes (in line 3) and comes to an end in line 5. Then silence follows and Jaeson enacts the meeting closing. In two out of a total of three formal meetings at company N, following a short pause, the chair says "thank you", which indicates the meeting closing, and nobody responds to it.

The following is an example of closing at company J's formal meeting.

Example 4.11 [JFM03_07, 05:05]

1	Ashizawa:	はい ちょっとスタートの時間もちょっと遅れて
		hai chotto sutaato no jikan mo chotto okurete
		okay the starting time was a little late
2		時間もおしまして申し訳ないんですけど
		jikan mo oshimashite mooshiwake nai n desu kedo
		sorry time's up
3		一応次回は8月の24日を
		ichioo jikai wa hachigatu nijuu yokka o
		next meeting will be on 24th on August
4	XM:	来月ね
		raigetsu ne
		next month
5	Ashizawa:	予定してます
		yotei shitemasu
		we are planning
6	XM:	来月ですね
		raigetsu desu ne
		next month isn't it?
7	Ashizawa:	ということで よろしいでしょうか (6.0)
		to iukoto de yoroshii de shoo ka (6.0)
		is it fine?
8	Komeda:	時間は？
		jikan wa?
		time?
9	Ashizawa:	いつもと同じ6時から
		itsumo to onaji rokuji kara
		at six o'clock as usual
10	XMs:	はい
		hai
		okay
11	Ashizawa:	よろしいでしょうか ++

		yoroshii de shoo ka++
		are you happy about that?++
→	12	はい じゃあ すみません お疲れ様でした
		hai jaa sumimasen otsukaresama deshita
		okay then thank you
	13 Others:	お疲れさまでした
		otsukaresama deshita
		thank you
→	14 Komeda:	ご苦労さんでした。
		gokuroosan deshita
		well done

In the formal meetings at company J, at the end of the discussion section, the chair does not request other business but confirms the next meeting's schedule from lines 3 to 11. Checking the next meeting serves as the preclosing. A difference from company N's formal meetings is that company J's formal meetings end with some acknowledgement among meeting members. Ashizawa, the chair, finishes the meeting with saying, *otsukaresama deshita* 'thanks, that's enough for today'[10] in 12 in example 4.11, or *arigatoo gozaimasita* 'thank you very much' found in other formal meetings. Other meeting members' responses include the same expressions as the chair. Another noteworthy point is the CEO's final remark in line 14. Following meeting members' acknowledgment of one another's efforts, Komeda, the CEO, responds with *gokouroosan deshita* 'well done'. *Gokuroosama/-san* is the expression that is likely to be used by people of higher status to those of lower status (the *Daijisen*, Japanese-Japanese dictionary, Shogakukan, 2006, translated by the researcher). The CEO's behaviour explicitly enacts the power difference between the CEO and other members, i.e. that he is of higher status than other meetings members.

As examples 4.10 and 4.11 demonstrate, the closing phases at both CofPs consist of the four components. The words in these phases tend to be formulaic in each CofP and, especially at company J, sound somewhat ceremonial. These characteristics are similar to those of the opening phases.

Post-meeting

At post-meeting sections, small talk occurred in both New Zealand and Japanese formal meetings.[11]

To summarise, in terms of the structure of formal meetings, they share common features across the CofPs. The formal meetings consist of the five sections, the procedures of opening and closing sections generally corresponding to the literature, and largely following a linear pattern. Both the opening and closing phases are typically managed by the chair and the words and procedures tend to be rationalised in each CofP. During the main discussion phases, smooth topic transitions are co-constructed between the chair and the meeting members with the assistance of transitional markers. These transitional markers are also similar across the CofPs. Typical transitional markers include "okay" and "alright" in English, and their counterparts, *hai* and *jaa* in Japanese. Silence also serves as a transitional marker across the CofP. There are, however, differences between the two CofPs in the manifestations of the formal meetings. For example, the openings and closings are more formal at company J.

Through the analysis of the structure of formal meetings it could be argued that meeting management is mostly conducted by the chair, but it cannot be managed without the cooperation of meeting members. It is interesting however to find that the CEOs enact power through their linguistic behaviour in the openings. It also can be argued that some aspects of formal meetings such as the opening and closing are routinised and their procedures are predetermined, but others such as main discussions are more dynamically constructed by meeting members.

4.7.2 Informal meetings

The informal meeting data is all audio-recorded and includes catch-ups, brain-storming, and briefings. As expected, in both informal meetings at company N and company J, the atmosphere is more casual and there are more occurrences of laughter than in the formal meetings. For example, to my ear, in company N's informal meetings, casual conversational phrases such as "you know", "eh", and "blah blah blah" are prominent.

As noted by Boden (1994) and Bargiela-Chiappini and Harris (1997a) in terms of the meetings they investigated, the opening and closing sections of the informal meetings at both CofPs are not marked clearly. Each phase of the five sections is thus not as clear as those at formal meetings. In line with the analysis of formal meetings, here, the structural characteristics are discussed in the five sections.

Pre-meeting and opening

There is no official chair in the informal meetings and the meeting opening is not marked explicitly. Since sound recording was entrusted to a target person, in most informal meetings, utterances for starting to record serve as the meeting opening as shown in the following example:

Example 4.12 [JIF02_02, 00:00]

1	Tanimoto:	[レコーダーを準備しながら] うん よし 株主総会 録音しといたったら 良かった ほんま
		[while turning on the recorder]un yoshi kabunushi sookai rokuon shitoitattara yokatta homma
		[while turning on the recorder]okay then I should have recorded the general meeting of stockholders really
→ 2		じゃあ すいません ちょっと あらためて 付けさせていただきまして
		jaa suimasen chotto aratamete tsukesasete itadaki mashite
		okay excuse me but let me turn on the recorder and record [the interaction]
3	Others:	[笑いがおこる]
		[laughter]
4		(4.0)
→ 5	Tanimoto:	ええ それでまあ 趣旨はだいたい あのー わかりました
		ee sorede maa shushi wa daitai anoo wakarimashita
		okay then I think I understand what you want
6		2つですね…
		futatsu desu ne …
		there are two aren't there?…

In example 4.12, Tanimoto is preparing to record. He accidentally turns on the recorder and his monologue is recorded. In his monologue, he regrets not to have recorded the general meeting of stock holders that he attended just before coming to this meeting, and he was not allowed to record the general meeting. Then, Tanimoto announces that he is starting to record in line 2. His way of speaking is humorous and other meeting members laugh in line 3. There is silence following general laughter, and the meeting topic starts in line 5.

In the informal meetings at company N, after comments about starting to record, small talk and/or humour tend to occur. The following is an example of the opening of an informal meeting at company N.

Example 4.13 [NIF03_10, 00:00]

1	Sharon:	it's quite strange when you listen to
2		your own voice on tape
3	Jaeson:	well we never get to hear these
4		+ okay I'm talking to sharon +++
→ 5		so um what do you think it was then +++

6	Sharon:	[laughs] [laughs]: I don't know: I don't know
7		I think she just had had a few beers
8		and so she was bold enough to 1/come\1 up and
9		2/say\2 something to me
10	Jaeson:	1/yeah\1
11	Jaeson:	2/yeah\2
→ 12	Jaeson:	but anyway so you they you said they had a meeting

In example 4.13, Sharon and Jaeson's discussion of the recording process lasts until line 5, which indicates the meeting opening. Then digression occurs. From line 5 to 11, they are talking about someone they both know. This topic is considered to have been continued before the recording started. In line 12, a transitional marker "but anyway so" returns the discussion to the meeting topic. In some meetings, digressions often last a long time.

Main discussion

Overall, topic transitions and topic progressions are very difficult to follow in the informal meetings at both CofPs. In most cases, a topic changes abruptly without any signal as shown in the following example:

Example 4.14 [JIF02_02, 13:00]
1	Manabe:	…その次の週となると またこれがですね
		…sono tsugi no shuu to naru to mata kore ga desu ne
		… the week after next it will be
2	Tanimoto:	うーん
		uun
		well
3	Manabe:	全くない状態が うーん それが あの
		mattaku nai joootai ga uun sore ga ano
		no time well um well
→ 4		セミナーの準備もしないといけない/しないといけない\ですけどね
		seminaa no junbi mo shinai to ikenai /shinaito ikenai\desu kedo ne
		actually I have to prepare for the seminar
→ 5	Ashizawa & Yoshioka:	/[笑]\
		/[laugh]\
6	Tanimoto:	セミナーの資料が そうですね 今回、資料++ ちょっとだけ あのー
		seminaa no shiryoo ga soo desu ne konkai shiryoo++ chotto dake anoo

	as for the handout for the seminar this time the handout well
7	まあほんま [会社名] で話した資料を *maa homma* [company name] *de hanashita shiryoo o* the handout for the seminar at [company name]
8	ちょっとアレンジしてお渡ししますので *chotto arenji site owatashishimasu no de* actually I think I will revise it and give it
9	少しボリュームを あのう 削って… *sukoshi boryuumu o anoo kezutte …* a little cut down the amount well …

In example 4.14, while they are talking about the date for the next meeting, in line 4, Manabe says that it is difficult to find a day for it because he is busy with preparing a seminar at company J, where he is an instructor for the company's clients. Following Manabe's turn, the topic changes to the seminar. In line 5, Tanimoto talks about the seminar's handout. There is no explicit transitional marker between the topics.

There are cases, though not so often, where transitional markers are employed as illustrated in example 4.13, where "but anyway so" in line 12 serves as a transitional marker. In the informal meetings at company N, transitional markers such as "okay", "but anyway", "um", "alright", and "so" are employed at topic transitional points. Silence also sometimes serves this function. On the other hand, in the informal meetings at company J, in most cases, silence indicates topic transitions. Explicit transitional markers such as *hai* 'yes/okay', and *jaa* 'then' are rarely employed.

One conspicuous, common feature in the informal meetings at both CofPs is that small talk and accompanying humour are finely interwoven with business talk.[12]

Closing and Post-meeting

As with meeting openings, the meeting closings are not explicitly marked. In two out of the six informal meetings at company N, the recording is cut off suddenly since recording is completely up to a target person. In other meetings, there is no clear signal to indicate the meeting closing and interaction finishes and meeting members leave the meeting place. In one meeting, the two meeting members explicitly farewell each other: "Thank you, Rob", and "See you then."

In the informal meetings at company J, too, in one out of the four, interaction finishes without any noticeable closing and meeting members leave the room without any farewell or saying *kaerimasu* 'I'm leaving.' In another meeting, Tanimoto says *dewa miitingu syuuryoosimashita ijoo* 'This is the end of the meeting. That's all.' Since he switches the recording off at this point, we cannot know whether this is the end of the meeting or the end of recording. In two meetings, a person who is in charge of the meeting says farewell to other members by saying something such as *doomo* 'thank you' or *arigatoo gozaimashita* 'thank you very much.'

In sum, the informal meetings at company N and company J are similar in general regarding meeting structures. The section duration is not clearly distinguished. Meeting openings and closings are short and not as ritualised as those of the formal meetings. In the discussion section, meeting topics and other topics including humour and small talk are interwoven. These analysis findings illustrate that management of informal meetings is not pre-determined and routinised across the CofPs. They indicate that meeting management is a dynamic process in which every participant plays a part.

4.8 Summary

In this chapter, the rationale for conducting contrastive analysis between formal and informal meetings has been explained with reference to previous research on meetings. The previous research agrees that formality is the most prominent categorisation, and formal and informal meetings have common features respectively. The importance of the categorisation between formal and informal meetings is also supported by there being different terms to refer to formal meetings and informal meetings in Japanese. However, so far, most research on meetings has paid little attention to this formal/informal categorisation, and there has been little research focussing on informal meetings. This supports the rationale for a contrastive analysis between formal and informal meetings in this research.

Then, after presenting a working definition of these two kinds of meetings, the structural characteristics of formal and informal meetings have been summarised, drawing on the previous literature. Previous studies of formal meetings have indicated that there are similar components of meeting structures in formal meetings (e.g., Marra 1998; Chan 2005). On the other hand, there are few previous studies on informal meetings and the analysis of them has been based on limited data (Boden 1994; Bargiela-Chiappini & Harris 1997a).

In the last half of this chapter, the meeting data for this study has been presented, along with selected analysis results in terms of meeting structures in formal and informal meetings, as a preliminary step to facilitate the analysis of small talk and humour. The analysis results have revealed that formal and informal meetings are different in terms of meeting structures, and that there are many similar structural characteristics in the same meeting category across the two CofPs. The structures of the formal meetings in both CofPs were similar at the macro level. Corresponding with the analysis findings of Chan (2005), formal meetings consisted of five sections. The openings and closings consisted of similar components to those found in the previous literature (e.g., Boden 1994; Marra 1998) and were routinised, and their procedures were generally predetermined. In the main discussion phases, smooth topic transitions were co-constructed between the chairperson and the meeting members with the assistance of transitional markers such as "okay" and "alright" in English, and their counterparts, *hai* and *jaa* in Japanese. Silence also served as a transitional marker across the CofPs. In terms of topic progression, a linear pattern was found across the CofPs.

Based on the results of the analysis of the structure of formal meetings, it could be argued that while meeting management is mostly conducted by the chairperson, it cannot be managed without the cooperation of meeting members. It also can be argued across the CofPs that some aspects of formal meetings, such as the opening and closing, are routinised and their procedures are predetermined; however, others such as main discussions are more dynamically constructed by meeting members. At the micro level, however, differences were found among each CofP. For example, the openings and closings were more formal at company J. And the chair's expressing gratitude to reporters after they finished their reports served as a transitional maker at company N.

Yet the informal meetings were similar, in general, when considering the meeting structures across the CofPs. In both CofPs the section durations were not clearly distinguished. Meeting openings and closings were short and not as ritualised as those of the formal meetings. In the discussion sections, meeting topics and other topics — including humour and small talk — were interwoven. These findings indicate that the management of informal meetings is not pre-determined and routinised but follows a more dynamic process than formal meetings.

These analysis findings have revealed that the structural features in formal meetings generally support the existing literature and thus are common across workplaces and nations. They also have revealed that the structural characteristics of informal meetings are clearly distinct from those of formal meetings, and that more and more research on informal meetings will be necessary. The results of this study clearly indicate that the contrastive study of formal and informal meetings is valuable, and that paying attention to the formal/informal dimension is necessary when examining meeting discourse.

If the meetings are similar in general regarding meeting structures, what about Relational Practice? This question is addressed in the following chapters

– in Chapter 5 regarding small talk and in Chapter 6 regarding humour.

Notes
1 Yamada (1997a: 151) lists all her recorded meeting data. Though there are 10 meetings including these four, the other six meetings are not analysed in detail in her reported research.
2 See Chapter 3 for more detail regarding LWP.
3 See Chapter 3 for detailed information about the participants (including the target participants).
4 See Chapter 3 for detailed information about the participants (including the target participants).
5 Details of small talk will be discussed in Chapter 5.
6 Adapting Chan's (2005) ways of showing Chinese, in this book, Japanese words/phrases are shown as the style of Romanisation accompanying the English translations marked with single quotation marks.
7 In my personal experience and interviews with friends, in Japan formal meetings tend to start with the meeting name's introduction.
8 In my personal experience and interviews with friends, in Japan in formal meetings, the previous meeting's minutes are checked either at the opening section or at the closing section.
9 Humour will be addressed in Chapter 6.
10 *Otsukaresama* is the expression to show one's appreciation for one's colleagues and is translated as "Thanks! That's enough for today" and "Thanks for all your hard work" (*Shin Wa-ei Dai Jiten*, Japanese-English Dictironay, the fifth edition, Kenkyusha, 2004).
11 Details of small talk will be addressed in Chapter 5.
12 This will be discussed in Chapter 5 and Chapter 6.

CHAPTER 5

Small talk

In Chapter 4, the structural characteristics of formal and informal meetings have been examined. The results indicate that formal and informal meetings differ in terms of structure, and that there are many similar structural characteristics in the same meeting category across the two CofPs, i.e. company N in New Zealand and company J in Japan. This leads to the next issue: if the meetings are similar in terms of meeting structure, what about Relational Practice? This is the focus of the second research question introduced in Chapter 1. It concerns the manifestations of small talk and humour in New Zealand and Japanese formal and informal meetings. Small talk in the meetings is analysed in this chapter and humour is the focus of Chapter 6.

In workplace discourse, transactional or work-related talk is highly valued because of its obvious relevance to workplace objectives. However, relational or social talk also plays an important role by enhancing rapport among co-workers and thus contributing to good workplace relationships. Small talk is a typical example of this relational talk (Holmes & Stubbe 2003). However researchers of workplace discourse have only recently begun to pay attention to small talk in various workplaces, and the amount of literature in this area is still very limited. The first half of this chapter is devoted to a review of the relevant literature and the theoretical examination of small talk. The second half describes the results of the analysis of small talk in the meeting data, also demonstrating the target participants' linguistic behaviours in terms of small talk.

5.1 Approaches to small talk

It is generally agreed that Malinowski (1923/1927)[1] first introduced and identified the concept of "phatic communion", which is "the earliest and the prototypical formulation of small talk as a communicative mode" (Coupland 2000b:

2). Since then, phatic communion has received attention in anthropology, sociolinguistics, and sociology. In sociolinguistics, it has been typically taken to refer to conventionalised, desemanticised, marginal, and non-transactional talk (e.g., Coupland et al. 1992). This has tended to lead to a negative perception of small talk as the "small" in small talk implies. However, recent researchers have begun to pay attention to small talk in authentic interactions, placing positive value on the relational aspect of interaction (e.g., Coupland 2000a; Holmes & Stubbe 2003; Mullany 2006).

Major works reviewing the small talk literature are Schneider (1988), Cheepen (1988), Coupland et al. (1992), and Coupland (2000a). In this section, on the basis of these literature reviews, I describe how the major approaches toward small talk have changed – categorising them into the *classic approach*, the *discursive approach*, and the *negotiative approach*. Finally I consider which approach is appropriate for analysing manifestations of small talk in the meeting data I am analysing.

5.1.1 Classic approach

As noted above, the first usage of the term *phatic communion* is attributed to Malinowski (1927), who defined phatic communion as "a type of speech in which ties of union are created by a mere exchange of words" (Malinowski 1927: 315). According to the author, one of the major motivations behind phatic communion is to avoid silence. He regards silence as follows:

> [T]o a natural man, another man's silence is not a reassuring factor, but, on the contrary, something alarming and dangerous. ⋯ The breaking of silence, the communion of words is the first act to establish links of fellowship
> (Malinowski 1927: 314)

Malinowski (1927) contends that phatic communion is a way of avoiding the threat of silence and of establishing human bonds. He continues that "there is in all human beings the well-known tendency to congregate, to be together, to enjoy each other's company" (1927: 314). He also argues that phatic communion "serves to establish bonds of personal union between people brought together by the mere need of companionship and does not serve any purpose of communicating ideas" (Malinowski 1927: 316). Coupland (2000b: 3) criticises Malinowski's treatment of phatic communion as "a systematically ambivalent view of small talk, talk which is aimless, prefatory, obvious, uninteresting, sometimes suspect and even irrelevant, but part of the process of fulfilling our intrinsically human needs for social cohesiveness and mutual recognition".

The negative perception of phatic communion results from Malinowski's attitudes toward it. First, for Malinowski, phatic communion is merely the avoidance of silence for the sake of the social bond and thus he classifies it as meaningless because it does not transmit any information. This traditional treatment of phatic communion may reinforce the notion that talk is either giving information (transactional) or simply serving to establish human relationships between participants. Talk primarily serves to express content or information and this is a major purpose of communication. Thus, when analysed in terms of the transactional aspect, phatic communion is evaluated as "referentially deficient and communicatively insignificant" (Coupland et al. 1992: 209).

Another reason why Malinowski's perspective results in a negative perception of phatic communion is his examples of phatic communion. Greetings, inquiries about health, comments on weather, aimless gossip, and affirmations of some extremely obvious observations are given as examples. These examples reflect that "hallmarks of phatic communion are its ritualised and apparently purposeless character" (Coupland 2000b: 2).

Building on the notion of phatic communion, Laver (1975, 1981) explored the discourse structure and social function of phatic communion in the opening and closing phases of interaction. Drawing on "informal observation of everyday social encounters" (1975: 216) by himself and his students, Laver found a sequential organisation of interactions. The author divides the temporal structure of interactions into three major phases: the *opening phase*, the *medial phase*, and the *closing phase*. Considering phatic communion as a limited set of stereotyped phrases of greeting, parting, commonplace remarks about the weather, and small talk, his analysis focusses on the opening and closing phase, because they are strongly characterised as the marginal phases of interaction.

According to Laver (1975, 1981), phatic communion at the margins of conversations serves two functions. One is to establish and maintain the interpersonal relationship between the two participants, which is consistent with Malinowski (1927). The other function of phatic communion is to achieve the transition from non-interaction to full interaction comfortably, as well as the return from interaction to non-interaction. In the opening phase of interaction, "it [phatic communion] allows the participants to cooperate in getting the interaction comfortably under way" (Laver 1975: 221). In the closing phases of an interaction, phatic communion facilitates a cooperative parting, assuaging "any feelings of rejection by the person being left" (Laver 1975:231).

As Jaworski (2000) points out, for Laver (1975, 1981), along with Malinowski (1927), the primary motivation of phatic communion is to "defuse the potential hostility of silence in situations where speech is conventionally anticipated" (Jaworski 2000: 111). Moreover, Laver (1975, 1981) takes the same position as Malinowski (1927) that phatic communion at the margins of conversations does not transmit chiefly referential information. Instead, it exchanges between conversational participants "indexical information about aspects of the participants' social identity relevant to structuring the interactional consensus of the present and future encounters" (Laver 1975: 236).

While Malinowski's (1927) and Laver's (1975, 1981) approaches toward small talk are different, they have some characteristics in common. First, there seems to be a clear dividing line between phatic talk and non-phatic talk, i.e. between relational talk and transactional talk, in their approaches. Both also assume that phaticity in the talk is inherent, predictable, and identifiable from its surface form (Coupland et al. 1992; Chan 2005).

5.1.2 Discursive approach

While Malinowski's (1927) and Laver's (1975, 1981) studies are both based on their fieldwork and not on analysing authentic interaction, Schneider (1988) and Cheepen (1988) extended the analysis of small talk to natural conversations.

Schneider (1988) provides a perspective on small talk that aims at making his study relevant for the development of sociopragmatic competence in the language learning context. Thus, Schneider's (1988) analysis focuses mainly on describing small talk based on such things as forms, structures and topics rather than the explanation of social functions that small talk achieves for interlocutors. Analysing 52 natural conversations of small talk in encounters with acquaintances at a party and at a café, Schneider (1988) considers small talk as a discourse type, whose characteristic is simply having minimal information content. By demonstrating typical forms, structures, and topics of small talk, he attempted to provide a predictable model of the structure of small talk.

Cheepen (1988) argues that certain patterns of topic change and development depend on the status relationships of discourse participants, drawing on data consisting largely of five social chats and two job interviews. The author categorises two different types of speech encounters according to the predominant goals of the interactants. Transactional encounters are those whose goal is to communicate a message and interactional encounters are those whose goal is to achieve rapport between speakers and hearers. Describing the relative status of the participants as an important component of conversation, Cheepen (1988) relates it to these two encounters. She claims that the acknowledgement and expression of relative status plays an important role to define the type of conversational encounter. Her major claims are that all interactional encounters have the same macro-structure and that "this structure is designed so as to allow participants to pursue the interactional goal of the maintenance and development of their interpersonal relationships" (Cheepen 1988: 48).

While both approaches attempt to analyse small talk at the discourse level, they consider that whether an utterance is small talk or not depends on predictability according to its surface form. In this sense, both approaches take a top-down approach. They also maintain that there seems a clear dividing line between phatic talk and non-phatic talk.

5.1.3 Negotiative approach

Coupland (2000a: 13) criticises the previous research on small talk, or phatic communion, for "defining small talk too rigidly as a bounded mode of talk", and for considering phaticity as the degree of communicative predictability. Coupland et al. (1992) regard small talk as situated practice and a local creative construction, and propose a negotiative approach to small talk.

Adopting this approach, the function of particular sequences of talk as phatic or otherwise is not predetermined, but negotiated dynamically and discursively among the participants. The phatic function of talk is "contingent upon its local sequential placement in particular contextualised episodes and on the momentary salience of particular interactional goals" (Coupland et al. 1992: 215, italics in original). The phatic mode of talk surfaces whenever relational goals become salient – even *within* sequences of transactional, instrumental, or task-oriented talk. That is, "phatic communion may be negotiated *relationally*, and *in real time*" (Coupland et al. 1992: 215, 217).

The characteristics of the negotiative approach to small talk can be summarised as follows: (1) phaticity is not inherent but negotiated discursively; (2) small talk is non-predictable and constructed dynamically; (3) the phatic function of talk depends on "the momentary salience of particular interactional goals" (Coupland et al. 1992: 215); and (4) talk is inherently multifunctional and there is no clear division between transactional and interpersonal.

Developments in approaches to small talk discussed so far can be summarised in the following table:

	Classic approach	Discursive approach	Negotiative approach
Analysis focus	Observation	Authentic interaction	Authentic interaction
Function: Transactional / relation talk	Clear line	Clear line	No clear line
Direction	Top-down	Top-down	Bottom-up
Phaticity	Predictable	Predictable	Discursive and dynamic construction

Table 5.1: Changes in approaches to small talk

As table 5.1 shows, while the classic approach is primarily based on the researchers' observations of people's linguistic behaviours regarding small talk, both the discursive and the negotiative approaches analyse small talk in authentic interaction at the discourse level. There is, however, a difference between these two approaches. The discursive approach takes a top-down approach, considering that phaticity of talk is predictable according to its surface form. On the other hand, the negotiative approach conceptualises that any talk is multifunctional and phaticity of talk is constructed dynamically in interaction.

Which of the above three approaches is the most appropriate for the current study? This study employs Relational Practice as the analysis framework. This framework takes a dynamic view of interaction from the perspective of Relational Practice, recognising small talk as a discursive Relational Practice strategy. In other words, the current study explores how the relational aspect of talk is negotiated discursively at the discourse level. Given these considerations for the analysis of the data, it is evident that the negotiative approach is the most appropriate for the current study.

Since the present research addresses small talk in business meetings, the next section is devoted to a literature review of workplace small talk.

5.2 Small talk in workplace discourse

Research on small talk in workplace discourse began only in the last decade and remains limited (Coupland 2000a). First, I outline the recent major research on workplace small talk, focussing on empirical studies based on the analysis of authentic workplace interactions.

The first substantial contribution to research in this area is the book *Small Talk* (2000) edited by Justine Coupland. This book includes research on small talk in a variety of work situations such as a hairdresser's salon and a driving lesson (McCarthy 2000), travel agencies (Coupland & Ylanne-McEwen 2000), supermarket checkout counters (Kuiper & Flindall 2000), women's health-care centres (Regan 2000), and call centres (Cheepen 2000).

As noted by Mullany (2007), one significant contribution to research on workplace small talk has been conducted by researchers from the LWP project.[2] The LWP team members have conducted research on workplace small talk in a wide range of workplace settings, drawing on a large number of authentic workplace interactions (e.g., Holmes 2000a, 2000b; Holmes & Stubbe 2003).

Another important contribution to research on small talk in workplace discourse is Mullany (2006, 2007). Working primarily within gender studies, the author explores female and male managers' verbal performance in six recorded meetings including small talk. Despite the stereotypical expectation that small talk is feminine gendered discourse, the meeting data analysis revealed that it was employed by managers of both sexes.

In the following sections, features of small talk in the workplace are summarised from the previous literature, considering definition, distribution, topics, and functions.

5.2.1 Definition

According to Holmes (2000a: 36), small talk is located on a continuum between core business talk and phatic communion. At one end, *core business talk* directly serves the organisation's goals; it is relevant on-topic talk, maximally informative, context-bound, and transactional. At the other end of the continuum is *phatic communion*, which is irrelevant in terms of workplace business; it is atopical, minimally informative, context-free, and social or interpersonal. Small talk can be placed between social talk and phatic communion although interactions may move back and forth along this scale as shown below:

Figure 5.1: Locating small talk on the continuum

(from Holmes 2000a: 38)

A similar continuum is identified by McCarthy (2000). He analysed talk between hairdressers and their clients, and that between driving instructors and their students. In doing so, he distinguishes four broad types of talk, ranging from phatic exchanges through relational talk and transactional-plus-relational talk to transactional talk.

Both Holmes (2000a) and McCarthy (2000) argue that workplace talk is highly context dependent and that it is impossible to draw a clear line anywhere along the continuum. This perspective is also noted by other researchers (Candlin 2000; Coupland 2000b; Mullany 2007). In particular, in workplace settings where the major goals are to fulfil a range of transactional purposes, small talk "cannot be segregated from the 'mainstream' concerns of talk at work" (Coupland 2000b: 6). Mullany (2007: 92) also observes the crucial point that "[c]onceptualizing small talk on a continuum should make clear that the analytical aim is not to look for a categorical decision as to whether talk is transactional or affective." As Coupland et al. (1992) noted, the phatic mode of talk appears whenever relational aspects of interaction become salient even within sequences of transactional talk. This perspective corresponds to the discursive approach to small talk as well as Relational Practice, and I adopt this position for the analysis of small talk in this study.

5.2.2 Distribution

In terms of the distribution of small talk, researchers on workplace small talk agree that small talk is found at the boundaries of interactions, especially before and/or after a transactional task. For example, drawing on interactions between clients and their travel agents, Coupland and Ylanne-McEwen (2000) found that the transaction generally starts and/or closes with small talk. In meetings, small talk tends to occur around boundaries of meetings, or the topic transitional points, as well as the opening and closing phases of meetings (Chan 2005; Mullany 2007). Small talk also arises at the boundaries of the working day and is used as a punctuation of interaction (Holmes & Stubbe 2003). It is common to have greetings in many workplaces for the first meeting of the day among co-workers. It is also common that they farewell each other when parting (Holmes 2000b).

5.2.3 Topics

The topics of small talk range from ritualised formulaic greetings and farewells to broader personally oriented talk (Coupland 2000b; Holmes & Stubbe 2003). They include "the weather, ritualized enquiries about health, out-of-work social activities, sport, generalized complaints about the economy or personal complaints about work, mentions of family, positive comments on appearance, work, and so on" (Holmes 2000b: 129).

Coupland and Ylanne-McEwen (2000) analysed weather talk between clients and their travel agents by drawing on two different corpora of travel agency talk. The weather is one of Malinowski's (1927) examples of safe, ritualised topics available even between non-familiars. However, the analyses revealed the variety of ways in which weather is treated by participants. They range from phatic ritual, and shared experience, to arching as a bridge to more intimate, personal self-disclosure, and as a commercialised topic within the transactional talk of the travel industry. Coupland and Ylanne-McEwen (2000) found that through weather talk, travel agency staff and their clients can exchange information about their personal lives and feelings, thereby facilitating friendly relationships. This indicates that even small talk about topics that are considered ritualised and not expected to develop is constructed dynamically among interactants.

5.2.4 Functions

Researchers agree that workplace small talk is multifunctional and can serve transactional and relational goals simultaneously (e.g., Coupland 2000a; Holmes 2000a, 2000b, 2006a; Holmes & Stubbe 2003; Chan 2005). From a transactional perspective, small talk serves discourse functions within workplace communication, marking the boundaries and transitions of interactions – such as a meeting's phases, or topics within a meeting – serving as a link to business talk. From a relational perspective, small talk is an essential part of workplace interaction, helping to oil the wheels of workplace communication, and contributing to good workplace relationships. It can be used to enhance rapport among co-workers, expressing solidarity and collegiality (Coupland 2000a; Holmes & Stubbe 2003; Chan 2005; Mullany 2007). It can also serve to promote good relationships with clients, which results in positive outcomes in each workplace (Cheepen 2000; Coupland & Ylanne-McEwen 2000; Kuiper & Findall 2000; Regan 2000). Small talk also helps one to exercise power (e.g., Holmes & Stubbe 2003; Mullany 2007). It is often superiors who control small talk and decide when to start and finish it, what subjects are acceptable, and how much time is spent on it in an interaction. From subordinates to those in authority, small talk can be employed to challenge or reduce social distance.

Acknowledging that there are various relational functions in small talk, researchers of small talk in workplace discourse argue that it is primarily employed to avoid silence, as a time-filler (e.g., Coupland 2000a; McCarthy 2000; Homes & Stubbe 2003). A typical example of this is when a number of people gather together for a meeting. Sitting around in silence would be socially embarrassing and it is expected that people who work together should have topics to talk about. Thus small talk helps to avoid uncomfortable moments of silence, filling the gap while people are waiting for a meeting to start (Holmes 2000a, 2000b).

In sum, it is generally agreed that small talk plays a significant relational role in workplace discourse, helping staff to avoid embarrassing moments of silence, to promote good relationships with customers, and to facilitate good relationships among co-workers. All of these result in positive outcomes in each workplace. It is also agreed that there is no clear line between transactional talk (business- or task-oriented talk) and interpersonal talk (participant-relationship-oriented talk), and that any talk is inherently multi-functional and serves transactional and interpersonal goals simultaneously.

5.3 Small talk from Asian perspectives

While it is agreed that small talk is sociolinguistically universal, there are significant cross-cultural differences in its use and perception (e.g., Coupland et al. 1992; Clyne 1994; Jaworski 2000). However, almost all literature on small talk has addressed English interactions only. To date and to the best of my knowledge, there is only a handful of research projects on small talk that focus on Asian languages including Japanese interactions. Since this research focusses on small talk in meetings, cross- and inter-cultural research on small talk in business meetings from Asian perspectives is introduced in this section.

Spencer-Oatey and Xing (2003) conducted a contrastive study of two Chinese-British welcome meetings that were held by the same British company. Analysing the video-recorded meetings, field notes, and interviews with the participants, the authors make various observations regarding the opportunity to engage in small talk. There was a 15 minute pre-meeting phase when the participants had to wait for the meeting to start. During this pre-meeting phase, the meeting participants took the opportunity to engage in small talk such as introducing themselves to each other. There were many occurrences of silence during this time and the British seemed very uncomfortable and actively initiated small talk. From the British point of view, this was primarily a gap-filler to avoid embarrassing silence. From the Chinese point of view, however, it gave a valued opportunity for relationship building.

The most detailed and extensive empirical study on small talk in business meetings is Chan's (2005) cross-cultural research in New Zealand and Hong Kong. She drew on data from authentic business meetings in both countries. Focussing on small talk during the pre-meeting phase, she found that the most common topics of small talk in both data sets tended to relate to three particular areas: participants, physical context, and the immediate task. Chan (2005) also maintains that the small talk in her data serves the function of time filling and rapport building. However, her data reveals a big difference between the New Zealand and Hong Kong meeting discourse — the degree of tolerance for silence. The participants in Hong Kong had greater tolerance for silence than those in New Zealand.

A series of research projects by Yamada (1990, 1992, 1994, 1997a, 1997b) explored Japanese and American conversational styles by analysing intra- and inter-cultural meetings.[3] In her research, Yamada (1997b) addresses small talk. She compares a tape-recorded weekly *kachookai* — or section head's meeting — with three Japanese (20 minutes-long), and a tape-recorded weekly manager meeting with three Americans (27 minutes-long). While in the American meeting the participants started with business talk, in the Japanese meeting the first third of the whole meeting was "nontask-sounding talk" surrounding topics which were not related to the business at hand at all. Following this long episode of small talk, the participants switched to more work-related topics, then finally concluded with the meeting topic. Yamada (1997b) argues that "the non-task sounding talk is a strategic prelude and buffer to the more task-related talk that follows" (1997b: 127). She concludes that long non-task sounding talk is essential in the Japanese meetings to establish the cohesiveness of the group and to confirm goodwill among members. Comparing the same pair of meetings, Yamada (1992) points out that there were many more occurrences of long silence (pauses greater than 1.5 seconds) in the Japanese meeting than in the American meeting (103 cases vs. 20 cases), and that an average pause in the Japanese meeting was longer than that in the American meeting (8.2 seconds vs. 4.6 seconds). She explains that the Japanese devalue talk and idealise silence while the Americans value talk or explicit communication.

The above research suggests that perspectives on silence might be different from an Asian perspective. In the following section, attitudes toward silence are addressed.

5.4 Small talk and silence

Researchers on small talk in English speaking societies mentioned in the previous sections argue that the primary motivation behind engaging in small talk is avoiding silence. It can be argued that in English speaking societies, people are likely to feel uncomfortable when silence occurs and thus small talk serves to break the awkward silence. However, the discussions in the last section indicate that this would not be applicable to Asian contexts.

This difference in the attitude toward silence is also reported by other researchers. Jaworski (1993) points out that people from some non-Western cultures were more tolerant toward silence than those from other Western cultures. For example, Lehtonen and Sajavaara (1985) have observed that during mealtimes Finnish families engage in relatively less small talk than Anglo-American families. They also report that the Finns often put a positive value on silence in social occasions.

In terms of Chinese interactors, Giles et al. (1991) examined beliefs about talk and silence in a questionnaire-based study from university students. They found that the Anglo-American students placed more positive value on talk than the Chinese students while the Chinese students viewed silence more positively. Moreover, in a different questionnaire-based study, Giles et al (1991) found that Hong Kong students were more disposed towards small talk than their Beijing counterparts, and that the latter expressed a greater tolerance for silence than the former. On the other hand, both groups of Chinese respondents (from Hong Kong and Beijing) appeared to perceive silence as more important, and more enjoyable, than Americans.

Analysing authentic conversations in Japanese, Nakane (2006) found that silence can be used as a positive politeness strategy when it functions as a sign of solidarity and rapport, while it can also be a negative politeness strategy if it functions as a distancing tactic. In addition, it is also possible to use silence as an off-record strategy when it serves as the most indirect form of a speech act (Saville-Troike, 1985; Tannen, 1985).

These examples suggest that in some communities, when there is no urgent need for talk, silence is not always perceived as awkward or uncomfortable to the extent that it is perceived by members of other communities. They also suggest that different levels of requirement of small talk are employed in different communities and that non-talk or maintaining silence resulting from such norms is not necessarily awkward or unsociable. In Asian contexts, it could be argued that small talk and silence can function as communicative tools, as well as sometimes functioning in opposition to each other as found in English society. I now turn to an analysis of how small talk and silence function in the New Zealand and Japanese meeting discourse.

5.5 Analysis of small talk

In this section, findings of an analysis of small talk in meetings are reported with reference to the previous literature. The ways in which small talk is manifested is presented first in terms of formal meetings and then informal meetings. As noted in section 5.4, the analysis employs Holmes' (2000a) definition of small talk.

5.5.1 Small talk in formal meetings

This section explores the manifestations of small talk in formal meetings of company N and company J, describing the topics, distribution, and functions of this small talk. The analysis results are reported for the five sections of meetings discussed in Chapter 4: the pre-meeting, opening, main discussion, closing, and post-meeting.

Pre-meeting
Consistent with Chan's (2005) analysis, small talk is the most frequently occurring type of interaction in the pre-meeting phases. Topics of small talk in the pre-meeting phase are mostly consistent with Chan (2005). That is, the

most common topics at both CofPs are: (1) greetings; (2) participants; (3) physical environment; and (4) the immediate tasks that are relevant to what the participants are engaging in. Though all the examples cannot be shown because of the restriction of space, illustrative examples along with their topic categories are described below.

The following excerpt is an example in the category of "greetings" from company N. At the very beginning of the recording, Evan is greeting Veronica.

Example 5.1 [NFM01_02, 00:00]
1 Evan: morning Veronica
2 Veronica: [singsong]: morning:
3 Evan: I've got my finance notes here
4   I'll give them to you /after the meeting\
5 Veronica: /oh good\ that'll be good

There are examples where participants greet each other in the pre-meeting sections at company J, too. For most meeting members, the formal meeting is their first encounter of the day and it is reasonable to greet one other.

Another common topic is "participants" as illustrated in the following example.

Example 5.2 [NFM02_04, 04:50]
1   Seamus: hey Darryl
2   Darryl: hey +
3   Seamus: what's Darryl talking about today
4   All   [laughter]
5   Evan   are we having a formal
6   are we having a formal welcome
7   Jaeson: yes we are
8   Evan: oh okay
9   Harry: your shout Darryl [laughs]
10 Jaeson: Maori # Paul- Paul's doing the Maori welcome
11 Paul: why me
12 Jaeson: [laughs]

In example 5.2, the topic is a new staff member, Darryl. This meeting is his first management meeting at the organisation. The participants are talking about how they should welcome the new staff member. They are talking about a formal Maori welcome ceremony that is popular in New Zealand. Talking about what can be done with the new staff member as well as the other meeting members can function to facilitate collegiality among meeting members. Moreover, talking about how they would welcome the new staff explicitly shows consideration toward him. It is evidence that small talk has a positive function from a relational perspective.

"The physical environment" is also a common topic of pre-meeting small talk in company N and company J.

Example 5.3 [JFM02_01, 03:00]

1	Yoshioka:	どうしよう
		dooshiyoo
		what shall we do?
2	Ashizawa:	いただいたんやろ？
		itadaita n ya ro?
		have we got them?
3	Yoshioka:	うん １人ずつ
		un hitori zutsu
		yes [one box] for each
4	Ashizawa:	うん メールが おれもいただいた
		un meeru ga ore mo itadaita
		yes I've got an e-mail too
5		(2.0)
6		でもう /行かれた？\
		de moo /ikareta?
		already? /has she left?\
7	Yoshioka:	/出られた\ どうしたらええやろ
		/derareta\ dooshitara ee ya ro
		/she has gone\ what shall we do?
8	Ashizawa:	いや ぼ あの 会議のときに僕が言うって
		iya bo ano kaigi no toki ni boku ga iu tte
		well I'll tell about them [=chocolates] at the meeting

In example 5.3, the participants are looking at boxes of chocolates that I left for each meeting participant, and talking about them. Their physical environment has been changed by the chocolates, and this has lead to small talk.

Another common topic involves "the immediate task".

Example 5.4 [NFM01_02, 07:00]

1	Seamus:	who is it who's /who sent you a text\ Kevin
2	Harry:	/I don't understand\
3	Seamus:	I don't understand half these texts I get
4		++ people abbreviate them +
5	Sharon:	mm ++

6	Harry:	that's why kids /can't spell\
7	Sharon:	/it's a new language\
8	Harry:	mm

In example 5.4, when Seamus is using his cell phone, his immediate task, the participants are looking at it. This motivates the commencement of small talk. They are talking about young people's ways of writing text messages. In company J's meetings, there is a scene where a participant is checking the video camera that I put in the room, and the participants are discussing how the camera shows the participants, while watching him.

The examples discussed so far all correspond with those identified in Chan (2005). However, not all the topics of pre-meeting small talk are consistent with it. In company N's meetings, another category, i.e. a topic triggered by the previous topic, is found as shown in the following example.

Example 5.5 [NFM01_02, 01:50]
1	Harry:	and we've got a demo as well I think haven't we
2	Evan:	a demo?
3	Paul:	oh we got a demo
4	Evan:	have we + great
5	Harry:	(oh just the)
6	Paul:	retail
7	Harry:	yeah
→ 8	Paul:	oh play it on that
		[*with pointing to the projector that he will use at the meeting*]
9	Evan:	actually Wendy brought home a data projector
10		from [organisation] yesterday
11		/+\ cos she's she's having a hui [= *gathering*]
12		at home this morning
13		with a number of the staff from [organisation]

In example 5.5, three participants are talking about a demonstration to be conducted during the meeting. Harry is asking whether a data projector will be used for someone's presentation, pointing to the projector in line 8. Then Evan starts to tell an anecdote about helping his wife set up a projector the previous night for this morning's gathering (hui) at their house from line 9. Though not directly related to "the projector" pointed to by Harry in the meeting room, Evan's anecdote is triggered by "the projector" because it reminded him of having enjoyed watching DVDs using a different projector the previous night. In company N's pre-meetings, the participants speak fast and continuously with topics developing one after another. Business related topics trigger small talk topics and, in some cases, that topic triggers another topic.

In company J's pre-meetings, on the other hand, the participants' talking speed is not so fast and, in most cases, when one topic (related to business) ends, silence occurs, and then small talk, then back to the business topic.

Example 5.6 [JFM03_01, 15:00]

1	Yoshioka:	[after drinking a bottled tea, giving a deep sigh] (24.0)
2		[after 24 second silence, the two participants start to talk looking at the canned drink which Chida has been drinking]
3	Chida:	カロリーゼロのやつ 前飲んだやつ 味なかった
		karorii zero no yatsu mae nonda yatsu aji nakatta
		the calorie free one which we had drunk before had no taste
4		そんなことないですか？
		sonna koto nai desu ka?
		don't you think so?
5	Oka:	あんまりな
		anmari na
		well not so much taste
6	Chida:	ああそうそう ダイエット
		aa soosoo daietto
		well yes diet
7	Oka:	ふーん 何の情報やろ ふーん
		fuun nanno joohoo ya ro fuun
		well what kind of information? well
8		(2.0)
9	Chida:	[笑]( ) 全然 ( )
		[laughs] ( ) zenzen ( )
		[laughs] ( ) not at all( )
10	Oka:	何がつながってんねん
		nani ga tsunagatte n nen
		what links to?
11		(2.0)
12		シュガーシロップ？ 違う？ シュガーシロップ
		shugaashiroppu? chigau? shugaashiroppu
		sugar syrup? different? sugar syrup
13	Chida:	甘いんでしょうね 甘い 甘いすね ( )しょう [笑]
		amai n de shoo ne amai amai su ne ( ) shoo
		it might be sweet sweet sweet isn't it ( ) [laughs]

In example 5.6, after talk about a business topic with Yoshioka and another meeting member, a long silence occurs, and then other members, Chida and Oka, start a new topic (small talk). They are talking about the canned drink that Chida has been drinking. The drink is calorie free and they are discussing the taste of calorie free drinks. As will be discussed later in this section, it is interesting that while some members are talking other members remain silent.

In terms of topic transitions, in company N's pre-meeting phases, both business topics and small talk topics are developed continuously and it is difficult to draw a clear line between work-related and non-work-related topics. In the pre-meeting sections at company J, silence occurs between topics and it is not difficult to identify small talk. These differences are evident from analysing interaction at the discourse level.

Keeping this difference in topic transition between company N and company J in mind, in order to explore the distribution of small talk in more detail, topic flow at the pre-meeting phase is examined. The following table shows an example of topic flow of pre-meeting sections, one from company N and the other from company J.

Company N/ NFM01_02 8 minutes (business topic: 26 seconds)	Company J/JFM02_01 12 minutes (business topic: 7 minutes 10 seconds)
greetings work-related document **meeting food** today's meeting projector **hui** { projector { **a participant's car** **meeting food** **someone's seat** **a participant's clothes** { projector { **text message** { indecipherable Meeting opening	**chocolates from the researcher** today's seminar held at company A a computer software business travel cost agenda **chocolates** (distributing to each member) this morning lecture held at company A **a participant** Meeting opening

Table 5.2: Topic flow of pre-meeting phase
Bold font for topics of small talk and { for overlapping section

A prominent difference is that there are more topics in the pre-meetings at company N than in company J (N: 14 vs. J: 8) although the duration of the pre-meeting is longer in company J (N: 8 min. vs. J: 12 min.). Another difference is that there is more small talk than business related talk in company N, while business related talk occupies most of the pre-meeting section in company J. The other difference is that there are occurrences of overlapping talk only in company N. That is, when there are more than three people, more than two groups form and there are different conversations which occur simultaneously. In each group people are engaging in different episodes of small talk. It can be argued that while in company N meeting members engage in talk more actively and there is more small talk, in company J, silence is considered acceptable and there is less talk including small talk. It is worth noting that this result is counter to Yamada (1997b), who contends that long episodes of small talk are essential in Japanese meetings to establish group cohesiveness. Thus it is dangerous to generalise about manifestations of small talk based on limited data, and that as discussed in Chapter 4, it is important to take meeting type into consideration when analysing meeting discourse.

Opening, main discussion, and closing

Through the opening, main discussion, and the closing sections, there are only two occurrences of small talk (one each from company N and company J) during the main discussion part. The following is an example from company N.

Example 5.7 [NFM01_02, 11:40]

1	Jaeson:	right Evan financial report
2	Evan:	me first woohoo okay um
3		(4)
4		[*Tommy has just entered the meeting room*]
		just in time Tommy
5	Evan:	I'm just about to cut loose mate good timing
6	Paul:	grab a chair
		[*Tommy has to go and get a chair*]
7	Evan:	he's turned up for the exciting stuff
8	XM:	[laughs]
9	Paul:	is the other meeting table # [louder]: Tommy: #
10		tell Tommy that the meeting table
11		with the other chair is there
12		Seamus: hey it's probably there's more chairs
13		there there's a small ( )
14	XM:	oh there's one here he wants a big chair
15	Tommy:	comfy for the extra weight
→ 16	Jaeson:	um yeah ##(Evan)
17	Evan:	okay I think Jaeson's got some comments
18		about the print result

In example 5.7, when Evan is about to start his report, Tommy happens to come into the meeting room. Then, the meeting members start to talk humorously about Tommy and the table and chair that he goes to look for. After a short period of small talk, Jaeson, the chairperson, initiates a return back to the meeting topic by employing the topic shift marker "um yeah" and a short pause in line 16.

The following example is an instance of small talk which occurred during the discussion phase in company J's formal meeting.

Example 5.8 [JFM02_01, 23:25]

```
    1  Ashizawa:  … 積極的に 積極的に動くというところは
                   … sekkyokuteki ni sekkyokuteki ni ugoku to iu tokoro wa
                   …[negotiations with clients] actively actively progressing
    2             あー 今んところはないという状況になってます
                   aa ima n tokoro wa nai to iu jookyoo ni natte masu
                   well, there is nothing [no actively progressing sales nego-
                   tiations] now
    3             えー 私の方からは以上です
                   ee watashi no hoo kara wa ijoo desu
                   that's all for my report
 → 4              で すいません ちょっと順序逆になりましたけど
                   de suimasen chotto junjo gyaku ni narimasita kedo
                   excuse me this is the opposite order but
    5             あのー [人名] さんの方から
                   anoo [name]san no hoo kara
                   well from [name]
    6             えーと ええ あのー お土産ということで [笑]
                   eeto ee anoo omiyage to iu koto de
                   well hmm souvenirs
    7             チョコレート 皆さん いただいてますんで
                   chokoreeto minasan itadaite masu n de
                   we've got chocolate for each of you
    8             えー また あのー 顔合わすことございましたら
                   ee mata anoo kao awasu koto gozaimashitara
                   when you have an opportunity to meet her
                   [Following this utterance, several members say thank you
                   to Tanimoto who is the researcher's acquaintance]
    9  XM:        ありがとうございます
                   arigatoo gozaimasu
                   Thank you
   10  XM:        /ありがとう\ございます
                   arigatoo gozaimasu
```

		Thank you
11		/お礼を言うといて＼いただけたらと思います
		orei o iutoite itadake tara to omoimasu
		express your gratitude to her
12	(2.0)	
→13	Ashizawa:	はい#
		hai #
		okay #
14	Wada:	えーと [取引会社名] なんですけども...
		eetto [client's name] *na n desu kedo mo...*
		well regarding [client's name] ...

As Ashizawa finishes his report in line 3, he starts to talk about the boxes of chocolate that I gave Ashizawa and that have already been distributed at each member's place (on the meeting table). It is worth noticing Ashizawa's utterance in line 4. Before he starts to talk about the chocolate, he apologises and says that the topics are out of order. It is reasonable that his apologies suggest that he considers that non-business talk should not occur during the main discussion. Moreover, it can be also argued that the reverse order would mean that according to the right order, non-business talk should be placed before the main discussion, i.e. pre-meeting phase. This corresponds to a typical characteristic of Relational Practice. That is, the small talk is considered peripheral. Following talk about the chocolate, Ashizawa, the chair, returns to meeting talk by employing the topic shift marker *hai* 'okay' and a pause in line 13.

What is common in small talk during the main discussion sections is that small talk "accidentally" occurs (implying that it should not be there), is regarded as marginal, and that the chair initiates a return to the meeting topic.

Post-meeting

During the post-meeting, meeting members begin to leave the room, so it is sometimes difficult to catch exactly what they are talking about. While the meeting participants generally talk about business topics related to the meeting which has just finished, there are three occurrences of small talk, one from company N and two from company J. All are related to the meeting that has just finished. In one example from company N, the meeting members are talking about the food that was served at the meeting. In one example from company J, a participant, Manabe, is asking another member, Wada, what made the *shinkansen* (bullet train) late. Wada works at company J's branch in another region and takes the bullet train to company J's head office for the monthly meeting. On that day, there was an accident along the railway line and he had to wait for a long time in the train. Following Wada's explanation about why the bullet train was late, Manabe is saying *taihen desita ne* 'that's too bad,' which shows sympathy. The other example from company J is also noteworthy from a relational perspective.

Example 5.9 [NFM01_05, 21:30]
1   Tanimoto: 不安ですけどね　がんばってください
                fuan desu kedo ne ganbatte kudasai
                I understand your nervous feeling take it easy

In example 5.9, Tanimoto is talking to a new staff member. In the meeting, the new member spoke in a voice which signaled a lack of confidence. Tanimoto cheers him up after the meeting, explicitly showing consideration toward the new member. This plays an important role in facilitating team work (Holmes & Stubbe 2003; Chan 2005). The two examples of small talk at the post-meeting section at company J are worth noting from a relational perspective. Both serve as moral support.

The ways in which small talk is manifested has been examined according to each phase of formal meetings. I now turn to consider functions of small talk in formal meetings.

Function

As noted in section 5.6, it is generally agreed that in Western contexts people feel uncomfortable when silence occurs. Small talk serves to break the silence, i.e. fill the embarrassing moment (e.g. Jaworski 2000; McCarthy 2000), which is also applicable in pre-meeting small talk (Chan 2005). This is consistent with the results of meetings at company N. In formal meetings of this CofP, all instances of silence last less than 10 seconds except one which lasts 36 seconds.

The following is the example of the longest silence at company N's meetings.

Example 5.10 [NFM02_04, 00:00]
1   Evan: just you and me Veronica
2   Veronica: yep /it'll be a\ quick meeting won't it
3   Evan: /be a quick meeting\
4   Veronica: um can I have your notes ++
5   Evan: yeah
6   Veronica: or (unless) you're doing /(just) a really brief\
7   ++ just (to really brief them) ++
8   Evan: /just in there\
9   Evan: that'll be fine
10   (36)
                [*while Veronica is reading documents, Evan looks*

			embarrassed.]
11	Veronica:		how's (month end) going up there
12			with financial year end
13			would it be easier with sage

In example 5.10, a 36 second silence occurs while one participant, Veronica, reads some documents. It is worth noting that the silence occurs for a reason. That is, there are two people and when one of them is focussing on doing something and cannot talk, the other has no option but to keep silent. It is also worth noting that observation of the video indicates that Evan, who might have no option but to keeping silent, looks somewhat embarrassed.

In company J's meetings, on the other hand, silence occurs frequently and most stretches of silence last more than 10 seconds. The following example is the longest silence in company J.

Example 5.11 [JFM03_02, 05:50]
[*In the next excerpt, the two participants are murmuring with each other and unintelligible parts are shown as ( )*]

1	Ueki:	来られた
		korareta
		came
2		(112.0)
3	Emoto:	( )
4	Ueki:	合わないですよね 合わないですよね。( )
		awanai desu yo ne awanai desu yo ne
		it doesn't match doesn't match ( )
5	Emoto:	お金と( )お金と( )社会保険が( )
		okane to ( ) okane to ( ) shakaihoken ga ( )
		with money ( ) with money ( ) social insurance
6	Ueki:	うん？
		un?
		Yes?
7	Emoto:	社会保険事務所に確認したら( )[会社名]( )何を基準に( )
		shakaihokenjimusho ni kakunin sitara ( ) [company name] ( ) nani o kijun ni ( )
		checking it at a social insurance office( ) [company's name] what is a standard ( )
8	Ueki:	( )
9	Emoto:	( )
10	Ueki:	( )

11	Emoto:	( )
12	Ueki:	( )
13		(160.0)
14	Emoto:	( )
15	Ueki:	( )
16		(120.0)
17	Ueki:	( )
18	Emoto:	[笑] [laughs]

Figure 5.2: Japanese meeting participants' waiting for other members

In example 5.11, two participants are waiting for other participants to arrive. During the long period of silence, the participants look at the wall or fold their arms as seen in figure 5.2. While the two participants are murmuring with each other, there are long stretches of silence lasting 112 seconds, 160 seconds, and 120 seconds. At company N, small talk is employed as a device to break the silence or to fill the time. This, however, is not the case in company J. In this CofP, remaining silent with colleagues could be a way of signalling that members are comfortable and at ease with each other. In my experience, such a scene where participants wait in silence for other participants to arrive is not uncommon in Japan.[4] It could be argued that silence might serve beneficially as a Relational Practice strategy in Japan.

Another major function of small talk is building rapport (e.g., Holmes & Stubbe 2003; Chan 2005). This claim appears consistent with the data in both CofPs. For example, in example 5.2 from company N, selecting a topic that can be shared not only by regular meeting members but also by a new staff member explicitly shows consideration toward the new member. In example 5.9 from company J, too, a meeting member is talking to a new member to encourage him. As these examples demonstrate, small talk effectively functions as a Relational Practice strategy, creating team spirit and showing collegiality.

Creating team spirit with small talk is shown syntactically. The following example is from company J.

Example 5.12 [JFM032_02, 15:20]

1	Hosoi:	まだ 誰も 来てないですね *mada dare mo kite nai desu ne* no one is here.
2	Tanimoto:	そうですね さっき来たとき 何人かいらっしゃったんで すけど *soo desu ne sakki kita toki nannnin ka irasshatta n desu*

		kedo
		well when I came here there were some.
→ 3	Hosoi:	誰かおれが座ろうとしている席
		dare ka ore ga suwaroo to siteiru seki
		someone the seat where I'm going to sit
→ 4	Tanimoto:	[笑]押さえてる人が
		[laughs]osaeteru hito ga
		[laughs] [*someone*] is holding
→ 5	Hosoi:	押さえている人がいた
		osaeteiru hito ga ita
		someone holding [my seat] is here
6		ずらしとこ [笑] よいしょっと
		zurashi toko [laughs] yoisho tto
		I'll put this to other place [laughs] yo-ho!

In example 5.12, Hosoi and Tanimoto are constructing a sentence cooperatively. This is called "co-construction" (Mizutani 1993), where participants co-construct an utterance, and it serves to show affiliation.[5] Another feature of this example is humour and laughter in small talk. Analysing authentic meetings, Mullany (2007) points out that small talk often accompanies humour. In my meeting data from both CofPs, too, there are many occurrences of humour in small talk. Humour is also a paradigmatic Relational Practice strategy expressing solidarity and collegiality (Holmes & Schunur 2005), and it is understandable that it occurs in small talk. In the pre-meeting phases at company N, humour is also often accompanied not only by small talk but also business related talk, and it is difficult to clearly distinguish the two. Considering that humour serves a relational role, it can be argued that business related talk also serves a relational function, and that any talk is multifunctional.

While humour accompanies small talk in both CofPs, there is a clear difference between company N and company J. The difference is the tone of talk. The following example is from a pre-meeting at company N.

Example 5.13 [NFM03_05, 05:30]

1	Harry:	[goofy voice]: oh: +
2	Sharon:	no they're /all mine\
3	Veronica:	/no that's for\ Sharon
4		/(as we're) going through the meeting\
5	Sharon:	/[laughs]\
6	Paul:	good grief
7	Sharon:	no they're not
8		[laughter]

9	Jaeson:	oh chocolate oh dude /[drawls]: oh:\
10	Harry:	/happy birthday\ Sharon

In example 5.13, Sharon brings a box of chocolates to the meeting. The meeting members are excited to open it and pretend that they are celebrating Sharon's birthday though it is not her birthday. Everyone actively engages in talk in a humorous tone and laughter occurs repeatedly, showing the participants' enjoyment. Their talk is lively and animated and the atmosphere is relaxed and casual.

The following example is from a pre-meeting of company J, which is an almost identical context as in the above example.

Example 5.14 [JFM02_01, 15:00]

1	Ashizawa:	住吉 これ 席にこれ 配ってくれる？
		Sumiyoshi kore seki ni kore kubatte kureru?
		Sumiyoshi could you distribute them to each place?
2	Sumiyoshi:	はい
		hai
		yes
3	Ashizawa:	[名前] さんからお土産 みんなに 1個ずつチョコレート
		[name]san kara omiyage minnna ni ikko zutsu chokoreeto
		They are souvenirs from [name] one box of chocolate for each
4		あのー 終わった後 これ お礼言うといてよ ...
		anoo owatta ato kore orei iutoite yo ...
		well, after the meeting, you should say thank you to her. ...

In example 5.14, Sumiyoshi is distributing to each meeting member a box of chocolate that I left for them. While being given the chocolates, no one is excited, no one opens the box, and everyone remains silent. These two examples clearly show the difference of the tone of talk – the animated and high tone in company N and the rather quiet tone in company J.

To summarise, consistent with Chan (2005), small talk in formal meetings is concentrated in the pre-meeting sections in both CofPs. While acceptable topics of small talk mostly correspond to Chan (2005) across these two CofPs, at company N, topics triggered by the previous topics are found. Corresponding to the previous literature on small talk in the workplace (e.g., Holmes & Stubbe 2003; Coupland 2000a), the main function of small talk in formal meetings is building rapport and creating a sense of team spirit across the two

CofPs. One large difference between these two CofPs is the interpretation of small talk and silence. Another difference is the ways members contribute to talk.

5.5.2 Small talk in informal meetings

This section moves on to focus on the analysis of the manifestations of small talk in the informal meetings of company N and company J, describing their topics, distribution, and functions. In line with the previous section, the analysis results are reported following the five sections of meetings discussed in Chapter 4: the pre-meeting, opening, main discussion, closing, and post-meeting.

Pre-meeting

As discussed in Chapter 4, informal meetings at both companies mostly start with utterances signalling the start of the recording. As opposed to the pre-meeting sections of formal meetings, small talk is not found except these utterances associated with recording.

Opening, main discussion, and closing

While in formal meetings small talk rarely occurs during the opening, main discussion, and closing, in informal meetings, small talk occurs even in the main discussion. There are occurrences of small talk where topics correspond to the five most common topics at pre-meeting small talk (Chan 2005): (1) greetings; (2) participants; (3) physical environment; and (4) the immediate task involved. Though greetings are not found in the pre-meeting section, in some informal meetings, at the closing or when participants leave the meeting place, they exchange short farewells such as "thank you" and "see you then" at company N, and *arigatoo gozaimasu* 'thank you very much' and *jaa* 'see you' at company J.

The following is an example in the category of "participants". It is the beginning of an informal meeting at company N.

Example 5.15 [NIFM02_07, 00:00]

```
   1                  [interaction starts]
→  2   Jaeson:        yeah I'm talking to Rob Bellinger
→  3   Rob:           I- I broke it down [coughs]
   4                  what I what I figured was
   5                  what I thought was the most logical
→  6   Jaeson:        what happened to the small talk
   7   Rob:           [laughs] [laughs]: just I love the col- I love
   8                  what you're doing with your hair
```

9		/these days: [laughs]\
10	Jaeson:	/[laughs]\ oh you're just [distortion] I mean
11		you're so /straight into it you know [laughs]\
12	Rob:	/[laughs]\ um when we talked about [sighs]
13		the style of operation o- of of the type of buyer
14		...

In example 5.15, Jaeson and Rob are having a catch-up meeting. Rob would like to propose a new franchise system in this informal meeting. As soon as Jaeson's utterance to start recording finishes in line 2, Rob immediately starts to explain his proposal in line 3. Jaeson interrupts this by asking him what happened to the small talk in line 6. This tongue-in-check utterance by Jaeson makes Rob laugh and relax and he starts to talk humorously about Jaeson, the "participant". Following his "small talk", Jaeson explains that why he asked about the small talk is because Rob was very intense. Jaeson attempts to make Rob, who is too serious and intense about his proposal, relax by pointing to the absence of the normal small talk in a humorous tone. This shows Jaeson's consideration toward Rob. Small talk serves a positive function from a relational perspective. It is also noteworthy that the absence of small talk at the beginning of the meeting results in the explicit comment in line 6. It could be argued that small talk is expected at the beginning of a meeting.

The following is an example of what Chan (2005) would label "physical environment".

Example 5.16 [JIFM01_01, 04:10]

1	Tanimoto:	ここね　結構いろいろなもんあって
		koko ne kekkoo iroiro na mon atte
		here [at this restaurant] there is a variety of food
2		たまにね　一応 [町の名前]/ だったんで\
		tamani ne ichioo [name of this town] /datta n de
		sometimes I used to live in this town
3	Ashizawa:	/ はいはい \ はいはい
		/hai hai\ hai hai
		/yeah yeah\ yeah yeah
4	Tanimoto:	社会人のおっちゃんばっかりで /[笑]\
		shakaijin no otchan bakkari de /[laughs]
		businessmen only /[laughs]\
5	Ashizawa:	/ はいはい \ はいはい
		/hai hai\ hai hai
		/yeah yeah\ yeah yeah
6	Tanimoto:	帰り 飲みに / 行って \

		kaeri nomi ni /itte
		on the way home we used to go out for drink
7	Ashizawa &	/[笑]\
	Nio:	/[laugh]\
8	Tanimoto:	なつかしい思い出です
		natsukashii omoide desu
		it's my nostalgic memory

In example 5.16, Tanimoto, Ashizawa, and Nio are having a review meeting about a client whom they visited on that day. After visiting the client, they decided to have a meeting somewhere in the town over dinner. Since Tanimoto used to live in that town, he proposed this restaurant where he often went when he lived there. In the example, he is talking in a humorous tone about how nostalgic he feels at this restaurant. The other members are responding with positive remarks that show understanding. The small talk in this example also serves a positive function from a relational point of view, building rapport among meeting members.

The following example is from company N. The topic of this small talk is "immediate task involved".

Example 5.17 [NIFM04_13, 09:20]

	1		[putting CD into CD player]
	2	Jaeson:	we can listen to this
	3	Sharon:	yeah
	4	Anna:	yeah that's what I thought I thought to remind us
	5		what was what /so I put a big star by the um +\
	6		by the Strauss one
	7		cos that's the um that's number nine +
	8	Sharon:	/be inspired [laughs]\
	9	Jaeson:	oh /oh yeah the other one I love is Tchaikovsky\
	10		um ++
	11	Anna:	/so we'll keep those tickets for us [laughs]\
	12	Sharon:	I've only heard number /nine\
	13	Anna:	/I've got\ a star by that one too [laughs]
	14		/they're they're\ the stars yeah
	15	Jaeson:	/number five?\
→	16	Sharon	who who do you think of our clients
	17		would want to go ...

In example 5.17, Jaeson, Sharon, and Anna are talking about inviting their clients to classical concerts. Company N is an official sponsor of this orchestra and regularly gives its clients tickets to concerts. In order to decide which concerts' tickets to take, they start to listen to a CD of this orchestra. While listening to the CD, they are talking about their favourite music and composers. Then Sharon returns to the business related topic in line 16. In addition to the kinds of topics in this example, it is interesting to point out the common features found in small talk in informal meetings at company N. The first is the lack of topic transitional markers between small talk and business-related talk. This results in it being difficult to draw a clear line between small talk and meeting talk. Another common feature is that everyone contributes to small talk and small talk is constructed cooperatively and rhythmically with overlaps occurring, which can be described as "polyphony" (Coates 1996: 133).[6] These characteristics are discussed in more detail later in this section.

Similar to the pre-meeting sections of company N's formal meetings, during the main discussion phase of company N's informal meetings, participants speak quickly and continuously with topics developing one after another. Figure 5.3 shows the topic flow of the first twelve minutes at an informal meeting between Jaeson and Paul.

Figure 5.3: Topic flow of the first 12 minutes of an informal meeting

The underlined parts in figure 5.3 indicate associations between topics. As they show, topics are continuously triggered by the previous topics. Both business topics and small talk topics are developed complexly. Example 5.18 is an excerpt from the final part of the above figure.

Example 5.18 [NIFM06_0214, 10:30]

1	Jaeson:	I mean I'll I would always watch the All Blacks
2		but didn't really follow it
3	Paul:	yeah
4	Jaeson:	super twelve was a sort of really lift-
5		lifted the profile of it eh you know
6	Paul:	it has it's made it a bit er
7		more of a spectacle as it would being um
8	Jaeson:	( )
9	Paul:	um [tut] yeah more money in it now
→ 10		um also er + I'm going to get Anna
→ 11		to organise a a group for um sevens next year ···
12	Jaeson:	oh that's a good idea
13	Paul:	yeah
→ 14	Jaeson:	and the [client] girls will love that eh /([names])\
15	Paul:	/oh it just depends\ on what numbers
16		we're sort of talking about
17		and what it's going to cost is the concern
18		but Seamus said oh just like the normal
19		the the same as the Dunedin thing
20		it's sort of select a um /+\ crew
21		the [client] guys will probably be there anyway
22	Jaeson:	/yeah\ that's right yeah
23	Paul:	yeah cos I think er
→ 24	Jaeson:	are they still talking about going to Hong Kong
25		those girls
26	Paul:	they are going
27	Jaeson:	they are /yeah\ are you going to go with them
28	Paul:	/yeah\
29	Paul:	no no just [laughs] too much grief [laughs]
30	Jaeson:	yeah
31	Paul:	yeah um no Sue just um I think
32		she sort of came to the realisation
33		that I was going to be travelling with six women

34		/and er was not not very happy about it\
35	Jaeson:	/[laughs] when you told me when you told me
36		I was thinking\ jeez mate
37	Paul:	well er yeah er but /the other thing is\
38	Jaeson:	/there's no way\ I would be allowed to do that
→ 39	Paul:	yeah the other thing is
40		I'll um I'll er probably try to take a bit of er
41		leave without pay at some stage during next year

In example 5.18, Jaeson and Paul are talking about the All Blacks, which is New Zealand's national rugby team. In lines 10-11, Paul moves the topic to company N inviting their clients to a rugby game. Then in line 14, Jaeson mentions their female clients, saying that they want to go to the game. Paul continues to talk about the invitation, and then Jaeson moves to a new topic about the client "girls'" travelling to Hong Kong (line 24).[7] Jaeson and Paul are talking about this topic in humorous tone, and then Paul again returns back to another business-related topic, paid leave, from line 39. In this example, topics are rapidly and continuously changing but all topics are triggered by and associated to previous topics. Business related topics and small talk are finely and subtly interwoven without any explicit topic transitional markers. The participants move backwards and forwards between small talk and business-related talk. In this example, too, it is difficult to draw a clear dividing line between small talk and business-related talk. Moreover, humour is incorporated not only into small talk but also into business-related talk. This indicates that business-related talk also serves a relational role and that any talk can be multi-functional as argued in the negotiative approach to small talk (e.g., Coupland 2000a).

In terms of distribution, an interesting characteristic is found. That is, in informal meetings in both CofPs, small talk occurs abruptly without any prologue. The following example is from company J.

Example 5.19 [JIFM01_01, 48:50]

1	Tanimoto:	ゴールに持ち込まれたら　動けない　というのがありますから #
		gooru ni mochikomare tara ugokenai to iu no ga arimasu kara #
		we cannot move if they come close to goal
→ 2		何か飲みますか？　日本酒おいしいですよ
		nanika nomimasu ka? nihonshu oishiidesu yo
		would you like something to drink? *Sake* [here] is delicious

	3		まあ　焼酎もありますしね

maa shochuu mo arimasu shi ne
well they have *shochu* too

	4	Ashizawa:	はい　何でも

hai nan demo
yeah anything you recommend

In example 5.19, Tanimoto, Ashizawa, and Nio are having an informal meeting at a restaurant over dinner. Just before the excerpt (until line 1), they are intensely discussing how they can make company J's staff more efficient. Tanimoto in line 2 suddenly asks Ashizawa and Nio whether they would like to have another drink. This indicates Tanimoto's consideration toward the other members. This abrupt occurrence of small talk is also often found at company N's informal meetings as shown in the following example.

Example 5.20 [NIFM05_14, 02:30]

	1	Rob:	\1/I mean logistics in terms of the workflow\1
	2	Jaeson:	\2/it's finished\2
	3	Rob:	and who manages that process now
	4	Jaeson:	[drawls]: um: Joe downstairs
	5		but it's under Marshall's umbrella if you like
	6		/er but\ there's the reason this has come up
	7	Rob:	/(his pervey)\
→	8		oh I've ordered a boat by the way
	9	Jaeson:	woohoo can you show me a picture of it
	10	Rob:	yeah I can yeah yeah
	11	Jaeson:	on the internet or
	12	Rob:	[drawls]: er: yeah I've got pictures of THE boat
	13	Jaeson:	THE boat
	14	Rob:	on my up on my thing
	15	Jaeson:	well I'll have to come and have a look
	16	Rob:	yeah
	17	Jaeson:	awesome when's it coming
	18	Rob:	hopefully by next weekend
	19	Jaeson:	great
	20	Rob:	it's got to come from Christchurch
	21	Jaeson:	yeah yeah
→	22	Rob:	anyway sorry
	23	Jaeson:	I mean I don't if you pay me
	24		I'll go down and bring it up /[laughs]\
	25	Rob:	/[laughs] it's only going to cost me\

26		a hundred and fifty bucks to get it here
27	Jaeson:	okay /I'll\ pay you [laughs]
28	Rob:	/they'll\
29		they'll deliver it to
30		they'll deliver it to the
31		they'll deliver it to the ferry terminal
32		and put it on the straitsman
33	Jaeson:	yeah
34	Rob:	and the straitsman
35		people will take it off and store it here
36		until I pick it up
37	Jaeson:	yeah yeah
38	Rob:	[coughs] hundred and fifty bucks
39	Jaeson:	fantastic that's nothing eh costs ++
40		yeah I mean it costs basically
41		that's what you're paying for what it costs
42		to bring a car over aren't /you yeah\
43	Rob:	/yeah yeah\ (well that's factor) yes
44		/that's right that's all this it's a seven metre thing\
45	Jaeson:	/and you'd normally be driving on yourself\
46		yeah yeah
47	Rob:	that's all it is
48	Jaeson:	[drawls]: s-: so what is it
49	Rob:	it's a bonito five eight five
50	Jaeson:	five eight five
51		which is effectively a nineteen footer?
52	Rob:	yeah it's five point six metres on the water
53		and five point eight nine five point nine metres
54		of overall length yeah
55		so nine nineteen footer is what you'd call it
56	Jaeson:	yeah great cool
57	Rob:	so
58	Jaeson:	you'll enjoy that
59	Rob:	yeah
60	Jeason:	yeah [laughs] lucky thing [laughs]
61	Rob:	now all I've got to do
62		is find some time to use it
63	Jaeson:	green with envy
→ 64		# okay um now so but but part of the reason
65		of course for this coming up is that
66		I'm just not happy with the way

67 that's working at the moment anyway

In example 5.20, Rob and Jaeson are talking about the delivery system for company N's products. Suddenly Rob in line 8 starts talking about his boat, which he has just bought, and Jaeson is also contributing to this talk. Then, Rob in line 22 apologises, which indicates that his small talk should not occur here, or during the discussion section, as found in example 5.8. However, ignoring Rob's apology, Jaeson continues this small talk in a humorous way, and finally in line 64, Jaeson returns the discussion to a business-related topic. Similar to example 5.17, in this example, too, both Rob and Jaeson construct small talk cooperatively and "polyphonically" (Coates 1996). From this stretch of discourse alone, it is hard to know why Rob suddenly starts to talk about his new boat. However, within a wider scope of discourse, drawing on ethnographic information, the reason why he starts small talk can be conjectured. The previous topic, company N's delivery system, reminds him of his new boat because when he bought the boat, its delivery system was good. Thus it is understandable that he suddenly started small talk (in line 8).

It can be argued that in both CofPs, small talk (even if it is abrupt) would be tolerated during the informal meetings' main discussion sections.

Post-meeting
In the post-meeting section of an informal meeting at company J, an interesting example was found.

Example 5.21 [JFM02_02, 64:30]
1   Tanimoto: 足ももうほぼ？
                ashi mo moo hobo?
                is your leg fine already?
2   Ashizawa: ちょっとまだ
                chotto mada
                well not yet actually
3   Tanimoto: 少しまだ＃　お大事に
                sukoshi mada # odaiji ni
                not yet completely # look after yourself
4   Ashizawa: 長い間座ってると　動き出しが痛いんです
                nagai aida suwatteruto ugokidashi ga itai n desu
                after sitting for a long time, I feel pain when i start to move

In example 5.21, Tanimoto asks how Ashizawa's broken leg is when he is about to walk on crutches to leave the room. This explicitly shows Tanimoto's consideration toward Ashizawa. Similar to small talk at the formal meetings' post-meeting sections at company J, this example also serves as moral support.

In informal meetings, since small talk primarily occurs during the main discussion section where talk is required, and it is integrated with business-related talk, it would be difficult to say that small talk is employed to break the silence. As found in all the examples in this section, small talk serves a relational function, creating team spirit and building rapport among meeting members.

5.5.3 Target participants' linguistic behaviours regarding small talk

In this section, the target participants' linguistic behaviours in terms of small talk are discussed. A common feature regarding small talk across the two CofPs is who manages small talk and meeting talk at formal meetings. In the main discussion sections of formal meetings, Jaeson and Ashizawa, the two chairpersons, initiate a return from small talk to the meeting agenda, or meeting talk. In other words, in both CofPs, moderators manage small talk and meeting talk.

One large difference is the way small talk is constructed. At company N's formal meetings, every meeting member starts small talk and cooperatively constructs small talk, while in company J, Ashizawa, the moderator, actively contributes to small talk and others merely respond to it. In informal meetings at company N, too, every meeting participant, including Jaeson, actively contributes to small talk, and small talk is constructed by everyone cooperatively and "polyphonically" (Coates 1996). On the other hand, at company J's informal meetings, Tanimoto actively contributes to small talk and Ashizawa responds it. It could be argued that at company N everyone equally contributes to small talk, while at company J, a particular person is in charge of contributing to small talk and the person who serves this role might change.

Considering that not only small talk but also business-related talk are often accompanied by humour and laughter across these two CofPs, it is reasonable that small talk and humour are closely related from a relational perspective. It would clearly be useful to explore the target participants' linguistic behaviours by combining the analysis results in small talk with those in humour. Keeping the differences in this section in mind, differences in the target participants' linguistic behaviours are discussed in Chapter 6 in more detail.

5.6 Summary

In this chapter, previous research on small talk has been reviewed. Approaches to small talk have developed from the classic view, taking phaticity as predetermined, to a negotiative view, considering phaticity as negotiated dynamically and discursively. Adopting the new negotiative approach to small talk, researchers of workplace discourse have paid attention to small talk in authentic workplace interactions including meetings. These researchers argue that small talk plays an important role from a relational perspective in the workplace, serving to facilitate smooth human relations among colleagues. Research on small talk in English speaking societies leads us to consider avoiding silence as the major motivation behind small talk. On the other hand, non-Western researchers, especially from Asian perspectives, do not always attach a negative value to silence, and they agree that silence would not necessarily have to be avoided by starting small talk.

In the second half of this chapter, results of the contrastive study on small talk have been outlined. That is, manifestations of small talk have been explored in formal and informal meetings at company N and company J, describing acceptable topics, distribution, and functions. The results are summarised in table 5.3.

	Company N	Company J
Topics	greetings, participants, physical environment, the immediate task involved	
	topics triggered by previous topic	
Distribution	Formal meetings: mainly at pre-meeting section Informal meetings: mainly at main discussion (abrupt occurrence, interwoven with business related talk)	
Function	positive function from a relational perspective (creating team, building rapport)	
	silence avoidance	no silence avoidance (silence serves positively like small talk)
Other features	accompanying humour and laughter	
	constructed by everyone cooperatively and rhythmically	not constructed by everyone
	animated tone	
		long silence
		back support at post-meetings

Table 5.3: Features of small talk in formal/informal meetings at company N and company J

Comparing small talk in formal and informal meetings, a difference regarding distribution is found across the two CofPs. In formal meetings, corresponding to the findings of Chan (2005), small talk is concentrated in the pre-meeting sections. On the other hand, in informal meetings, small talk mostly occurs during the main discussion sections where there are many more occurrences of small talk than in formal meetings. One reason is that, in informal meetings, small talk would be tolerated and has the potential to occur anywhere even in the main discussion phases. Another reason is that in informal meetings, small talk is finely interwoven into meeting talk during the main discussion phase. These findings regarding formal and informal meetings are common across the two CofPs. It is evident from the analysis results, however, that manifestations of small talk are different between formal and informal meetings. This indicates that the contrastive study in this research is warranted and considering the formality of meetings is necessary when examining meeting discourse from a relational perspective.

Comparing small talk at company N's meetings with small talk in company J's meetings, the following characteristics of its manifestations are evident from the analysis. First, small talk topics are largely similar across the two CofPs, and these common topics corresponded to Chan's (2005) analysis results. However, in addition to these common topics, in the meetings at company N, topics were triggered by previous topics and often developed in new directions.

Secondly, small talk is almost obligatory at company N's meetings in such cases where no urgent talk is necessary at the pre-meeting phases. At company J's meetings, on the other hand, silence is tolerated. From a relational perspective, small talk plays an important role at company N's meetings, while keeping silent as well as small talk makes a contribution at company J's meetings. The difference in attitudes toward silence between these two CofPs corresponds to previous literature (e.g., Chan 2005; Nakane 2006). That is, in English speaking societies, a negative value is placed on silence, whereas it is not necessarily considered this way in Asian society.

Thirdly, a unique finding in this research is that the ways of contributing to talk, or the way small talk is constructed, is different. At company N's meetings, the meeting members speak continuously and with overlaps, and topics develop one after another. Small talk is constructed by the meeting members cooperatively and "polyphonically" (Coates 1996). At company J's meetings, by contrast, some participants talk but others remain silent. They speak with no continuity and new topics seldom develop.

In terms of the distribution of pre-meeting small talk, the results reported here contrasted with those of Yamada (1990, 1997b). She points out that a prominent feature of her Japanese meeting data is the long non-task sounding talk with which a meeting begins. She argues that the initial period of long small talk is essential to the organisation of Japanese meetings, and that Japanese meetings are relationship driven. In this research, the results contrasted with hers. There is no occurrence of the initial long period of small talk at formal and informal meetings. This indicates that it would be dangerous to generalise directly the analysis findings based on a limited amount of data and apply them to all Japanese meetings. As Chan (2005) also points out, interaction is dynamically and discursively negotiated among participants and any generalisations must be interpreted carefully.

Without generalising, the data analysis indicates the following: While there are differences in the manifestations of small talk between formal and informal meetings as well as between the two CofPs, the analysis indicates that small talk functions as Relational Practice because it serves to create team spirit and to build rapport among meeting members across these two CofPs and kinds of meetings. There were many examples where small talk was finely interwoven in meeting talk. This suggests that any talk including social talk and work-related talk is multifunctional and should be analysed at the discourse level.

Considering that small talk is often accompanied by humour and laughter in the data, it is clear that small talk and humour are closely linked from a relational perspective. Keeping the manifestations of small talk in mind, the following chapter focusses on humour.

Notes

1 Malinowski (1923/1927) indicates that Malinowski (1923) is the first mention of small talk but in this research, Malinowski (1927) which is the second edition is used as a reference. Hereafter, Malinowski (1927) is employed in order to avoid complexity.
2 See Chapter 3 for detailed information about LWP.
3 See also Chapter 4 for more detail.
4 This is also supported in Chapter 7.
5 This syntactic co-construction is also found in company N's meetings (example 6.9 in Chapter 6).
6 Coates (1996) compares collaboratively constructed utterances with overlapping to polyphony where several musical instruments play different tunes harmonically.
7 The mention of Hong Kong refers to the rugby team's tournament held there (the Hong Kong Sevens).

CHAPTER 6

Humour

Chapter 5 examined small talk in the meeting data. The analysis indicated that the importance of small talk, a Relational Practice strategy, is recognised across both the CofPs and both kinds of meetings, formal and informal, and that its manifestations differed in each CofP and in each type of meeting. It was also noted that small talk often accompanies laughter and humour. This suggests that small talk and humour are interrelated and that the manifestations of both Relational Practice strategies would be similar. These issues are addressed in this chapter.

Humour is another typical example of relational talk and plays a crucial role by contributing to good relations among colleagues in the workplace where transactional or work-related discourse is highly valued because of its obvious relevance to workplace objectives (e.g., Fletcher 1999; Holmes & Stubbe 2003; Schnurr 2005). In parallel to the previous chapters, this chapter first examines the previous literature on humour, in particular focussing on workplace humour, describing various aspects of humour including definitions, types, categories, distribution, and functions. The second part of this chapter explores the manifestations of humour in the meeting data, describing the target participants' linguistic behaviours regarding humour. In the final part of the chapter, I draw on the analysis findings with respect to small talk and humour together and attempt to interpret then from an emic perspective. [1]

6.1 Humour

Humour has received attention from various disciplines such as psychology and philosophy (e.g., Morreall 1983; Provine 2000; Hayakawa 2003). Best known are traditional philosophical studies of humour, which have been conducted over many centuries. The three major theories of humour from a philosophical perspective include *superiority theory*, *incongruity theory*, and *relief theory*. Superiority theory derives from the work of the philosophers Plato and Aristotle, and more recently Hobbes. It is based on the idea that laughter is caused by the feeling of triumph of one person over another person (Morreall 1983). Incongruity theory is derived from the work of Kant and Schopenhauer. It focusses on the cognitive processes of perceiving humour as the sudden perception of incongruity (Morreall 1983). Finally, relief theory is most closely associated with Freud, in which he hypothesised that laughter is the release of repressed energy (Hay 1995).

While traditional research on humour was concerned with what is perceived as humorous, recent researchers have started to be concerned with interactional aspects of humour, or what people accomplish with humour. From a discourse perspective, pragmatic research on humour has been conducted relatively recently. For example, Mulkay (1988), Chiaro (1992), and Norrick (1993) discuss the communicative functions of humour; Bell (2009a, 2009b) and Priego-Valverde (2009) address failed humour; Hay (1995) examines types of humour in conversations between friends. In the field of conversational analysis, the social meanings expressed by humour are further illuminated (e.g., Sacks 1989; Pizzini 1991). There is also a good deal of recent research examining the social meaning of humour (e.g., Kotthoff 2006; Tracy et al. 2006; Norrick & Chiaro 2009). Since the present research addresses humour in business meetings, the next section is devoted to a literature review of workplace humour.

6.2 Workplace humour

Over the past twenty years, research on humour in the workplace has been undertaken in such disciplines as business management, social psychology, and communication. In recent years, a focus has been the analysis of humour in authentic business interaction (Westwood & Rhodes, 2007). Research on workplace humour includes: humour in business organisations (Decker 1987; Davis & Kleiner 1989; Duncan et al. 1990; Morreall 1991); humour for improving productivity (Caudron 1992); humour for defusing conflict among workers (Duncan et al 1990; Fry 1992); humour as a component of the complexity of the workings of business organisations (Hatch & Ehrlich 1993); humour as social cohesion at work (Blau 1955; O'Quin & Arnoff 1981; Holdway 1988), leadership and humour (Schnurr 2005, 2009); humour and gender (Mullany 2004; Schnurr & Holmes 2009; Vine et al. 2009); and so on.

The research literature indicates that humour plays a particularly important role in the workplace from a relational perspective. However, most of the research focusses on workplace humour in English speaking societies. By contrast, the amount of literature on workplace humour in Japanese is very scarce. As one rare example, Takekuro (2006) conducted a contrastive study on humour in Japanese and in English and showed that there were no occurrences of humour in Japanese formal business settings while there were many occurrences of humour in similar settings in English. These findings suggest that humour may not be considered appropriate in Japanese workplace settings. The current study addresses this issue. I begin with a consideration of different definitions of humour.

6.2.1 Definition

Humour is a "complex and paradoxical phenomenon" (Linstead 1985: 741). Workplace humour is context bound and often cannot easily be understood by non-group members (e.g., Pogrebin & Poole 1988; Holmes & Stubbe 2003; Schnurr 2005). Researchers have provided various definitions of (workplace) humour. For example, drawing on a significant amount of authentic workplace interaction, Holmes (2000c) defines humour as follows:

> Humorous utterances are defined as those which are identified by the analyst, on the basis of paralinguistic, prosodic, and discoursal clues, as intended by the speaker(s) to be amusing and perceived to be amusing by at least some participants' (Holmes 2000c: 163).

In her definition, the role of the analyst is considered. Holmes (2000c) points out that deciding whether an utterance is humorous depends on the analyst's point of view. In analysing humour, a variety of interactional clues such as "the speaker's tone of voice and the audience's auditory and discoursal response" (2000c: 163) play important roles.

Mullany (2004) criticises Holmes' (2000c) definition for not covering unintentional or failed humour, and for being speaker-oriented. Mullany (2004: 21) expands Holmes' (2000c) definition in the following way:

> Humour is defined as instances [of utterances] where participant(s) signal amusement to one another, based on the analyst's assessment of paralinguistic, prosodic and discoursal clues. These instances [of utterances] can be classified as either successful or unsuccessful according to addressees' reactions. Humour can be a result of either intentional or unintentional humorous behaviour from participants.

Within the definition above, Mullany (2004) includes failed or unsuccessful humour and unintentional humour where a listener laughs at an utterance that is not intended to be amusing. Her definition includes hearers' perspectives as well as speakers' perspectives.

Schnurr (2005) takes hearers' emotions into consideration in adopting Brown and Keegan's (1999) approach to humour. It is reasonable to think that humour and responses to humour are emotion-involving activities which can be constructed discursively and jointly between speakers and hearers. From the speakers' points of view, there are successful and failed attempts at humour. From the hearers' points of view, on the other hand, there are possible varieties of responses "such as the prototypical laughter or smile, as well as the lift of an eyebrow, the production of more laughter or the expression of offence" (Schnurr 2005: 44). This means that the hearer's perception of humour depends on a variety of situations and their emotions are not limited to amusement but also other different feelings. Schnurr (2005: 44), thus, defines humour as:

> ... [U]tterances which are intended and/or perceived as being funny, and which result in a change of emotions in the audience, which then triggers some kind of response.

Schnurr's (2005) definition includes not only failed or unsuccessful humour but unintentional humour and also a variety of responses involving hearer's feelings. Her definition considers hearers' perspectives as well as speakers' perspectives. That is, her succinct definition considers humour as being jointly constructed in ongoing interaction. In this research, thus, I take Schnurr's (2005) definition.

6.2.2 Classification

Regarding a taxonomy of humour, Hay (1995) classifies humour into 12 types by analysing authentic conversations among friends. By analysing humour in authentic workplace interaction, Schnurr (2005) develops Hay's taxonomy into 13 types of humour including anecdote, fantasy, self-denigrating, teasing, and wordplay. With reference to other research on workplace humour, some of the most relevant types are described below.

Hay (1995) found that anecdotes and fantasy are by far the most frequently occurring types of humour in her data. *Anecdote* is defined as "a story which the speaker perceives to be amusing" (Hay 1995: 65) and is about "the experience or actions of either the speaker or someone they are acquainted with" (1995: 65-66). *Fantasy* is similar to anecdote in that both are story telling but different in that anecdote is based on an event that actually took place. Fantasy is "the construction of humorous, imaginary scenarios or events" (Hay 2001:

62). It encourages participation and is usually a collaborative construction of humor with a number of participants contributing (Marra 1998; Hay 2001; Holmes & Marra 2002a).

Self-denigrating or *self-deprecating* humour is "an insult directed at oneself" (Hay 1995: 78). This kind of humour could be employed as a defence strategy when making a mistake by showing one's admission of the mistake (Hay 1995, 2001; Zajdman 1995). In her research on leadership and humour, Schnurr (2005) found that self-denigrating humour is often employed by leaders to minimise status differences. By laughing at themselves, leaders show their willingness to admit their own weaknesses and failures and this makes them "seem more human and approachable" (Barsoux 1993: 112).

A *tease* is "a potentially insulting/aggressive comment but simultaneously provides/relies upon cues that the utterance is to be understood as playful/non-serious" (Alberts, 1992: 155) and includes jocular abuse, where "the speaker jokingly insults a member of the audience" (Hay 1995: 70). Teasing has a dual nature (Alberts, 1992) and is thus ambiguous. It may function as playful and as an expression of solidarity (e.g., Hay, 1994, Schnurr 2009a) but at the same time "display(s) and reinforce(s) the speaker's power and control" (cited in Schnurr 2009: 1127; see also Boxer & Corte's-Conde, 1997; Eisenberg, 1986; Hay, 1995).

Drawing on interviews, participant observation, and document collection involving four business organisations in New Zealand, Plester (2007) explored how workplace humour is affected by workplace culture. She found that verbal banter is the most common type of humour in all the organizations she researched. *Banter* is defined as "verbal humour that involved a *put-down*, a tease, 'taking the piss' and enjoying humour at the expense of others or even at one's own expense" (Plester 2007: 178).

According to *Collins COBUILD Advanced Learner's English Dictionary New Digital Edition* (2004), banter "is teasing or joking talk that is amusing and friendly", while to tease someone means "to laugh at them or make jokes about them in order to embarrass, annoy, or upset them". The difference between tease and banter is whether the humorous utterance has possibilities to hurt the respondents' feelings. Teasing has a negative connotation as well as positive connotation while banter seems to have a positive effect.

Wordplay is defined as "any humorous statement in which the humour derives from the meanings, sounds or ambiguities of words" (Hay 1995: 79). A typical example of this type is a pun where a speaker uses "words that are either identical in sound (homonyms) or very similar in sound, but are sharply diverse in meaning" (Abrams, 1993: 172).

Another categorisation of humour is based on style of construction. Holmes & Marra (2002a) and Holmes (2006b) classified humour into two construction types, *single* and *extended contributions*. Single contribution, e.g., a quip or one-liner, means a scene where a single participant says something humorous but another humorous utterance does not follow. On the other hand, extended contributions are sequences of humorous utterances and called *conjoint humour* by these authors. Conjoint humour is divided into a continuum from *collaborative* (supportive) to *non-collaborative* (contestive) types of humour. The continuum depends on how participants link their humorous contributions to the contributions of others, with very different effects in terms of the overall style of interaction

One end of the continuum has very collaboratively supportive, jointly constructed humour sequences where participants "integrate contributions tightly, using devices such as echoing, mirroring or completing another's utterance" (Holmes & Marra 2002a: 1688). This type of humour sequence represents "an obvious means by which people 'do collegiality' at work" (Holmes & Marra 2002a: 1688). This is also described by Coates as "'all-together-now' (ATN) talk – talk in which participants' turns supportively overlap with each other or are sensitively synchronized with participants' echoing, mirroring, or completing each others' turns" (Cited in Holmes 2006b: 38, see also Coates, 1989:120). The other end of the continuum is labelled "competitive" where "participants each [make] independent autonomous contributions to the construction of the overall sequence" (Holmes 2006b: 39) with little overlap. Participants compete with each other to "produce succinct quips or brief, witty one-liners, which are relatively loosely semantically linked" (Holmes 2006b: 38). This type corresponds to "a sparky 'one-at-a-time' (OAAT) style of talk (to use Coates' term, 1989: 120)" (Holmes 2006b: 38).

Conjoint humour can be summarised as in the following table:

Collaborative, supportive		Non-collaborative, competitive
• Humorous sequences constructed using a more collaborative style • Stylistically cooperative (collaborative) • Conjoint humour / jointly constructed • Maximally collaboratively constructed = a cohesive contribution to a single shared floor	⇔	• Humorous sequences developed more competitively/challengingly (non-collaborative) • Minimally collaboratively constructed or competitive floor = an independent often more competitive contribution to the floor

Table 6.1: Features of a collaborative, supportive type of humour and a non-collaboratively constructed competitive type of humour

6.2.3 Distribution

In terms of distribution, most workplace humour researchers argue that humour frequently occurs at the boundaries of interaction. The opening and closing phases of meetings are favourite sites for humour (Holmes & Stubbe 2003). Humour also occurs within meetings, often during transitional phases such as around topic transition points and just after decisions have been reached (Consalvo 1989; Brown & Keegan 1999; Holmes & Stubbe 2003; Marra 2003; Schnurr 2005). These characteristics of the distribution of workplace humour correspond with those of Relational Practice, which is considered as typically peripheral in workplace discourse. It is reasonable to assume that they are similar, considering that humour is generally analysed as a typical example of Relational Practice.

6.2.4 Function

Nobody will deny that humour serves to amuse or entertain at one level. In business discourse, however, humour does not only serve this function but is multifunctional, playing an important role in contributing to good workplace relations (e.g. Brown & Keegan 1999; Holmes & Stubbe 2003; Schnurr 2005; Holmes 2006b).

Humour in the workplace is identified as an exemplary Relational Practice strategy (Holmes & Schnurr 2005) and helps to create team spirit [2] by expressing solidarity or a sense of belonging to a group (e.g., Duncan et al. 1990; Morreall 1991; Caudron 1992; Barsoux 1993; Clouse & Spurgeon 1995; Fletcher 1999). Shared humour in particular reinforces common ground and shared norms. Humour contributes to achieving both "social bonding" (Eisenberg 1986: 360) and "the glue that bonds" (Ross 1992: 2) and "constructs participants as equals, emphasising what they have in common and playing down power differences" (Holmes & Stubbe 2003: 109-110).

In workplace discourse which is "seldom neutral in terms of power" (Holmes et al. 1999: 354), humour can be used to manage power relationships among team members by de-emphasising power differences (e.g., Pizzini 1991; Brown & Keegan 1999; Holmes 2000c). For example, when producing unwelcome messages or performing face-threatening acts such as criticisms and directives from superiors to subordinates, humour can serve as a softener or hedge. It expresses concern for maintaining good workplace relationships by those who are in positions of power and can attenuate the power difference (Holmes 2000c; Holmes & Stubbe 2003). Humour is used as "an effective way of 'doing power' less explicitly, a subtle device for getting things done in a socially and professionally acceptable manner" (Holmes & Stubbe 2003: 122). Thus, because humour can minimise status differences and avoid hurting respondents' feelings, it can be employed as an effective leadership tool (e.g., Yukl 1989; Schnurr 2005)

On the other hand, humour can also be employed by subordinates to challenge power differences when expressing disapproval and resistance. Humour is considered as an acceptable means for expressing subversive attitudes or aggressive feelings (Rodrigues & Collinson 1995; Ackroyd & Thompson 1999; Holmes 2000c, Holmes & Marra 2002b). These findings indicate that humour may be employed by everyone regardless of their position or power.

In addition, in terms of identity work, Schnurr (2009) and Mullany (2007) analysed humour in authentic workplace interaction and argue that humour contributes to the construction of various social identities including leader, manager, and gender identities.

Another function of humour is defusing tension and "thus facilitate[s] dealing with difficult situations and stress" (Schnurr 2005: 52). According to Holmes (2000c), in some meetings, humour occurs during difficult negotiations. Because of this function, humour effectively is employed in some workplaces such as in police offices (Pogrebin & Poole 1988), in hospitals (White & Howse 1993), and in emergency rooms (Rosenberg 1998). Holmes and Stubbe (2003: 71) identify a marker of "tension release" as one of the functions of meeting humour and point out that humour occurs "after difficult discussion sections in meetings, especially in work places where participants' face needs and work relationships were given attention".

6.2.5 Workplace humour and culture

It is generally agreed that not only the use of humour but also the perception of humour are affected by socio-cultural factors (e.g., Apte 1985; Hayakawa 2003). In terms of workplace humour, from a CofP approach, it has been pointed out that the manifestation of workplace humour is different according to each CofP (e.g., Holmes and Marra 2002a; Holmes and Stubbe 2003; Holmes 2006a). Holmes and Marra (2002a) found that such dimensions of humour as the amount, type (single utterance or extended sequence), and construction (collaborative vs. competitive) help to characterise a distinctive workplace culture.

On the other hand, Marra and Holmes (2007) compared workplace humour between a Maori organisation and a Pacific Island factory team and pointed out that not only the culture of the CofP (i.e. workplace culture) but also ethnic cultural norms or underlying expectations affect the manifestation of humour. Moreover, in their empirical cross-cultural study on workplace humour in

New Zealand and Hong Kong, Schnurr and Chan (2009) suggest that the manifestation of humour is influenced by expectations of "several layers of culture" from micro-level (i.e. workplace) to macro-level (the wider society where the workplace belongs)" (2009: 152). This issue is worth examining in the current cross-cultural study.

6.3 Responses to humour and laughter

Before analysing the data on humour in this study, it is useful to consider ways of responding to humour, and laughter in particular.

Humour and laughter have long been strongly linked. It is generally recognised that laughter is the most common response to humour. However, many researchers, who focus on humour and laughter in real interaction, have questioned the assumption that they are inseparable (e.g., Provine 2000; Haakana 2002; Glenn 2003; Hayakawa 2003). In series of studies on humour, Hay (1994, 1995, 1996, 2001) analysed responses to humour in authentic interaction. Her research results indicate that "different types of humour are responded to in different ways by the audience at which they are directed, and the appropriateness of the support strategies depend on the context in which the humour occurs" (Hay 1995: 187). A variety of humour responses include not only laughter but also smiling, nodding, producing more humour, echoing some of the words, and so on. The strategy that hearers adopt for responding to humour depends on the situational context.

Given that laughter is one of the major ways of responding to humour, research on laughter in interaction gives an interesting insight from a relational perspective. For example, Glenn (2003) focusses on the production and interpretation of laughter in English interactions, while Hayakawa (2003) examines laughter in Japanese interactions. Both argue that laughter plays an important role in the creation and maintenance of interpersonal relationships. However, differences are apparent in their focuses of types of laughter. Glenn's (2003) main focus is laughter associated with things which are laughable or funny, while Hayakawa's (2003) main focus is laughter which does not indicate amusement or humour.

In earlier research (Murata 2005), I analysed intercultural conversations conducted in English between American and Japanese participants on their first encounter. The results indicated interesting differences. While the Americans laughed only at comments which were obviously intended to be funny, the Japanese not only laughed at humorous comments but also at more general and neutral comments. The Americans did not seem to know how to interpret the Japanese laughter following utterances not intended to be funny, and this caused misunderstanding between the Americans and the Japanese. Based on this analysis, it appears that Japanese laughter sometimes reflects amusement or enjoyment like American laughter, while sometimes it does not.

It can be argued that laughter is not only a response to humour, or a constituent of a conversational sequence, but also an independent component of conversants' communicative behaviours, serving particular discourse functions in interaction, especially in Japanese interaction. Since the current study addresses the Japanese data, it is important to take these functions of laughter into consideration when analysing the data. It will be interesting to explore how humour and laughter function, especially in Japanese meeting discourse, from a relational point of view.

6.4 Analysis of humour

In this section, the manifestation of humour is presented first in regard to formal meetings and then informal meetings. The findings of previous research on humour discussed in the previous sections are drawn on to shed light on the humour in the New Zealand and Japanese meeting discourse.

6.4.1 Humour in formal meetings

This section explores the manifestations of humour in formal meetings of company N and company J, describing its distribution, instigators, types, and functions.

Distribution

In terms of distribution, corresponding to the previous literature, humour generally occurs at the boundaries of interaction including opening and closing phases. As noted in Chapter 4, because the five sections of formal meetings are clearly divided, it is easy to confirm that humour typically occurs at the section boundaries as shown in the examples in this section. As discussed in Chapter 5, humour is often accompanied by small talk especially in the pre-meeting phases at both companies. However, that is not always the case. Especially during discussion phases, business related topics also accompany humour as shown in the examples in this section.

As discussed in Chapters 4 and 5, the overall tone of talk is different in formal meetings between the two CofPs. In particular, there are more occurrences of humour at company N's formal meetings. For example, in two out of three formal meetings at company N, humour and laughter follow the chairperson's opening remarks. On the other hand, in formal meetings at company J, the sales staff's reports start just after the chair's opening remarks without any laughter or humour. This suggests that humour contributes to the difference in the tone of the meeting.

Instigators

A significant difference is found regarding the instigators of humour in the two CofPs. In company N's formal meetings, everyone contributes to the humour. In company J's formal meetings, on the other hand, the moderator and CEO mainly initiate the humour. Overall, the moderator or CEO offers humour and other meeting members respond to it.

Example 6.1 is from a formal meeting at company N and takes place just after the meeting starts. As discussed in section 6.2.3, the opening phase is one of the typical potential sites for humour. Jaeson, the chairperson, introduces a new member and a new manager who is the current pre-production manager.

Example 6.1 [NFM02_04, 08:45]   (Cf. Example 4.3)
```
    1   Jaeson:   okay ++ get into it + okay
    2             thanks everyone for coming along
    3             just like to welcome our newest member
    4             to the management team + Darryl
    5             who's now serving as the er pre-production manager
→   6             and um we have a new i s manager
    7   Paul:     i s?
    8   Jaeson:   /i s\ + how's that
    9   Harry:    /i s\
   10   XM:       apparently
   11   XM:       is that
   12   Paul:     the information system sounds better than than
   13             in- in- infoma- info /i t\
   14             /[laughter]\ [laughter]
   15   Evan:     [laughs]: waiting for that one:
   16             [laughter]
   17   Sharon:   i s
   18   Jaeson:   eh
   19   Paul:     i s
→  20   Jaeson:   yeah 1/it's twenty\1 first century now it's called i s 2/(  )\2
   21   Sharon:   1/i s\1   2/i\2 s
   22   Paul:     oh okay
   23   Harry:    i t comes after i s
   24   Jaeson:   is it [laughs]
   25             … [about 1 minute deleted]
```

→ 26 Jaeson: okay just going back over the previous minute

Jaeson mistakenly says "I S" instead of "I T" in line 6. These acronyms for a concept create an opportunity for the team members to tease one another, using linguistic play around the term "I S", and laughter occurs. The meeting members, regardless of status, jointly tease Jaeson, the chair and general manager, who has higher status than other members, by constructing humour cooperatively. Jaeson, the target of the teasing, does not keep quiet but responds with humour to defend himself, as seen in line 20. It is evident from this example that everyone actively contributes to humour and constructs humorous sequences collaboratively and "polyphonically" (Coates 1996), which was also found in the construction of small talk in Chapter 5. It is worth noting that after the sequence of humour the chair returns to the meeting talk by employing the topic transitional marker "okay" in line 26.

Example 6.2 is from a formal meeting at company J. Ueki, a development staff member, is talking about a code for a client. He is reporting that the client found a strange number on a note, which is written in *kana* (a Japanese syllabary).

Example 6.2 [JFM03_03, 23:40]

 1 Manabe: カナの手形ナンバー
              kana no tegata nambaa
              the note's kana number
 2 Ueki: ええ 手形についてる番号自身が 普通は英数字できますよね
              ee tegata ni tsuiteru bangoo jishin ga futsuu wa eisuuji de kimasu yo ne
              yes on the note the number usually is written in letters of the English alphabet and numbers
 3   振出銀行から
              furidashi ginkoo kara
              from a selling bank
 4 Tanimoto: うん うん カナで
              un un kana de
              Uh huh kana[a kind of letter: the Japanese syllabaries]
 5 Ueki: カナです
              kana desu
              kana
→ 6 Manabe: 見たことあるような気がしますね 小切手とか手形で
              mitakoto aru yoona ki ga shimasu ne kogitte toka tegata de

7		I think I've ever seen it on checks and notes for example
		カタカナの シ テ みたいなものが 古―いもの
		katakana no shi te mitai na mono ga furuui mono
		something like "シ" "テ" in kana Very old ones
→ 8	Komeda:	明治時代？
		Meiji jidai?
		the Meiji era?
9		[笑いがおこる]
		[laughter]
10	Ueki:	今回たまたまあった
		konkai tamatama atta no wa
		the note I happened to see
11		あの ABC[銀行名]の名古屋支店のほうの発行分だけだったんで
		ano ABC[=bank name] no Nagoya shiten no hoo no hakkoobun datta n de
		is from that ABC[=bank name] 's Nagoya branch, only from that office
12		そちらに問い合わせをしてみたんですね
		sochira ni toiawase o shite mita n desu ne
		and I've asked the branch
13		そうすると その その番号管理自身は
		soosuruto sono sono bangoo kanri jishin wa
		then, they said, managing numbers on notes
14		あの 支店で独自でやられて されてるらしいんですね
		ano shiten de dokuji de yararete sareteru rashiin desu ne
		depends on each branch they said
15		ですから あの 実際には起こり得るみたいなんですけど
		desukara ano jissai ni wa okoriuru mitai na n desu kedo
		so this can happen actually
16		… [about 20 seconds deleted]
17	Komeda:	それは何 地銀かなんか？
		sore wa nani chigin ka nanka?
		is this a local bank?
18	Ueki:	いえ ABC[笑]
		ie ABC [laughs]
		no ABC [laughs]
→ 19	Komeda:	ABC か[笑]自分とこの会社は ABC って言うてるくせにな
		ABC ka [laughs] jibun toko no kaisha wa ABC tte iuteru kuse ni na

		ABC isn't it? [laughter] you know the name of the bank is ABC isn't it?
20		[笑いがおこる] [laughter]

Manabe, another meeting member, says that he thinks he has seen *kana* on an old note in line 6. Following Manabe's turn, in line 8, Komeda asks an intentionally foolish question: "The Meiji era?" and general laughter occurs. The *Meiji* era is more than 100 years ago and nobody can see the currently available notes made in those days. Later Ueki explains that the note is from a nationwide, popular bank in Japan. Komeda makes another comical remark in 19. His utterance means the letters on the note from their branch are written in *kana* that looks very old-fashioned and strange while the bank's name is in the English alphabet and looks modern and fashionable. As this example and example 6.8 later in this section show, a typical pattern of humour in formal meetings at company J is that the CEO or the chair instigates the humour and other members respond with laughter.

Types

The first difference between the two CofPs regarding types of humour is how humour is constructed. In both CofPs, there are occurrences of conjoint humour, but the way of constructing humour is different. As found in Example 6.1, in formal meetings at company N, humour is often co-constructed by meeting members. In formal meetings at company J, there are also occurrences of conjoint humour as seen in the following example. Example 6.3 takes place shortly before a sales staff member, Chida, finishes reporting to the group, which is a topic transitional phase and an exemplary site of humour.

Example 6.3 [JFM01_02, 17:30]

→ 1	Komeda:	デモしたときに、その中で [O 社] の人 [笑]: いなかった : ? *demo shita toki ni sono naka de* [company O] *no hito* [laughs]: *inakatta :?* when you made a demonstration [*of company J's product (computer software)*] wasn't there someone from company O?
2	Chida:	いました *imashita* there was
3	Komeda:	やっぱり *yappari*

CHAPTER 6 HUMOUR   137

		it figures
4	Chida:	[O社]の あの [O社] から来てる監査法人なんですけども
		[company O]no ano [company O] kara kiteru kansahoo-jin na n desu kedo mo
		Company O well the auditing company affiliated with company O
5		その監査法人はまったくもう +
		sono kansahoojin wa mattaku moo +
		that auditing company completely
6	Ashizawa:	えっ/監査法人?\
		e /kansahoojin?\
		what? auditing company?
7	Manabe:	/コンサル\
		/konsaru\
		consulting company
8	Chida:	コンサル 監査法人じゃなく コンサルで
		konsaru kansahoojin ja nakute konsaru de
		consulting company not auditing company but consulting company
9		私はもうこっちとか こっちという [O社] から来てるけども
		watashi wa moo kocchi toka kocchi to iu [company O] kara kiteru kedo mo
		[the man from company O said] though I'm from some company which is affiliated with company O
10		[O社の製品名] を押すとかしません/あくまでも\
		[company O's product's name] o osu toka simasen / akumademo\
		I don't mean to push [company O's product's name] really
→ 11	Komeda:	/そりゃ言うわ\そりゃ
		/sorya iu wa\ sorya
		he's sure to say so
12		[笑いが起こる]
		[laughter]
13	Ashizawa:	おれでも 言う [笑]
		ore demo iu [laughs]
		if I were he I would definitely say so [laughs]
14	Yoshioka:	そりゃそうです
		sorya soo desu

		that's right
15	Manabe:	われわれでも言います
		ware ware demo ii masu
		we're sure to say so
16	Tanimoto:	言うよ言うよ
		iuyo iuyo
		sure to say sure to say
17		[笑いがおこる]
		[laughter]
18	Ashizawa:	そうか
		sooka
		I see
19		(4.0)
20	Chida:	私の担当分は以上です ++
		watashi no tantoo bun wa ijoo desu ++
		that's all from me ++

The meeting members together deduce that Chida's client company might be under the umbrella of an IT company called company O in the example. This company is a rival of company J. When Chida made a demonstration of his company's product, computer software, at the client company, he met someone from company O's affiliated consulting company. Being asked by Komeda, the CEO, whether there was someone from company O (or its related company) in line 1, Chida answers "yes" and then talks about the man's comment after the demonstration that he doesn't mean to push company O's product though he is from a firm related to company O in lines 8 to 10. Then, in line 11, Komeda makes fun of the client person, saying in a humorous tone "he's sure to say so [= *he's sure to say that he is not pushing his related company's product*]", implying that although he is saying so he must push the product. Then, other members, one after another, humorously and strongly support him by agreeing with his remark, and these agreements contribute conjoint humour which is constructed dynamically and discursively.

It is interesting to observe that there is a subtle shift in register in the sequence from lines 11 to 16. That is, Komeda in line 11 speaks colloquial Kansai daialect (/*sorya iu wa sorya*\). Ashizawa in line 13 also employs "*ore*", a colloquial form of *I* and ends his utterance with plain form. Yoshioka in line 14 uses Kansai dialect "*sorya*" and Tanimoto's utterance ends with plain form. These shifts could be regarded as functioning to frame the sequence as humorous.

Conjoint humour in this CofP is all initiated by the CEO and then followed by other members, not vice versa. From a CofP approach, or social constructionist perspective, it could be argued that the use of humour in this way contributes to the construction of the status relationships and affirms the CEO's superior status. It is also worth noting the order of responses with the humour. Ashizawa first responds with humour, and then Yoshioka, Manabe, and Ashizawa follow him. Ashizawa, the chair, is in charge of the interaction and thus in a powerful role, so it is reasonable that he initiated the responses to the CEO's humour. While Yoshioka and Manabe are both directors, Yoshioka is an in-house director but Manabe is an outside director. This difference is apparent in the speaking order. Finally Tanimoto is neither director nor a staff member at this company, so his turn is the last. This order thus both reflects and contributes to the creation of the power relationships in this interaction. Manabe and Tanimoto are professional accountants and are of higher social status. This is evident from the fact that the meeting members call both of them "*sensei*" which refers to someone respected. According to this social status, Manabe or Tanimoto should respond to the CEO's humour before Ashizawa and Yoshioka. Nevertheless, in this excerpt, they do not initiate the humorous responses but follow the other two members. It could be thus argued that Tanimoto and Manabe are not showing identities as professional accountants but other aspects of their identities such as outside director and (outside) business consultant. This indicates that various aspects of identities are discursively and dynamically negotiated with other conversational participants, and power relations are also not static but constructed dynamically and discursively among the participants.

Another difference is found in the use of teasing. In company N's meetings, one of the salient types of humour is teasing. The following is an example of a typical type of teasing at company N.

Example 6.4 [NFM03_05, 01:50]

→	1	Veronica:	can you (keep) your financial notes Evan
	2		Evan: um there won't be many
	3		but 1/yes what there are\1 I'll give you 2/+\2
	4		it's going to be brief and to the point today
	5		I've been told off about waffling on about crap
	6		that no one cares about so
	7	Veronica:	1/oh okay\1
	8		2/[voc]\2
	9		[laughs]
→	10	Evan:	I'm not looking at you particularly Harry
	11	Veronica:	[laughs]
→	12	Harry:	no I don't don't mind you waffling
	13		I just want it in English /[laughs]\

14		not accountant not accountant talk
15	Veronica:	/[laughs]\
16	Paul:	three words it's all good
17	Harry:	yeah something like that
18	Evan:	we made money thr- or we didn't three or two
19	Harry:	three or two

In example 6.4, Veronica asks Evan if she can get the financial notes, in line 1. Evan says there aren't any notes that day, and he is going to keep the meeting brief as he has been told off for "waffling", directing this at Harry in line 10. Harry says he does not mind waffling; it just needs to be in English, not accountant talk, in line 12 to 14. Evan teases Harry because Harry always complains that Evan's talk on financial issues is too long and tiring. Harry responds with reciprocal teasing. This kind of mutual teasing is often found at this CofP also seen example 6.1.

In company J's formal meetings, on the other hand, teasing is conducted one-way from those who are in authority to those who are of lower status. The following is an example of teasing at company J.

Example 6.5 [JFM03_06, 19:10]

1	Wada:	… そこら辺は　結構まともな人なんで　やってる人が…
		…*sokora hen wa kekkoo matomona hito na n de yatteru hito ga …*
		…so the man who is in charge at the company would be reliable …
2		[クライアントの担当者名] さん 終わった後何か言っていたの？
		[the client company's responsible person's name] *san owatta ato nanika itte ita no?*
		[the client company's responsible person's name] said something after the meeting?
3		すごくニュアンスが違うんやけど [笑]
		sugoku nyuansu ga chigau n ya kedo [laughs]
		what he said is different from [*what Kanda said*] [laughs]
→ 4	Komeda:	お客さんまともやのに 営業まともじゃないみたいやな
		okyakusan matomo ya no ni eigyoo matomo ja nai mitai ya na
		the client would be reliable, but the sales staff member[=*Kanda*]does not seem reliable
5		[笑いがおこる]

			[laughter]
6	Ashizawa:		何か言えよ
			nanika ie yo
			say something
7			[笑いが起こる]
			[laughter]
8	Ashizawa:		返せよ おまえ
			kaese yo omae
			you should make a response
→ 9	Komeda:		営業は大丈夫か？
			eigyoo wa daijoobu ka?
			is the sales staff[=*Kanda*]all right?
10			[笑いが起こる]
			[laughter]
11			[*After this general laughter, Wada, who is in charge of Kanda's client company as a systems engineer, and Hosoi, Wada's boss who is in charge of system development section of company J, talk about the current situation with this client.*]
12	Hosoi:		…だから単純に まあやりたいんじゃないのかなっていう感じは受けたけど
			…dakara tanjun ni maa yaritai n ja nai no kana tte iu kanji wa uketa kedo
			…to speak simply I felt from them [*the client*] that he would like to do [*use company J's product*]
13			あのー　すぐね資料をコピーしてくれって言ってたよね
			anoo sugu ne shiryoo o kopii shite kure tte itta yo ne
			well they immediately asked us to give them a copy of our document didn't they
			(2.0)
14	Kanda:		はあ　そうですね
			haa soo desu ne
			yes, I think so, too.
15	Hosoi:		黙ってて微笑んでるのもいいのかな /(　)\
			damattete hohoenderu no mo ii no ka na /(　)\
			it might be good for you to remain silent and smiling/(　)\
16			/[笑]\
			/[laughter]\
→ 17	Ashizawa:		神田さんの営業力かな /[笑]\
			kanda san no eigyooryoku kana

18   that's because of Kanda's sales ability, isn't it? /[laughs]\
            /[笑]\
            /[laughter]\

In Example 6.5, Kanda, a sales person, has finished reporting to the group about his client company. While Kanda said in his report that the client is only worrying about the cost, Wada said that the client's main concern is not the cost but the content of the software and that the client is considering similar software developed by company J's competitors. His talk sounds diffident and as if it lacks confidence and everyone is worried about whether he can make a contract with the company. After Kanda's turn, Wada, who is in charge of Kanda's client company as a systems engineer, explains the situation to date in lines 1 to 3. Following Wada's comment, Komeda, the CEO, and Ashizawa, the chairperson, both of whom are in positions of power and higher status than Kanda, jocularly abuse Kanda in lines 4 to 9. As opposed to the teasing at company N, Kanda, the target of the teasing, does not say anything but simply remains quiet.

Teasing is an ambiguous strategy (e.g., Hay 2001; Schnurr 2005). It may indicate a feeling of solidarity among interlocutors, but at the same time, be a potentially face-threatening act. In line 18, after sequences of teasing by Komeda and Ashizawa, Ashizawa, the chair, tries to diminish his teasing's possible negative effect by giving a positive comment about his sales ability. Then other members respond to this utterance with laughter. It is plausible to propose that Ashizawa is worrying about whether his teasing hurt Kanda's feelings and is showing his consideration toward Kanda, a sales staff, by encouraging him and his humour contributes to constructing Ashizawa's identity as Kanda's superior and sales director. This functions as an important relational strategy to construct rapport and also as Relational Practice which advances the primary objectives of the workplace, i.e. selling their product.

This supports the suggestion that among meeting members in this CofP, only those who are in positions of power can use this strategy, teasing. However it is worth noting that Komeda, CEO, initiates the teasing and then Ashizawa, the chair, follows him. As found in example 6.3, this order helps to construct the status relationships or power relations and affirm the CEO's superior status. It is noteworthy that humour is employed in this CofP to reinforce power relationships, a finding that is counter to previous studies (e.g., Pizzini 1991; Brown & Keegan 1999), which argue that humour manages power relationships among team members by de-emphasising power differences.

Another difference between the two CofPs is the use of a particular type of humour. In company N's formal meetings, collaborative fantasy humour is often found.

Example 6.6 [NFM03_05, 36:30]

1	Jaeson:	now in the catalogue we we er have um
2		we got pictures on every page you know
3		showing the products in use
4		so if it's business cards or if it's folders
5		or anything like that
6		⋯ [*about 20 seconds deleted*]
7		well what I was gonna say 1/+ is\1 is that um
→ 8		some of you may be approached to to be models
9		in + 2/in this\2 um catalogue
10		1/[laughter]\1
11		2/[laughter]\2
12	Harry:	I /was\ and where was I
13	Sharon:	/yeah\
14		[laughter]
15	Jaeson:	1/(h-) holding a ( ) and a fosters\1
16		2/+ wasn't what we meant [laughs]\2
17	Sharon:	1/the photo the photos haven't been taken yet\1
18		2/[laughter]\2
19	Jaeson:	so um yeah you might be approached
20		and asked to be in
21		I know Paul has several engagements already
22	Harry:	[clears throat] 1/+ oh [laughs]: 2/god:\1\2
23	Sharon:	1/[laughs]\1
24	Jaeson:	2/(one of us is in)\2 [laughs]
25		we might [laughs]: have: we may have to pay
26		to have Paul on it /[laughs]\
27	Paul:	/yeah\
28	Sharon:	yeah
29	Harry:	book him /in\
30	Jaeson:	/yeah\
31	Paul:	not a bad rate

In example 6.6, Jaeson is talking about the pictures on the company's catalogue which they are going to produce. In line 8, he says humorously that some of the meeting participants may be approached to be models for the catalogue. Of course, no one actually was approached to be models for the catalogue, but the members talk humorously as if they were approached to be models. They jointly construct imaginary happenings.

This is a typical example of fantasy humour. Fantasy is defined as "the construction of humorous, imaginary scenarios or events" (Hay 2001: 62). It is one of the typical types of humour found in casual and informal conversations among friends (Hay 2001), and it encourages participation and is usually a collaborative construction with a number of participants contributing (Marra 1998; Hay 2001; Holmes & Marra 2002). As the transcription shows, there are many overlaps. Fast and witty repartee within a team seems to indicate that the members are not only very aware of the importance of the issue (the new catalogue) but can also make fun of it. The brevity and directness of the contributions increase the humorous effect and make the atmosphere informal and casual like conversations among friends.

In company N's formal meetings, fantasy humour constructed cooperatively and discursively is prominent, while in the meetings at company J, there are no occurrences of this type of humour. Considering that fantasy humour is typical in casual conversations among friends, it could be argued the atmosphere is more informal and relaxed in formal meetings at company N than in those at company J, as also discussed in Chapter 5.

In formal meetings at company J, while most humour is initiated by the CEO or the chair, there are several sequences of humour where the participants make fun of their client. In this type of humour, not only those who are in authority but also other members contribute to the humour.

Example 6.7 [JFM01_04, 09:00]

1   Nio: エクセルで作るのが大変なんで お手上げですということです
ekuseru de tsukuru no ga taihen na n de oteage desu to iu koto desu
they have trouble making document in Excel and are at a loss

2   Hosoi: エクセルもちゃんと図形とか全部つくのにね [笑]
ekuseru mo chanto zukei toka zenbu tsuku no ni ne
Excel has everything like figure [laughs]

3   [笑いがおこる]
[laughter]

4   Manabe: あのー 最初作るのはいいんですけど
anoo saisho tsukuru no wa ii n desu kedo
at the beginning it is OK

5   修正とかをし出すと やっぱりエクセルとかじゃ 本当大変なんですよ
shuusei toka o shidasu to yappari ekuseru toka ja hontoo taihen na n desu yo
but once a correction is made, after all it's hard to use Excel

6   Hosoi: 反対やで
hantai ya de

		opposite
7		一番心配なのは そこに書く文書が考えられないんじゃないかなとかね
		ichiban shinpai nano wa soko ni kaku bunsho ga kangaerarenai n ja nai kana toka ne
		what I'm worrying about most is that they cannot think about the document itself which is made [with Excel]
8	Nio:	まあ その 電話の話で その 1,000 もこうエクセルでつなげるところも
		maa sono denwa no hanashi de sono sen mo koo ekuseru de tsunageru tokoro mo
		well in a telephone conversation [the client] says 1,000 connected in Excel
9		画面ではつながっているけど印刷したらずれとるという
		gamen de wa tsunagatte iru kedo insatsu shitara zuretoru to iu
		in the screen it is connected but the print out is out of alignment
10		[笑いがおこる]
		[laughter]
11	Manabe:	なるほど
		naruhodo
		I see
12	Nio:	ほんまにエクセルで作ってんのっちゅう話
		homma ni ekuseru de tsukutte n no tchuu hanashi
		I'm wondering if they actually use Excel to make [documents]
13	Hosoi:	エクセルが使えないんじゃないんですか もともと
		ekuseru ga tsukae nai n ja nai n desu ka motomoto
		they cannot use Excel actually can they?
14		[笑いがおこる]
		[laughter]

In Example 6.7, the participants express doubts about whether a client can use Excel, Microsoft's spreadsheet application, by making fun of the client. Topics related to their clients can be shared among the meeting members and humour about them reinforces their bond and creates team spirit.

Functions

One common and salient function of humour in both CofPs is to contribute to solidarity and create team spirit. The following is from a formal meeting at company J. It is a scene where Sumiyoshi, a new sales staff member at company J, succeeded in making a contract with his client for the first time and is reporting his success.

Example 6.8 [JFM03_06, 27:30]

→	1	Ashizawa:	はい 大トリ
			hai ootori
			now Ootori
	2	Sumiyoshi:	はい えー [クライアント名] さんですね
			hai ee [client company's name]san desu ne
			OK as for [client company's name]
	3		えー あのう 最終的に あのう まずはじめに あのう
			ee anoo saishuuteki ni anoo mazu hajimeni anoo
			well finally well first of all you know
	4		アドバイザリーサービスのところで えー 注文書をいただきまして
			adobaizariisaabisu no tokoro de ee chuumonsho o itadakimashite
			regarding advisory service related you know I got the order
	5		で えー で今日なんですけど -
			de ee de kyoo na n desu kedo-
			and you know today
	6	Ashizawa:	うん
			un
			Uh huh
	7	Sumiyoshi:	あのう [製品名] のほうの注文書が昼 +
			anoo [product's name] no hoo no chuumonsho ga hiru +
			you know an order of the product [*from the client company*] this afternoon +
	8	Ashizawa:	もらった？
			moratta?
			did you get it?
	9	Sumiyoshi:	はい 届きました
			hai todoki mashita
			yes it has arrived
→	10	Ashizawa:	よかった / やん !\
			yokatta /yan!
			that's good news /isn't it\
	11	XM:	/ おおお !\
			/ooo!
			/wow!\
	12		[everyone clapping their hands]

13   [笑いがおこる]
            [laughter]

When introducing sales staff, Ashizawa, the chair, always uses his or her family name, but in this example, he calls Sumiyoshi *Ootori* in a humorous tone in line 1. *Tori* means the last and most important performer of the day and *Oo* is functioning as an intensifier. Ashizawa expresses his warm welcome to the new sales staff member by using *Ootori*, which means that he is a very important person. After Sumiyoshi reports his success, in line 10, Ashizawa says "that's good news" in an exaggerated, humorous, and loud voice which elicits another member's "wow" and is followed by applause and qeneral langhter. As observed in example 6.8, there is a shift in register in lines 10 to 11. Ashizawa in line 10 ends with a colloquial Kansai dialect sentence final particle "*yan*" and "*ooo*" expresses the speaker's joy (excitement) in the Kansai colloquial dialect. These shifts could be regarded as functioning to frame the sequence as humorous.

In this example, Ashizawa actively expresses that he wants to share the joy of the success toward Sumiyoshi and encourages Sumiyoshi as Ashizawa's subordinate, simultaneously making the atmosphere friendly and supportive. In other words, from a CofP approach, Ashizawa's identity as a superior for Sumiyoshi, as well as being the chair of this whole meeting, are discursively constructed in ongoing interaction, and his use of humour here functions effectively and positively to enhance the team spirit and it helps construct rapport among the meeting members. It also functions effectively as Relational Practice which enhances the objective of the workplace (i.e. selling their products) because being encouraged by one's superior can be seen as motivating the sales staff.

This function is also reflected stylistically as shown in Chapter 5 (for an example at company J, see example 5.12 in Chapter 5). The following example is from company N's formal meeting.

Example 6. 9 [NFM01_02, 05:40]

```
    1   Evan:     what we really need's a good data projector
    2   Jaeson:   just Harry
    3   Seamus:   mm mm
    4   XF:       [laughs]
→   5   Evan:     one that can be borrowed
    6   XM:       exactly
    7   XM:       yeah /[laughs]\
    8   XMs:      /[laughs]\
→   9   Seamus:   for the rugby
```

In example 6.9, the members are talking about what they need in their office. They all agree that they need a good data projector. It is expected that Evan will finish his utterance "one [a good projector] that can be borrowed (for) …" with a work-related activity such as a presentation or meeting. Contrary to this expectation, the projector is "for the rugby" (a pass-time enjoyment). As introduced in incongruity theory in section 6.1, this incongruence results in humour. In this way, Evan and Seamus co-construct an utterance cooperatively which results in humour.

Though creating team spirit is a common function of humour across the two CofPs, there is a clear difference in terms of the function of the humour between the two CofPs. Consistent with previous literature (e.g., Holmes & Stubbe 2003; Schnurr 2005), in company N's formal meetings, there are many occurrences of laughter accompanying humorous talk about a sensitive or a serious topic, where tension could occur. The following is an example of this kind of humorous talk at company N.

Eample 6. 10 [NFM02_04, 60:10]

1	XM:	so there's gonna be no more <company's old name>
2	Sharon:	/no\
3	Jaeson:	/correct\
4	Seamus:	no
5	Harry:	oh
6	Jaeson:	gone
7	Sharon:	gone
8	Harry:	ok, so we're back to plain brown
9	Sharon:	1/no\1
10	Evan:	1/[laughs]\1
11	Seamus:	1/[laughs]\1
12	XM:	/let's not (think this)\
13	Seamus:	there'll be no mistaking them
14	Sharon:	they'll be /orange and green now\
15	XM:	that was the whole idea +
16		of having all of our cartons
17		[laughter]

In example 6.10, the meeting participants are discussing their company's re-branding. They are discussing renaming the business and changing to bright colours. Re-branding is a serious matter for a company. Whether the company is going to succeed or not may depend on the decision made at this meeting. It seems reasonable to assume that some anxiety and tension may be generated by this topic. It can be argued that talking in a humorous tone cooperatively and discursively, and generating laughter, serves to mitigate this. Thus humour here serves a relational role by mitigating the tension to maintain good relationships among the meeting participants.

On the other hand, in company J's formal meetings, in similar situations where the members are talking about a sensitive or a serious topic which could cause tension, their ways of talking are very different from those found at company N. That is, they talk about serious or sensitive topics very seriously with laughter alone (not associated with humor) often added to general statements. As discussed in section 6.3, it is interesting to note that such laughter, which is called laughter for defusing tension (Murata 2009a), is not a response to humour but serves to mitigate tension independently.[3]

To summarise, corresponding to the previous research, humour in formal meetings at both CofPs generally occurs at the boundaries of interaction including opening and closing phases, which are also favourable sections for small talk. Humour is often accompanied by small talk, but there are many occurrences of humour in business-related talk. Differences between the two CofPs can be summarised as follows: (1) in company N's formal meeting data, everyone contributes to the humour and humour is constructed cooperatively by the members, while in company J's formal meeting data, the CEO and/or the chair mainly initiate the humour; (2) salient types of humour at company N include collaboratively constructed fantasy and mutual teasing; and (3) regarding functions, while creating team spirit or building rapport is common across the CofPs, humour serves to defuse tension at company N. Especially at company J, humour also contributes to the construction of identities and the affirmation of power relations. Counter to Takekuro (2006), who suggests that humour may not be appropriate in Japanese workplace settings, in this CofP in Japan, humour functions positively from a relational perspective even in formal meetings, i.e. formal business settings.

6.4.2 Humour in informal meetings

In this section the manifestations of humour in informal meetings of company N and company J are examined, describing its distribution, instigators, types, and functions.

Distribution
One difference between formal and informal meetings is the distribution of humour. In the informal meetings at both company N and J, humour occurs not only in topic transitional sections but throughout meetings. The following is an example from an informal meeting at company N.

Example 6.11 [NIFM06_0214, 10:30] (Parts from example 5.18)

1	Paul:	um also er + I'm going to get Anna
2		to organise a a group for um sevens next year ···
3	Jaeson:	oh that's a good idea
4	Paul:	yeah
5	Jaeson:	and the [client] girls will love that eh /([names])\
6	Paul:	/oh it just depends\ on what numbers
7		we're sort of talking about
8		and what it's going to cost is the concern
9		but Seamus said oh just like the normal
10		the the same as the Dunedin thing
11		it's sort of select a um /+\ crew
12		the [client] guys will probably be there anyway
13	Jaeson:	/yeah\ that's right yeah
14	Paul:	yeah cos i think er
15	Jaeson:	are they still talking about going to Hong Kong
16		those girls
17	Paul:	they are going
18	Jaeson:	they are /yeah\ are you going to go with them
19	Paul:	/yeah\
20	Paul:	no no just [laughs] too much grief [laughs]
21	Jaeson:	yeah
22	Paul:	yeah um no Sue just um I think
23		she sort of came to the realisation
24		that I was going to be travelling with six women
25		/and er was not not very happy about it\
26	Jaeson:	/[laughs] when you told me when you told me
27		I was thinking\ jeez mate
28	Paul:	well er yeah er but /the other thing is\
29	Jaeson:	/there's no way\ I would be allowed to do that
30	Paul:	yeah the other thing is
31		I'll um I'll er probably try to take a bit of er
32		leave without pay at some stage during next year

As discussed in Chapter 5,[4] in example 6.11, Jaeson and Paul are moving back and forth between business-related talk (company N inviting their clients to a rugby game) and small talk (client "girls'" travelling to Hong Kong). Humour is finely interwoven into the ongoing meeting talk by both Paul and Jaeson. This is also found in informal meetings at company J.

Example 6.12 [JIFM01_01, 25:00]

1	Ashizawa:	クライアントはもうほとんど東京のほうが多いですか今は？
		kuraianto wa moo hotondo Tokyo no hoo ga ooi desu ka ima wa?
		do you have far more clients in Tokyo now?
2	Tanimoto:	関東多いですね。増えてきましたね 5社ぐらいですか
		Kanto ooi desu ne fuete kimashita ne 5 sha gurai desu ka
		there are many in the Kanto area [*where Tokyo is*] probably 5 companies.
3	Ashizawa:	はいはいはい
		hai hai hai
		Yeah yeah yeah
4	Tanimoto:	上場企業ばっかりなんで。
		joojookigyoo bakkari na n de
		all of them are publicly traded companies
5	Ashizawa:	はいはいはい
		hai hai hai
		Yeah yeah yeah
6		(12.0) [*they are eating something*]
→7	Tanimoto:	[ホテル名]はうちの仮事務所なんです。/[笑]\
		[name of hotel]*wa uchi no karijimusho na n desu* /[laughs]\
		[name of hotel][= *a good city hotel's name in Tokyo*] is our temporary office [*in Tokyo*] /[laughs]\
8	Ashizawa:	/[笑]\
		/[laughs]\
9	Tanimoto:	借りるほどのことでもないし
		kariru hodo no koto demo nai shi
		not enough to rent an office [*in Tokyo*]
10	Ashizawa:	はいはい
		Hai hai
		Yeah yeah
11		(11.0) [*they are eating something*]
12	Tanimoto:	狭いとしんどいですよ あの 朝から仕事してたら
		semai to shindoi desu yo ano asa kara shigoto shitetara
		being small makes me tired if I do some business [*in office*] from the morning
13	Ashizawa:	そうでしょうね そうでしょうね
		soo deshoo ne soo deshoo ne
		that's right I agree

14   (3.0)
15   それは、絶対に駄目ですよ
              sore wa zettai ni damedesu yo
              that's completely bad
16 Tanimoto: うん でも あんまり贅沢すぎると遊びに行ってるような感じがするんで
              un demo anmari zeitaku sugiru to asobi ni itteru yoona kanji ga suru n de
              yeah but if a hotel room is too gorgeous I feel I've come to Tokyo for holiday
17   知人がとってくれるから 比較的安く
              chijin ga totte kureru kara hikakuteki yasuku
              my acquaintance [*who works for the hotel's group company*] he books a hotel for me and relatively reasonably
18   すみません 費用を負担していただいて -
              sumimasen hiyoo o futan shite itadaite-
              Thank you for covering the charges [*for my stay in the hotel in Tokyo*]
19 Ashizawa: いいえ とんでもない とんでもない
              iie tondemonai tondemonai
              no, don't mention it
→ 20 Tanimoto: それで請求するの忘れ/ました から\ 1カ月ずらして請求します
              sorede seikyuu suruno wasure /mashita kara\ ikkagetsu zurasite seikyuu shimasu
              I forgot to charge you and I will charge you one month later
21 Ashizawa: /[笑]\はいはいはい
              /[laughs]\hai hai hai
              /[laughs]\ yeah yeah yeah
22 Tanimoto: それはまあ あの ひとつの（　）として 東京って行ってやっぱりね
              sore wa maa ano hitotsu no ( ) to shite Tokyo tte itte yappari ne
              that is one of (　) when I go to Tokyo after all
23   東京がなんだかんだいって内部統制は仕事は多い
              Tokyo ga nanda kanda itte naibutoosei wa shigoto wa ooi
              in Tokyo, there are a lot of business [*chances*] related to internal control.

In example 6.12, Tanimoto and Ashizawa are talking about Tanimoto's recent work. Tanimoto says that the number of clients in the Kanto area, which includes Tokyo, is increasing. Then Tanimoto starts talking about the hotel in Tokyo where he always stays. The hotel is not a hotel for business but a good city hotel. He is talking about the hotel humorously by saying that the hotel is his temporary office in Tokyo, in line 7. He also says that he feels sorry for charging the hotel fee, which would be expensive, to company J in a humorous tone. In this example, too, humour is nicely interwoven with ongoing meeting talk.

It is evident from the examples that humour and ongoing meeting talk are interwoven, and humour may occur quite abruptly almost anywhere in informal meetings. This is similar to occurrences of small talk. As discussed in Chapter 5, small talk in the informal meeting data also has the potential to occur abruptly and is interwoven in meeting talk.

Instigators and types

In terms of instigators and types of humour, there are no differences between formal and informal meetings at both CofPs. The following is an example from an informal meeting at company N.

Example 6. 13 [NIFM01_05, 16:40]
→ 1   Seamus: now Rob's just um told Trevor he was a big wussie for not
   2   Jaeson: [laughter]
   3   Seamus: was he defensive
   4   Rob: no not really sort of but with a laugh
   5   yeah that's okay
→ 6   Jaeson: but I like I sai- we're from Wellington
   7   /wind big winds you know people get killed\
   8   in Wellington all the time with wind
   9   Rob: /[laughs] [laughs]: yes that's right:\
 10   I said to him
 11   what are 1/the chances what are the what\1 are
 12   the chances of being hit by a falling tree
 13   2/[laughs]\2
→ 14   Jaeson: 1/get over it you blouse\1
 15   2/[laughs]\2 [laughs]
 16   Seamus: he obviously couldn't come up on Friday

The ongoing meeting topic is a potential franchisee (Trevor) coming for a visit. The meeting members are talking about Trevor in a humorous tone, for example, by referring to him as "a big wussie" in line 1, humorous comments about

Wellington's wind in line 6 to 13, and good natured humorous insult in line 14. It is clear that Seamus, Rob, and Jaeson jointly construct this humour. In informal meetings as well as formal meetings at company N, collaborative humour is common and every participant contributes to the humour.

The following example is from an informal meeting at company J. In the extract, Hosoi, a computer system development manager, is demonstrating a new (software) product and Manabe is checking it.

Example 6.14 [JIFM03_05, 33:40]

→ 1	Hosoi:		そういう部分で　あのー　先生のそういった時間短縮には
			sooiu bubun de ano- sensei no sooitta jikan tanshuku ni wa
			in this point well this [the new software] will be helpful for spending less time for work
2			あー、役立つと思うんですよね
			a- yakudatsu to omou n desu yo ne
			well it will be helpful
3	Manabe:		役立つ、役立つと思いますね
			yakudatsu yakudatsu to omoimasu ne
			I think it will be helpful too
4	Tanimoto:		役立ちますね　ええ
			yakudachimasu ne ee
			yeah it will be helpful
→ 5	Manabe:		そしたらもっと　たくさん-
			soshitara motto takusan-
			in such a case you mean this software will make me
6			[笑いがおこる]
			[laughter]
→ 7	Manabe:		働けってことかー
			hatarake tte koto ka-
			work harder
8			[笑いがおこる]
			[laughter]
9	Ashizawa:		いえ
			ie
			no
10	Komeda:		効率的に働けますよ
			kooritsuteki ni hatarake masu yo
			you'll be able to work effectively

The new software is for accounting and Manabe, an accountant and outside director who helped them to make the software, is checking it and giving feedback and advice while Hosoi is demonstrating and explaining the new software. Hosoi emphasises that this new software is effective and reduces time doing accounting related work, in lines 1 and 2. Following his turn, Manabe humorously comments that this means that they have to work more and laughter occurs from line 5 to 7, especially because he slows down his speaking and talks in a humorous tone in line 5. From line 5 to 7, by employing an imperative form (*hatarake* "work") and a quotation marker (*tte*), he expresses company J's staff's voice ("work harder"), which is received as humour by the audience (company J's staff) whose organisational standing are different. In what follows, Ashizawa responds with "no" and Komeda adds his support for the software.

In general, the CEO is initiating humour in this informal meeting, too, but it is interesting to find that Manabe is also initiating humour as found in this example. Manabe's commitment to the new software, the main topic of this meeting, is the highest because he is in charge of checking and revising (if necessary) the software, thus in this respect, he is the expert and of the leading contributor in the ongoing interaction. This might be one reason why he is taking the initiative in producing the humour. Producing humour would contribute to the construction of his identities as a professional accountant and a person who is in charge of the software.

In informal meetings that a CEO attends, the CEO again generally plays an initiative role in producing humour, but Ashizawa, the chair of formal meetings, does not contribute to the humour. Instead, certain other people, such as Tanimoto and Manabe, do so actively. There is no appointed chair in informal meetings, but those who initiate the humour also play leading roles in the meetings.

Functions

As with formal meetings at both CofPs, humour in informal meetings at both companies also serves to build rapport and create team spirit. The following is an example from an informal meeting at company J.

Example 6. 15 [JIFM01_01, 27:15]
1   Tanimoto: 東京は もうやらなあかんというのはわかってますから-
              Tokyo wa moo yarana akan to iu no wa wakatte masu kara-
              the clients in Tokyo have already realised that they will have to do that
2   Ashizawa: はいはいはい
              hai hai hai

		yeah yeah yeah
3		(4.0)
4	Tanimoto:	だから セミナーした後の質問の内容が全然違うんですよ
		dakara seminaa shita ato no shitsumon no naiyoo ga zenzen chigau n desu yo
		that's why the questions after the seminar are totally different
5		(3.0)
6	Nio:	そうなんですよ
		soo na n desu yo
		that's right
7		··· [about 30 seconds deleted]
8	Nio:	当然、わかっているやろうと思って話をしても +
		toozen waka tte iru yaroo to omotte hanashi o shite mo+
		when I talk with them with expecting they have already known+
9	Tanimoto:	はい 実はわかってない可能性が高いですね
		hai jitsu wa wakatte inai kanoosei ga takai desu ne
		I see, the possibility that they don't know is strong
10	Nio:	でも まあ 私もその(　)商品の目的とか運用
		demo maa watashi mo sono ( ) shoohin no mokuteki toka unyoo
		but well about the importance our product's purpose and its application
11		(3.0)
12		その重要性を一生懸命とくんですけど なかなか伝わらないっていうか
		sono juuyoosei o isshookenmei toku n desu kedo nakanaka tsutawaranai tte iu ka
		though I make great efforts to explain about it it's difficult to make them understand what I want to say.
13		(1.0)
14		話が 話のキャッチボールができないというか
		hanashi ga hanashi no kyatchibooru ga dekinai to iu ka
		regarding our conversation I cannot play conversational catch with clients
15	Tanimoto:	そうですね
		soo desu ne
		I see
16		(4.0)

→ 17	Nio:	結局文書化ができても
		kekkyoku bunshoka ga deki temo
		even if they can make documentation
18	Tanimoto:	文書化ができましたと 喜んでたら
		bunshoka ga dekimashita to yoroko n de itara
		they are excited with being able to make documents
19		「じゃ テストは？」て言うたら
		ja tesuto wa te iutara
		then I ask "have you tested them?"
20		「えっ それは監査法人がするんじゃないですか」
		e sore wa kansahoojin ga suru n ja nai desu ka
		then they ask "isn't testing your job?"
21		/[笑いながら]ちゃうって\
		[with laughing] chau tte
		/[with laughing] no it's NOT!\
22	Nio & Ashizawa	/[笑いが起こる]\
		/[laughter]\
23	Tanimoto:	そんなレベルなんですね 本当に
		sonna reberu na n desu ne hontoo ni
		such a [*low*] level actually

In example 6.15, the meeting members are talking about their clients in Tokyo and Osaka. While the company's clients in Tokyo are always considering a new accounting system, those in Osaka are not and do not even attempt to become familiar with it. The participants are talking about how much easier it is to sell their accounting software in Tokyo than in Osaka. Nio, a salesperson in Osaka was not actively involved in the conversation at the time the excerpt started, but he starts to talk when the conversational topic (about clients in Osaka) is related to him. Following his complaints about his clients in Osaka, Nio mentions an accounting topic in line 17, and then Tanimoto makes supportive comments about his remark in a humorous tone and laughter occurs. Regarding this extract, in the follow-up interview, Tanimoto says that he intentionally tried to contribute to the humour in order to involve Nio in the conversation because he did not talk very much at the meeting. We can see from this that Tanimoto employs humour to construct solidarity and develop rapport with another meeting member, Nio.

In this meeting, there are seven occurrences of humour and all of them are produced by Tanimoto. Why does Tanimoto rather than Ashizawa initiate humour? This informal meeting is conducted in a restaurant that Tanimoto proposed. After Tanimoto, Ashizawa, and Nio visited their client, they decided to have a review meeting and Tanimoto proposed this restaurant. All through the meetings, Tanimoto is in charge of the interaction. It could be argued that giving supportive humorous comment toward Nio's remark on accounting contributes to Tanimoto's identity as a professional accountant, Nio's superior, and a person who is in charge of this meeting.

As found in formal meetings, humorous talk can occur when talking about a sensitive or a serious topic. The following is from an informal meeting at company N.

Example 6. 16 [NIFM03_10, 04:50]

1	Sharon:	but this morning I had a woman ring me
2		from um [project name]
3		and someone has died +
4		someone who's a quite significant figure
5		within the what's the word
6	Jaeson:	( )
7	Sharon:	that's it
8	Jacson:	I knew it was one of them /[laughs]\
9	Sharon:	/yeah\ and um + her name is mentioned in a lot of a lot of their products
10		cos she has a lot to do with the [project name]
11		and also her photograph appears in the products
12		and so everything with her name on it
13		or where her photograph appears has to be
14		destroyed and reprinted
15	Jaeson:	cool
16	Sharon:	yeah that's what I thought
17		/but I didn't say it to her + ( ) [laughs]\
18	Jaeson:	/[laughs] sorry oh that how sad [laughs]\
19	Sharon:	yeah /um\
20	Jaeson:	/okay\ yeah

In example 6.16, Sharon and Jaeson are discussing a client's needs in regards to the sudden death of a key member of the client's company whose photographs and/or name have already been printed on their products. They do not have any procedure for dealing with this kind of matter and do not know what to do with the products related to the client. Talking about serious matters would make these interactants feel uncomfortable. Perhaps to overcome their unease at their good fortune (i.e. extra funds to replace the products with the new staff member), they talk in a humorous tone cooperatively, and laughter takes place throughout the discussion.

To summarise, most of the features of humour in informal meetings are similar to those in formal meetings at both CofPs. One prominent difference, however, is distribution. Humour is found all through meetings without being limited to the topic transitional sections.

6.4.3 Discussion

In sections 6.4.1 and 6.4.2, results of the contrastive study on humour have been demonstrated. That is, manifestations of humour have been explored in formal and informal meetings at company N and company J, describing the distribution, instigators, types and categories, and functions. The results are summarised in table 6.2 below.

	Company N	Company J
Distribution	Formal meetings (FM): (mainly) around topic transitional phases including opening and closing sections Informal meetings (IFM): anywhere at meetings (abrupt occurrence, interwoven with business related talk)	
Instigator	every participant	FM: CEO, the chair IFM: CEO, Tanimoto, Manabe
Type/style	co-constructed humour	(mainly) instigators' single humour
Salient category	mutual teasing jointly constructed fantasy	one-way teasing
Function	positive function from a relational perspective (creating team spirit, building rapport)	
	mitigating tension	identity/power relation creation marker

Table 6.2: Features of humour in formal/informal meetings at company N and company J

Comparing the humour in formal and informal meetings, a difference in distribution is found across the two CofPs. In formal meetings, consistent with the previous research (e.g., Holmes & Stubbe 2003; Schnurr 2005), humour mostly occurs at the boundaries of interaction including opening and closing phases, however it also occurs in discussion phases. In informal meetings, however, humour may occur almost anywhere throughout the meetings. Both of these distribution features are similar to small talk. However, since humour is finely interwoven with ongoing meeting talk, including not only small talk but also business-related talk, it could be argued that humour would be more tolerated almost anywhere in meetings than small talk.

Comparing the humour in company N's meetings and company J's meetings, the following features of its manifestations are evident from the analysis. The first salient difference is who contributes to the humour. In meetings at company N, it appears that any participant is free to contribute, while in those at company J not everyone is free to contribute to the humour but particular people can instigate the humour.

This difference between the two CofPs about who instigates humour affects the type of humour. At company N, meeting members equally and jointly construct humour and thus cooperatively constructed humour sequences are prominent. At company J, on the other hand, particular people initiate humour and others respond to it. Thus most of the humour is a single contribution. Generally, those people who are in authority and/or who are in charge of the interaction, such as the chair, actively contribute to humour.

This difference in terms of who is instigating humour is also reflected in the categories of humour. Among the conspicuous categories of humour in company N's meetings are "mutual teasing" and "fantasy humour", both of which are constructed cooperatively by meeting members. In meetings at company J, on the other hand, teasing is conducted only by people in authority or in a higher status than the target. It is also interesting that there are instances of humour (though not many) where meeting members, regardless of status differences, make fun of their clients. This kind of humour serves to confirm shared knowledge among meeting members and to show the cohesiveness of the meeting group, or membership to the CofP.

As the humour research indicates (e.g., Duncan et al. 1990; Morreall 1991), creating team spirit is the major function of humour in both CofPs. However, the ways of creating team spirit among meeting members are different between company N and company J. In meetings at company N, a collaborative construction of humour by members serves to strengthen solidarity or a sense of belonging to a group. Thus active contributions to the construction of the humour are expected and welcomed. Moreover, an informal atmosphere and a spirited tone in a stretch of humorous discourse, both of which are features of conversations among friends (Hay 1995; Coates 1996), also help build team spirit in this CofP. On the other hand, in meetings at company J, in most cases it is those who are in authority and/or in charge of the interaction that serve as the main instigators of the humour. That is, in this CofP, those people would be atmosphere makers or initiators of team creating. By following their humorous remarks or responding to them with laughter, other members who are not in positions of power contribute to creating team spirit or expressing solidarity.

Moreover, humour serves a unique function for each CofP. In meetings at company N, consistent with studies of other workplaces in the previous literature (e.g., Holmes 2000c; Schnurr 2005), humorous talk is employed when talking about sensitive or serious matters and it could help mitigate tension. In meetings at company J, it is likely that through employing humour or various responses to humour, a range of aspects of identity and related issues of power are constructed discursively and dynamically. Against previous literature on workplace humour (e.g., Pizzini 1991; Brown & Keegan 1999), in this CofP, humour is employed to reinforce power relationships. Thus it could be argued that humour functions as a means to create identity and as a strategy to affirm power.

Through all the data, and across the CofPs, humour plays an important role as Relational Practice, as does small talk. Humour is finely integrated with ongoing meeting talk including not only small talk but also business-related talk. It is thus difficult to clearly divide transactional talk and relational talk. The analysis results verify that business related talk also serves relational functions, and once again that any talk is multifunctional.

6.5 Emic perspective

In this section, I attempt to account for the analysis results of two exemplary Relational Practice strategies, humour and small talk, from an emic perspective. I set the following questions in Chapter 2: (1) whether Relational Practice (or an etic dimension) would be applicable to the Japanese data; and (2) what would be the underlying expectations, or communicative norms, in the New Zealand data and the Japanese data respectively. In terms of the first question, it is evident from the analysis of humour and small talk that Relational Practice is applicable to meetings at company J, i.e. the Japanese data. In this section, through an examination of target participants' linguistic behaviours, the second question is addressed.

6.5.1 Target participants' linguistic behaviours regarding Relational Practice

There is a noticeable difference regarding the target participants' linguistic behaviours between the two CofPs. At company N, there is no clear difference in terms of humour between formal and informal meetings. At every meeting, meeting members are free to produce humour and humour is constructed cooperatively and jointly. This characteristic is also found in small talk. Everyone contributes to small talk and it is constructed cooperatively among meeting members in formal and informal meetings.

On the other hand, at company J, the target participants' communicative behaviours regarding humour are totally different in each meeting. Komeda, the CEO, actively initiates humour all through the meetings. However, other target people are different and their discursive behaviours can be summarised in the following way. Ashizawa, the chair of formal meetings, actively contributes to humour in formal meetings while in informal meetings, he never produces humour but plays an important role as a respondent by initiating loud laughter. Tanimoto is not active in formal meetings but initiates humour in those formal meetings whose location he proposed and where he plays an active role in managing the interaction. Manabe is not active at all during the meetings except one informal meeting where he is in charge of the meeting's main topic and actively initiates humour. The analysis of humour thus indicates that those who are in authority and/or in charge of the interaction actively contribute to humour and that those humour instigators are not fixed even among members in the same CofP, but changeable according to interactions. Thus employing humour contributes to create various aspects of identity and power-relations discursively and dynamically.

Though the target participants' linguistic behaviours regarding small talk are not as clear as those regarding humour, they are nevertheless shared with those of humour. That is, in terms of small talk, a particular person is in charge of contributing, and different individuals serve this role according to the meeting. In formal meetings, Ashizawa, the chair, takes an initiative role managing small talk while in informal meetings where Tanimoto is in charge, Tanimoto actively contributes to small talk.

Here questions arise. Why are linguistic behaviours of members at company N regarding Relational Practice so different from those at company J? It is reasonable to assume that underlying expectations, or communicative norms, shared among members of company N in New Zealand and among those of company J in Japan, affect their linguistic behaviours and thus these underlying expectations would be very different according to the two CofPs. This issue is explored further in the next section.

6.5.2 Interpreting the results from an emic perspective

Humour and small talk are two typical Relational Practice strategies and their common function is creating team spirit. From the analysis results in this chapter and in Chapter 5, it is evident that both small talk and humour help to create team spirit across the CofPs. However, it is also clear that the manifestations of creating team spirit through small talk and/or humour are very different in each CofP.

In meetings at company N, the collaborative and "polyphonic" (Coates 1996) construction of small talk and/or humour by members functions to "do collegiality" (Holmes & Marra 2002a). Thus active contribution to the construction of the humour and/or small talk is expected and welcomed.

Moreover, an informal atmosphere and a high spirit in a stretch of humorous discourse, both of which are features of conversations among friends (Hay 1995; Coates 1996), also function to create team spirit in this CofP. Everyone is equally entitled to engage in Relational Practice.

On the other hand, in meetings at company J, in most cases it is those who are in authority and/or are in charge of the interactions that serve as the main instigators of the humour and/or contributors to small talk. That is, in this CofP, those people act as atmosphere makers or initiators of team creation. By following their humorous remarks or responding to them with laughter, or employing back channels to show they are "listening to you actively", other members who are not in positions of power contribute to team creation or expressing solidarity. In other words, conducting Relational Practice would be decided according to their position or place in relation to the members of the interaction.

Considering that the major difference between these two CoPs is national background, I attempt to analyse the manifestations of Relational Practice from an emic perspective based on national identities.

The characteristic linguistic behaviours of members at company N regarding Relational Practice could be accounted for by the emic construct "egalitarianism". Researchers from various disciplines such as sociology, anthropology, and political science (e.g., Ashkanasy et al. 2004; Kennedy 2007; Bonisch-Brednich 2008) point out that *egalitarianism* is a key concept of New Zealanders' behaviours. They have all observed and described egalitarianism as the most essential cultural trend. Egalitarianism is defined as meaning that "everyone should be the same and if they are not they should, at the very least, pretend to be" (Bonisch-Brednich 2008: 6). Bonisch-Brednich continues:

> So there are very good reasons for this carefully developed Kiwi system of playing down differences, denying hierarchies or at least acting them out in a more backstage kind of way, applying various tactics of disguising difference and constantly creating a social plateau.
>
> (Bonisch-Brednich 2008: 6-7)

This strong sense of egalitarianism is considered to originate from the Treaty of Waitangi in 1840 (McLeod 1969; Trevor-Roberts et al. 2003; Ashkanasy et al 2004; Bonisch- Brednich 2008) and continues to be firmly entrenched in the New Zealand spirit. (Ashkanasy et al. 2004). This underlying cultural trend, egalitarianism, is manifest in the "Tall poppy" syndrome (e.g., Feather 1994; Jackson 2000; Kennedy 2007).

The New Zealand concept of egalitarianism is not restricted to the sense

> of equal opportunity; it extends to the idea that people should be considered as equal in all aspects of life: ··· The phrase 'tall poppy syndrome' refers to a tendency in New Zealand to find fault with high achievers, to 'cut them down to size' if they act as though their achievements make them better than anyone else. (Kennedy 2007: 399)

This cultural trend is also clearly manifested in the Globe project (Global Leadership and Organizational Behavior; see House et al. 2004) which is a cross-cultural research project comparing perceptions of positive and negative leadership attributes involving 62 countries. It is found that "New Zealanders tend to have the lowest power distance in the world – that is, we do not tend to accept or embrace the fact that power in institutions and organisations should be distributed unequally" (Jackson 2000: 3). In the analysis of workplace discourse in New Zealand, too, it is pointed out by researchers from LWP (Holmes 2000a; Holmes & Marra 2004; Schnurr & Chan 2009) that this cultural expectation is enacted in participants' linguistic behaviours. It is evident from the analysis results in this study that the salient manifestations of humour and small talk, collaborative construction by everyone, would be affected by "egalitarianism", the implicit, underlying, shared expectation among meeting members at company N. In other words, meeting members of this CofP are dynamically and cooperatively constructing Relational Practice in on-going interaction, responding to this cultural communicative expectation, or an emic construct of New Zealand culture.

What about in the Japanese data? With respect to the different linguistic behaviours regarding humour, Tanimoto made an interesting comment. I asked him why he did not contribute to humour in formal meetings. He answered that he was not in a position (*tachiba*, in Japanese) to do so because he is not a staff member at company J; he is simply attending formal meetings as an outside business consultant. It is evident from his remark as well as the analysis results of humour and small talk that people's position or their place among the members of an interaction influences linguistic behaviour. This can be paraphrased as group-orientation.

Politeness researchers interested in Japanese data point out that the Japanese self is group-oriented. There are a number of similar concepts to represent this collective orientation in Japanese culture. They include *amae*, interdependency (Doi 1971), *bun*-holder, belongingness (Lebra 1976), *kanjin* (Hamaguchi 1985), and *omoiyari*, empathy (Clancy 1986). Among them, I employ the logic of *ba*,[5] dual mode thinking (Shimizu 2003; Ide 2006) as an emic construct for the Japanese data. There are two reasons why I adopt this: (1) the logic of *ba* is comprehensive and well-theorised and (2) similar to *egalitarianism* for the New Zealand data, the logic of *ba* has began to draw attention not only in sociolinguistics but also other disciplines such as business administration (e.g., Yamazaki 2002) and policy studies (e.g., Hisa 2003).

The logic of *ba* was originally developed by Shimizu (1996), a biophysicist who worked to discover the complex system of life in its living state. He established the principle that every cell is equipped with a dual mode functioning capacity by which it functions as an individual cell and at the same time as an appropriate part of the whole body. Inspired by his idea, he has been developing the logic of *ba*, or dual mode thinking, to explain elements of Japanese society including ways of thinking and behaviour. Within this theory, dual mode thinking is understood to mean that each local part functions independently and at the same time as an appropriate part of the whole. This idea, or coexistence of the whole and the self, is closely connected to Buddhism, which has influenced Japanese culture. One of the fundamental ideas in Buddhism is *engi*, interdependent co-realisation, where life is integrated in a mutually dependent system and all living things including individuals and nature provide mutual support, and coexist and are maintained in harmony (Nabeshima 2007).

Ide (2006) contends that the logic of *ba* is the most appropriate motivation to explain Japanese linguistic behaviours based on *wakimae*, discernment. Everyone is equipped with dual mode thinking as an individual and at the same time as a part of *ba*, the situation of the interaction. This consists of participants, the nature of the settings, and the other contextual elements. As a part of *ba*, everyone interacts with others in harmony and makes a coherent whole. *Ba* can be explained as analogous to an improvised drama. Everyone plays their role in an improvised drama, while adjusting to the dynamically changing scene. Ide (2009) argues how action-oriented (strategic) use or non-use of honorifics (or polite forms) can be explained by the logic of *ba*. When engaging in interaction, everyone is embedded in the context. Everyone is equipped with dual mode thinking capacity, to intuit what is happening in the interaction from a relational perspective, and to manage the use or non-use of honorifics almost automatically, indexing the contextual construal (*wakimae*), i.e. the speaker's sense of place in *ba* which is dynamically changing in interaction. Until recently, research in this area approached the concept of *ba* as emically appropriate in Japanese. The possibility that the concept of *ba* could be considered as a component in a more universal framework has now begun to be explored.

Though Ide (2009) limits her focus to linguistic forms such as honorifics and polite/non-polite forms, the analysis results indicate that that the logic of *ba* could be extended to include discursive strategies such as humour and small talk. It could be argued that meeting members at company J automatically perceive where they are standing in *ba* and then choose a Relational Practice strategy according to their position or role among participants of a particular interaction. That is, they play their appropriate role as a part of the whole according to the dynamically changing *ba*. The results support the view that the harmonious parallel coexistence of individuals and parts of the whole is neither predictable nor static, but dynamic and negotiated discursively.

This section has shown that incorporating an emic perspective helps in understanding Japanese politeness and people's linguistic behaviours more adequately. It could be argued from the analysis results that "egalitarianism" for the New Zealand company N and the "logic of *ba*" for the Japanese company J would be shared among meeting members as implicit underlying communicative expectations.

6.6 Summary

In this chapter, previous research on humour, especially focussing on workplace humour, has been overviewed. The research literature agrees that humor in the workplace plays a particularly important role from a relational perspective, serving to create team spirit by expressing solidarity or a sense of belonging to a group (e.g., Duncan et al. 1990; Morreall 1991). It is also found that while the manifestation of workplace humour can characterise a distinctive workplace culture (e.g., Holmes & Stubbe 2003; Holmes 2006a), broader cultural norms or underlying expectations such as ethnic community and national group may also affect the manifestation of humour (Marra & Holmes 2007).

In the second part of this chapter, results of the contrastive study on humour have been presented, focussing on its distribution, instigators, and functions in formal and informal meetings at company N and company J. The analysis results have shown that humour functions as Relational Practice across the CofPs, serving to create team spirit and building rapport among meeting members. However, the manifestations of humour are distinctive in each CofP. It could be argued from the analysis results that meeting members are enacting Relational Practice through humour in ways that meet the underlying expectations of each CofP. The analysis results have also demonstrated the differences in the manifestation of humour between formal and informal meetings. These findings clearly indicate that as discussed in Chapter 5, the contrastive study in this research (New Zealand vs. Japan and formal vs. informal meetings) is justified and considering formal or informal meetings is necessary when examining meeting discourse from a relational perspective.

The data has shown that humour is finely integrated with on-going meeting talk, including not only business related talk but also small talk. It could be argued that any talk including social talk and work-related talk is multifunctional and should be analysed at the discourse level.

In the last part of this chapter, I have proposed an emic construct, or underlying communicative constraint, of each CofP: "egalitarianism" for company N in New Zealand and the "theory of *ba*" for company J in Japan. It is found that an emic interpretation would be useful in understanding cultural differences more adequately. However, I do not mean to contend that the emic constructs proposed in this chapter are the only communicative norms in these CofPs. There would be other communicative norms, too. As stated in Chapter 2, members of each CofP are not only members of ethno-linguistic or national group such as New Zealanders or Japanese, but also a particular CofP or workplace. Moreover, it is found from the empirical cross-cultural studies on Relational Practice (e.g., Chan 2005; Marra & Holmes 2007; Schnurr & Chan 2009) that workplace culture influences the manifestation of Relational Practice. Since the meeting data in this study is limited to that from one business organisation from New Zealand and one from Japan, it is impossible to compare different CofPs in the same national cultural group. Thus, in the next chapter, the perceptions of business people from different organisations in the same national group, i.e. Japan, will be explored.

Notes

1 Some sections of this chapter have appeared in Murata (2014a).
2 While Fletcher (1999) uses the term "creating team", I employ the more general "creating team spirit".
3 For more detailed discussion, see Murata (2007, 2008, 2009a).
4 See more detailed discussion in example 5. 18 in Chapter 5.
5 Ba can be translated as "the situation in which things happens (which is experienced by a person)" (Kita 2009), i.e. a large-scale contextual concept including atmosphere, tone, relationships among interactants, implicit cultural expectations in ongoing interaction.

CHAPTER 7

Perception task

Chapters 5 and 6 examined the manifestations of small talk and humour. The analysis of these two discursive strategies demonstrated that while small talk and humour served as Relational Practice strategies, their manifestations were distinctive in each CofP. This suggests that meeting members are enacting Relational Practice through small talk or humour in ways that conform to the underlying expectations of each CofP. It was noted in Chapter 6 that these underlying expectations can be interpreted from an emic perspective based on the participants' national identities.

This chapter moves its focus from manifestations to perceptions of these discursive strategies. The third research question, regarding perceptions of small talk and humour, is two-fold. The first sub-question asks what perceptions Japanese business professionals have about New Zealanders' use of small talk and humour in formal and informal meetings. The second sub-question is concerned with what influences these perceptions.

As discussed in Chapter 2, recent politeness research (e.g., Eelen 2001; Mills 2003; Holmes & Marra 2004; Spencer-Oatey 2008a) argues that no utterance is inherently polite or impolite, but rather that politeness is constructed among interactants, i.e. both speakers and hearers. Thus when analysing Relational Practice, it is important to pay attention to hearers' perceptions. How can the hearers' perception be assessed? In this chapter, this question is examined first, reviewing the relevant literature. After providing the rationale for selecting the particular research methods, I describe the procedures used in the perception task for this study. In the last half of the chapter, the results of the analysis are presented and the issue of what influences the participants' perceptions is discussed.[1]

7.1 Classic method for assessing language attitude from hearers' perspectives

The classic method for assessing language attitudes, referred to as the *matched-guise technique*, was introduced by social psychologists (e.g., Lambert et al. 1960; Lambert 1967). This method was developed in Montreal, to examine existing tensions between English Canadians (ECs) and French Canadians (FCs), and specifically to explore the different impressions and views about speakers of French and English. In the original conception of a matched-guise study (Lambert 1967), hearers' reactions towards tape-recordings of a number of bilingual speakers reading a two-minute passage in one of their languages (e.g., French) and, then a translation of the same passage in their other language (e.g., English) are examined. Hearers do not know that the two samples of speech are produced by the same speaker, thus are likely to judge the two "guises" as different speakers. They are asked to evaluate the personal qualities of speakers such as intelligence, physical attractiveness, and kindness along a 6-point scale ranging from "very little" to "very much" based on their voices alone. Lambert's (1967) matched guise research showed that ECs evaluated the ECs far more favourably than the FCs. The evaluations of FCs were also biased toward the ECs and against the FCs. This pattern of results is considered "a reflection of a community-wide stereotype of FCs as being relatively second-rate people, a view apparently fully shared by certain subgroups of FCs" (Lambert 1967/reprinted in 2003: 308).

This method was later used to investigate different accents (standard or prestige accents and regional accents) of British English and French users (Giles & Powesland 1975; Hawkins 1993; Honey 1998). In these experiments, similar findings emerged, associating "status/competence" features with the prestige accent of French and RP in Britain and "solidarity" qualities with the regional varieties of non-standard speakers. This method appears to be an effective way to investigate listeners' attitudes to different accents. However, it does not allow for the evaluation of discourse features where contextual information also needs to be provided in order for listeners to be able to make evaluations. As the current study's task focusses on the discourse features of the manifestations of small talk and humour, it is clear that the classic matched guise approach is not appropriate for this study.

7.2 Assessing participants' perceptions in authentic interaction

Typical methods to collect participants' perceptions and interpretations of discourse features include follow-up interviews, with participants involved in a given interaction, and questionnaires. Tannen (1994a), Bilbow (1997a, 1997b), and Spencer-Oatey and Xiang (2003) modify these methods for their purposes and data.

In examining cross-cultural and cross-gender differences in conversational styles that could cause misunderstandings in interaction, Tannen (1994a: 5-6) employs the following *interactional sociolinguistic* methodological approach. This approach involves five stages:

1. Tape-recording naturally occurring conversations.
2. Identifying segments in which trouble is evident.
3. Looking for culturally patterned differences in signaling meaning that could account for the trouble.
4. Playing the recording, or segments of it, back to participants in order to solicit their spontaneous interpretations and reactions, and also, perhaps later, soliciting their responses to the researcher's interpretations.
5. Playing segments of the interaction for other members of the cultural groups represented by the speakers in order to discern patterns of interpretation.

Tannen (1994a) contends that the last two steps, which are called playback sessions, serve important roles when analysing conversations in the interpretive methodological framework. She argues that:

> They are crucial to ensure that the scholar's work is grounded in the experience of the speakers whose behavior is the object of study ⋯ Attention to how participants experience conversations under analysis provides invaluable insight into the workings of interaction   (1994a: 6).

Bilbow (1997a, 1997b) investigated the natural spoken discourse in 11 intercultural business meetings in English (approximately 15 hours) between Chinese and Western members of staff in a large Hong Kong airline company, focussing on directive speech acts such as directing and suggesting. He analysed these speech acts regarding not only their lexico-grammatical and prosodic features, but also the participants' impressions of both Chinese and Western staff members.

Following Goffman's (1959) "self-presentation" — or *impression management* — Bilbow (1997a) contends that impression management is a universal function of discourse. He considers impression management as consisting of two parts: (1) speakers projecting impressions of themselves through their discourse, on the basis of their impression managing style, and (2) hearers interpreting the discourse and creating certain impressions of speakers. Important here is that the impressions of speakers that hearers create may or may not correspond with the impressions speakers expect that they are projecting. He extends this notion to intercultural communication and suggests a *Cross-Cultural Impression Management* (CCIM) discourse model. This model suggests:

> ··· (i) that the attribution process is significantly affected by the cultural backgrounds of both speakers and hearers, and (ii) that 'discordant' attributions may lead to the reinforcement of negative person-perceptions, which, in turn, may result in distorted communication
> (Bilbow 1997a: 461).

Bilbow (1997a) attributes potential causes of discord to differing cultural backgrounds. When interactional participants share a common cultural background, there is a high degree of correspondence between the impressions speakers think they are projecting and hearers' perceptions of speakers. This may result in harmonious impression management between speakers and hearers. However, in cross-cultural situations, Bilbow (1997a) argues that there would be more chances for speakers' expectations and hearers' actual impressions to differ. Therefore, he continues, "In order to understand intercultural person perception, one needs to understand certain of the cultural values that individuals bring to intercultural encounters" (1997a: 464).

In order to explore these cultural values, Bilbow (1997a) collected perception data from both Chinese and Western staff of a company. He employed the following procedures, adapting Tannen's (1994a) interactional sociolinguistic methodological approach.

1. Preliminary data collection
   - Video-recording of authentic interaction in intercultural contexts.
2. Identification of units of analysis.
   - Identifying discourse segments including directive speech acts that appear relevant regarding subjects' impression managing potential.
3. Preliminary analysis
   - Identifying culturally patterned differences within and between these segments, and suggesting possible effects on cultural groups' impression management in intercultural contexts.

4. Development of a diagnostic tool
   - Creating an introspective diagnostic tool that consists of 20 video- and audio-extracts from the recorded data where speakers were observed directing or suggesting.
5. Perceptual data collection
   - Collecting subjects' interpretations of the impression managing effects of discourse segments using an introspective diagnostic tool.

Bilbow (1997a, 1997b) analysed authentic intercultural meetings. A video-based questionnaire asked meeting participants and their colleagues to rank their impressions of speakers on the basis of their discourse using a 9-point rating scale (ranging from "high," to "low"). Bilbow (1997a) selected a small set of "impression managing categories" that he thought were particularly relevant to the target speech acts. These include: authoritativeness, manipulativeness, sensitiveness, frankness, and deference. The analysis uncovered differences in the interpretation of each discourse segment according to the subject's profile, i.e. their cultural backgrounds. That is, people's perceptions were considerably affected by their cultural backgrounds. Bilbow (1997a) acknowledges that culture is not defined exclusively with reference to ethnicity, rather it "embraces all groups of people whose behaviour may influence individual communicative behaviour" such as gender and status groups (1997a: 464). Nevertheless, what Bilbow (1997a, 1997b) actually did was to compare the Western participants' linguistic behaviours and evaluations to those of the Chinese ones, highlighting the differences between the two groups. This suggests that socio-cultural backgrounds, in particular national cultural backgrounds, affect people's linguistic behaviours and perceptions.

Regarding the procedure of the video-based perception task, Bilbow (1997a) notes two problems. One problem involves the development of analytical categories. These categories were selected by the researcher because he thought they were particularly relevant to the target speech act in the task. Therefore, this procedure does not allow subjects to create their impressions freely. In addition, the categorical terminology in impression managing categories does not lead to universal interpretations. For example, the term "authoritativeness" might have different meanings or interpretations according to different cultural groups or individuals. It appears that using scales might not always be meaningful to participants. However, using rating scales may provide subjects with an aid to help them formulate their impressions about the video clip.

Bilbow (1997a) also identifies a problem regarding participant-observers' prior acquaintance with the speaker. When subjects are familiar with the individuals observed in the video-based perception task, he admits that it was very difficult for the subjects to separate "discourse" and "speaker". It could be argued that collecting a third party's perceptions would be more objective and reliable in exploring how a particular discourse segment would be perceived or interpreted, as subjects can evaluate the discourse segment independent of the interactants' characteristics.

Spencer-Oatey and Xing (2003) compared two Chinese-British business meetings that took place in Britain and were held by the same British company to welcome their Chinese business partners. They analysed video recordings of all the meetings, field notes were made by one of the authors, and follow-up interviews were conducted with the participants. Despite many similarities between the two meetings (meeting one: four British and six Chinese; meeting two: seven British and six Chinese), both the British and the Chinese were very satisfied with the first meeting, while the Chinese were very annoyed by the second. Spencer-Oatey and Xing (2003) propose that the different impressions of the Chinese and British participants resulted from different evaluations of a particular discourse segment. Along with Bilbow (1997a, 1997b), this also suggests that socio-cultural backgrounds, in particular national cultural backgrounds, affect people's perceptions.

Spencer-Oatey and Xing (2003: 44) discuss reasons for the importance of perception data as follows:

> As Fraser and Nolan (1981, p. 96) point out, no sentence of linguistic construction is inherently polite or impolite. Rather, politeness is a social judgment, and whether or not an utterance is heard as being polite, is to a large extent, in the hands (or ears) of the hearer. This indicates that if we are to understand how relations are managed, we need to have insights into the social expectancies and judgments of the people involved.

Spencer-Oatey and Xing (2003) suggest interviews with participants and playing (parts of) the interaction as a useful way of collecting perception data. They contend that "the interlocutors can then give explanatory comments and/or interpretive reactions that can provide additional insights into the discourse/interaction" (Spencer-Oatey & Xing 2003: 44).

The results of the above research suggest that cultural backgrounds affect people's perceptions about discourse. More specifically, members of the same national or language group are likely to evaluate the same discourse segment in the same – or at least similar – ways. Moreover, different cultural groups have very different impressions of the interactions as a result of differences in the evaluation and interpretation of the same discourse segment.

However, Marra and Holmes (2007) and Schnurr and Chan (2009) point out that in workplace discourse, the norms and underlying expectations of the

CofP — i.e. people's workplace culture — also affect linguistic behaviours. It is expected that people's perceptions of workplace discourse would also be affected by their workplace culture. This indicates that considering "national culture" may not be enough.

Here questions arise. Following the claims by Bilbow (1997a, 1997b) and Spencer-Oatey and Xing (2003), Japanese business people should evaluate a particular discourse in the same or a similar way. Following the arguments presented by Marra and Holmes (2007), and Schnurr and Chan (2009), the participants' evaluations are also likely to be influenced by their workplace and they evaluate a discourse segment in different ways *according to their workplace*. In order to explore the hearers' perceptions and investigate these hypotheses, it is worth investigating how Japanese business professionals who are from different workplaces interpret manifestations of small talk and humour in New Zealand business meetings.

Bilbow (1997a) gave a questionnaire to participants and Spencer-Oatey and Xing (2003) mainly utilised interviews with participants plus a questionnaire. In order to collect a wide range of responses from task participants, the present study combined the above researchers' methods. The next section explores what kind of interviews are appropriate for collecting perception data from Japanese business professionals who are not participants of the interaction but third parties.

7.3 Assessing third party's perception: extended focus group interviews

There are various types of interviews according to the number of interviewees, ranging from dyadic interviews to large group interviews. Among them, the focus group interview was selected for the current research (Basch 1987; Stewart & Shamdasani 1990; Sussman et al. 1991). The focus group interview is defined as "an interview style designed for small groups" (Basch 1987; Lengua et al. 1992, cited in Berg 1998: 100). Focus group interviews enable researchers to "strive to learn through discussion about conscious, semiconscious, and unconscious psychological and sociocultural characteristics and processes among various groups" (Berg 1998: 100).

One advantage of employing focus group interviews is to reduce the pressure on participants. Sussman et al. (1991) state that small group interviews create less pressure for participants to respond and help elicit more comprehensive responses than self-report questionnaire methods. Another advantage is group dynamism — also described as a "synergistic group effect" (Stewart & Shamdasani 1990; Sussman et al. 1991). Interactions among group members encourage discussion where comments and reactions can build on each other. The synergistic group effect helps a group member to draw from other's comments or to brainstorm with other members of the group and to generate various ideas through group discussion. This group dynamism draws attention to the difference between group interviews and more conventional styles of one-to-one, face-to-face interviewing approaches (Berg 1998).

Discursive negotiation is also an advantage in the focus group interview. It enables participants to elicit shared views of the group where participants belong, and they are likely to be constructed and expressed more explicitly in focus group discussion (Sussman et al. 1991; Berg 1998). For example, De Cillia et al. (1999) document the development of the discursive production of national identity in focus group interviews where participants negotiate meanings.

Using focus group interviews alone may be sufficient to collect perception data. However, the above research suggests that integrating a questionnaire into the focus group discussion, referred to as "extended focus group interviews", would be even more effective. The procedures of the extended focus group interview include a pre-group interview session where participants are asked to fill out the questionnaire before the group interview starts (Berg 1998: 111). The questionnaire contains material which will be the basis of questions to the participants during the group session. The questionnaire is employed to help participants to prepare their ideas, in order to facilitate discussion during the group interview.

7.4 Perception task

For the perception task, extended focus group interviews were employed to collect a wide range of evaluations from discussion participants using video clips. In the following section, the perception task employed in the current study is described.

7.4.1 Overview

Adopting Tannen's (1994a) and Bilbow's (1997a) procedures, nine scenes were selected involving relational talk centring on small talk and humour. These clips highlight differences among these features in the New Zealand and Japanese meeting data.[2] Each scene lasted approximately 30 to 60 seconds. During the perception tasks, participants viewed each clip, responded to them according to a questionnaire, and then discussed their impressions in a group discussion.

The research questions relevant to this component of the study are:

1. How do Japanese business professionals evaluate the manifestations of small talk and humour in New Zealand business meetings?
2. What influences their perceptions and evaluations?

In order to investigate claims that perceptions may be affected by national cultural norms, and/or norms or expectations of each workplace, focus group interviews with participants from three different business organisations were conducted. Moreover, in order to obtain a wide range of perception data, a total of four group interviews were conducted, two with participants who had extensive international business experience ("the international group") and two with participants who had little or no international business experience ("the domestic group"). Each group interview involved four participants.

7.4.2 Participants

Sixteen participants, males and females ranging in age from 20s to 50s, were drawn from three business organisations willing to cooperate in the perception task: pseudonymed respectively "Globe"; "Y&T"; and "Sakura". As stated in Chapter 3, it was quite difficult to find companies to cooperate with the research. I asked as many of my acquaintances as I could to find potential business organisations for the perception task, and three companies accepted the offer. These three organisations, fortunately, were rather different in regards to their characteristics.

Globe is a large American-based production company (approximately 4,000 employees in Japan). About 30% of the employees in Japan are non-Japanese, from not only Western countries but also other Asian countries. The company's atmosphere is westernised and English is heard very often in the company building. Most people wear fashionable formal suits. All the participants of the perception task from this company use English in their daily work. This group is called "Globe (I)". "I" stands for "international group".

Y&T is a large Japanese-based advertising company that has international divisions (approximately 3,000 employees in Japan). Almost all employees are Japanese. The company's atmosphere is casual and most people do not wear business suits but wear casual clothes. Two group interviews were conducted at this company, one with participants who had worked in the international division but seldom use English at work now (Y&T (I)), and the other with participants who had never worked in the international division (Y&T (D)). "D" stands for "domestic group".

Sakura is a small, local consulting firm for small and medium sized businesses (approximately 150 employees in Japan). All employees are Japanese. This organisation is a typical traditional type of Japanese company with explicitly hierarchical relationships. Everyone wears a tie and dark-coloured suit. This group is called "Sakura (D)".

The characteristics of each business organisations are summarised in the following table:

	Globe	Y&T	Sakura
	American-based production company	Japanese-based advertising company which has international divisions	Local consulting firm
The number of employees	4,000	3,000	150
Nationality of employees	30% non-Japanese 70% Japanese	Japanese quite a few non-Japanese	Japanese
Language	Japanese and English	Japanese	Japanese

Table 7.1: Characteristics of the three business organisations

7.4.3 Video-clips and target discourse features

On the basis of the results of the analysis described in Chapters 5 and 6, nine scenes of approximately 30 to 60 seconds were selected from the New Zealand business meeting data. Seven out of the nine scenes highlighted *differences* between the discourse features of small talk and humour in the New Zealand and Japanese meeting data, and two showed *similarities*.

Ethical restrictions meant it was not possible to use the video-recorded business meeting data; in addition, the actual scenes would have been quite difficult for non-native speakers of English to understand. Thus, utterances in the scenes were simplified by editing slang and extraneous details.[3] In this process, I tried to retain as much of the meeting participants' communication as possible to show the target discourse features. The nine scenes were then re-recorded as simulation video clips using New Zealand actors and actresses.[4]

Small talk and silence
Five scenes from the New Zealand meeting data were selected for the perception task. The three scenes, labelled "uncomfortable silence", "overlapping", and "casual atmosphere", show features of small talk that differentiated the New Zealand data from the Japanese data (see Chapter 5). The other two scenes, "interwoven small talk" and "zero small talk", show common features

of small talk in the New Zealand and Japanese data. Each scene is briefly explained as follows:

"Uncomfortable silence"
The longest silence (36 seconds) found in the data was selected to elicit how the task participants reacted to silence (see example 5.10 in Chapter 5). In the scene, a meeting participant looks embarrassed while silence occurs because the other participant is focussing on reading meeting-related documents. The reason why this scene was chosen is, as pointed out in Chapter 5, instances of long silence were often found in the Japanese business meeting data, but seldom found in the New Zealand data.

"Overlapping"
A scene was selected from a pre-meeting phase of a formal meeting where the conversations of two groups overlapped and participants from one group joined the other group's conversation. This scene was selected because it shows a typical feature of small talk in the New Zealand meeting data. As stated in Chapter 5, in the New Zealand data, the participants actively contributed to talk and cooperatively constructed interaction, while in the Japanese data, the participants talked far less than the New Zealand meeting participants during the pre-meeting phase.

"Casual atmosphere"
A scene was selected from a pre-meeting phase of a formal meeting where everyone was talking in a casual way (see example 5.13 in Chapter 5). In the scene, one meeting member brought a box of chocolates and other members were excited to see it. They opened it and ate the chocolate. The intended target discourse feature of this scene was casual talking. This scene also shows a unique feature of the New Zealand pre-meeting phase. As illustrated in Chapter 5, there was a similar scene in the Japanese data where boxes of chocolate were distributed to everyone. In the Japanese example, no one opened the boxes or was excited; the participants remained silent.

"Interwoven small talk"
A scene was selected from an informal meeting where small talk was interwoven with business talk (see example 5.18 in Chapter 5). This interwoven small talk was found in informal meetings both in the New Zealand and Japanese informal meeting data.

"Zero small talk"
A scene was selected from the middle phase of a formal meeting where there

was no small talk and everyone focussed on business talk. This was a common feature both in the New Zealand and the Japanese meeting data. The intended target discourse feature of this scene was zero small talk or intense business talk.

Humour and laughter

This group includes "humour for defusing tension (1)", "humour for defusing tension (2)", "collaborative humour", and "complaining in a humorous way".

"Humour for defusing tension (1)"

A scene was selected from a formal meeting where members were discussing a serious topic – their company's re-branding – and where their talk included humour and laughter. There were many occurrences of humour and laughter when talking about serious matters in the New Zealand data, i.e. where there would be tension or anxiety. In the Japanese data, on the other hand, the meeting participants seldom talked about serious topics jokingly.

"Humour for defusing tension (2)"

The target discourse feature of this scene is also humour for defusing tension. Because there were many occurrences of this kind of humour, another scene was selected from an informal meeting. In this scene, two people are talking about the sudden death of their client (see example 6.16 in Chapter 6). They had created lots of advertising for this client, and she has her name and photo in the materials. They realise they need to be sensitive, but, at the same time, are happy since this means they will receive a lot of work from this company in reproducing materials. In my own experience, it is quite unacceptable that someone's death is talked about in a humorous way in Japan.

"Collaborative humour and making fun of the boss"

A scene was selected from the beginning phase of a formal meeting where everyone actively contributed to humour and made fun of their boss because he used an unpopular and old-fashioned term (see example 6.1 in Chapter 6). This scene shows prominent features of humour in the New Zealand data: they are that everyone contributes to the humour, and that humour is constructed cooperatively. There was no similar scene in the Japanese data where subordinates made fun of their boss.

"Complaining in a humorous way"

A scene was selected from an informal meeting where a subordinate is complaining in a humorous way. In the Japanese data, business related topics were not talked about cheerfully and animatedly. The intended target discourse feature is complaining in a high "key" accompanied by humour and laughter.

The order in which the video clips were used is shown in Table 7.2 below. They were randomly arranged in regards to: formal (F) or informal (IF) meeting type; pre- (Pre), beginning (Beg), or mid- (Mid) phase of meeting; and target discourse features' categories.

	Target discourse feature	Meeting type	Phase	Group category
1	Uncomfortable silence	F	Pre	Small talk and silence
2	Humour for defusing tension (1)	F	Mid	Humour and laughter
3	Overlapping	F	Pre	Small talk and silence
4	Humour for defusing tension (2)	IF	Mid	Humour and laughter
5	Collaborative humour and making fun of the boss	F	Beg	Humour and laughter
6	Interwoven small talk	IF	Mid	Small talk and silence
7	Zero small talk	F	Mid	Small talk and silence
8	Casual atmosphere	F	Pre	Small talk and silence
9	Complaining in a humorous way	IF	Mid	Humour and laughter

Table 7.2: Order of showing the video clips

7.4.4 Procedures

Before the actual perception tasks were administered, pilot-tasks were conducted with PhD students in New Zealand and with my university colleagues in Japan. Though the pilot-task participants were not business professionals, they provided useful advice regarding the task procedures. The pilot was also useful in estimating the time required for the interview.

The perception tasks were conducted between November 2008 and January 2009. For the task, a small meeting room at each company was provided, and the video clips were shown with a projector. Business organisations generally required that each group session finish within an hour.

During the perception tasks, participants viewed each clip, responded to them on a questionnaire, and then discussed them during a group discussion. In terms of a pre-interview questionnaire, a video-based questionnaire adapted from Bilbow (1997a) and Newton (2004) was used. The questionnaire was produced in booklet form. At the top of the left side of each two-page spread, the context of the target video clip is explained. The remainder of the left side is space for a participant to write their first impressions. On the right side of the two-page spread, the participant is asked to rate the clip on six different criteria including scales for polite/impolite, like/dislike, comfortable/uncomfortable using a 4-point rating system. Spaces were left next to each scale for participants to write comments.[5]

The whole procedure is as follow (procedures No. 5 to No. 9 are repeated for each video clip):

1. Brief introduction to the research.
2. Description of the working definitions in this research of formal and informal business meetings, i.e. *kaigi* and *uchiawase*.
3. Distribution of a questionnaire booklet and transcriptions to the participants.
4. Explanation of the procedure by using a practice video clip.
5. A short description of the context of the first clip.
6. The video clip is played.
7. The participants write their first impression.
8. The video clip is played again and the participants fill out an answer sheet.
9. The participants are asked for their impressions of the video clip.

At the end of each video clip (at procedure No. 9), the participant who finished writing the answer sheet first was asked what impression they had. Then after they gave their comment, another participant was asked the same question. An effort was made to let the participants answer freely, but when there was an unclear point, clarification was requested. There were cases where the participants did not understand the scene correctly, e.g., they mistook a pre-meeting scene as a meeting scene. On such occasions, an explanation about the scene was added and then participants were asked for their impressions again.

Some participants' English proficiency was not high enough to understand the video clips. Taking this into account, the following procedures were devised.

1. Just before showing a video clip, a short description of the context was read in order for the participants to watch the scene with as little intrusion as possible.
2. The scenario for each video clip was provided along with a diagram of the hierarchy of the company (including cast pictures) showing their relationships in order to aid understanding.[6]
3. At the beginning of the task, it was emphasised that the task was not a test of English proficiency and that the participants did not have to try to understand the English, per se, but needed to focus on how the people communicated in each video clip.
4. Each video clip was shown twice, and after each viewing the participants were given time to think about what they had watched.

It should be emphasised again that the reason the participants were given pre-interview questionnaires with the scales and places to comment was not for quantitative analysis. The questionnaire was employed to help the participants think through their perceptions about each video clip and put their thoughts into words, preparing them for discussion during the group interview. Acknowledging that participants' interpretations of each evaluative term might be different (Bilbow 1997a), the rating scales were used. The analysis focus is not on the scales of evaluative terms, but rather on the *qualitative data* from the group discussion. For the same reason, in the discussion section, the participants were asked to express their impressions as freely as possible in order to collect a wide range of evaluations and perceptions, rather than asking them only whether they assess the scene as polite or impolite.

The duration of the discussions are shown in the Table 7.3 below. The discussion times are different because each group was conducted at a different time of day. The discussion time of Y&T (D) is the shortest as I had been asked to conduct the whole session for Y&T (including the international and domestic groups) within two hours, and the session for the domestic group was conducted after belatedly finishing the international group. Regarding Globe (I), the session was conducted during working hours (in the morning). The discussion time of Sakura (D) is longer than the others because it was conducted after work.

		Globe (I)	Y&T (I)	Y&T (D)	Sakura (D)
1	Uncomfortable silence	2:40	1:55	1:31	4:34
2	Humour for defusing tension (1)	3:02	1:35	2:40	3:10
3	Overlapping	1:39	2:20	1:57	3:16
4	Humour for defusing tension (2)	2:30	2:17	1:25	2:02
5	Collaborative humour and making fun of the boss	2:19	3:02	1:29	2:41
6	Interwoven small talk	2:20	2:10	1:00	1:40
7	Zero small talk	1:42	2:48	1:24	4:25
8	Casual atmosphere	2:25	2:12	1:48	3:37
9	Complaining in a humorous way	1:10	1:37	1:00	1:54
	Total: 81:16 (average: 2:15)	19:47 (2:12)	19:56 (2:13)	14:14 (1:35)	27:19 (3:02)

Table 7.3: The duration of each group discussion

7.5 Analysis

The primary goal in the perception task is to explore how Japanese business professionals perceive the target discourse feature of small talk and humour. Thus, when analysing the data, the content of the participants' comments was focussed on. For the same reason, though discussions were conducted in Japanese, the equivalent translations by the researcher are shown.[7]

For several of the clips, there were participant comments in response to aspects of the clip other than the discourse features. For example, almost all participants responded to the clip "casual atmosphere" with comments on the appropriateness of bringing food to the meeting, not on the target discourse feature, which was the lively and casual pre-meeting talk. Because these and similar comments did not shed light on how the participants assess the target relational talk, they were removed from the analysis of section 7.5.1, i.e. how the task participants evaluate the target discourse features. Comments removed from the analysis in this section represented less than 20% of the total perceptions. However, these comments were taken into account in section 7.5.2 to examine what influenced peoples' perceptions.

7.5.1 Japanese business professionals' perceptions about Relational Practice in New Zealand business meetings

In this section, research question No. 1 – how Japanese business professionals evaluate the manifestations of small talk and humour in New Zealand business meetings – is addressed. The analysis results are discussed according to the discourse features of small talk and humour, referring to the aspects of relational talk discussed in the previous chapters.

Small talk and silence

In the features of small talk in the New Zealand and the Japanese formal and informal meeting data discussed in Chapter 5, *silence* was one prominent difference. Silence occurred more often and stretches of silence were much longer in the Japanese data. Most periods of silence lasted more than 10 seconds. There was a scene where there were long stretches of silence lasting 112 seconds, 160 seconds and 120 seconds while two participants were waiting for the arrival of other participants. During the long period of silence, the participants just looked at the wall or folded their arms as seen in the illustration (see example 5.11 in Chapter 5).

Conversely, in the New Zealand data, there was much less silence and all instances of silence lasted less than 10 seconds. The only exception (see example 5.10 in Chapter 5), there was an occurrence of silence that lasted 36 seconds while the participants were reading documents.

Another prominent difference was how much the participants contributed to talk. In the New Zealand pre-meetings, members actively engaged in talk. They spoke continuously and overlapped with topics developing one after another. This led to jointly constructed small talk by meeting members and also to less silence. Moreover, their talk was lively and animated. In the Japanese pre-meetings, by contrast, some participants talked but others remained silent. They spoke with no continuity and new topics seldom developed. While silence corresponds to no sound, in group situations such as meetings, there are cases where there is no absence of sound because one or more people are talking but others are not talking and remaining silent. This type of silence is categorised as "participatory silence" (Spencer-Oatey & Xing 2005: 56). In the participants' comments in the perception task, some people mentioned this type of silence. Thus, both no sound in interaction, i.e. nobody talking in group situations and participatory silence are regarded as silence.

Regarding the first prominent difference, the scene with the longest occurrence of silence (36 seconds in length) was selected from the New Zealand meetings, where a participant looked embarrassed while silence was occurring because the other participant focussed on reading a document.

Regarding silence, three participants from different organisations regarded it as normal and not uncomfortable. On the other hand, seven participants from among all the business organisations employed such terms as "uncomfortable", "tense", "serious", "awkward", and "uneasy". Though they had a negative feeling toward silence, they referred to some conditions when silence would be unremarkable or acceptable.

One condition for acceptable silence is certain human relationships. The following two Japanese individuals say that whether or not they stay silent depends on the social distance from other members:

> Y&T (D)-4: If it is someone who I know well, I would talk with them. But if **there is someone of higher status that I don't know well**, then I would not talk to them and keep silent.
>
> Globe (I)-4: Too much silence makes me nervous, but when I am with **a person I don't know very much**, I intentionally open my PC and work with it without talking to them.

It could be argued that silence would be acceptable when people who do not know each other are together, or when someone of a lower status is faced with someone of a higher status.

The other condition is the number of people present:

> Sakura (D)-1: If there are **around three people** and someone is talking, I would be silent.
>
> Y&T (I)-1: There are **only two people here**, aren't there? It's normal to talk to her to break the ice. I had a somewhat uncomfortable feeling.

It could be argued if there are people (at least two) engaged in small talk, others do not have to join the small talk but could keep silent. This corresponds with the business meeting data analysis in that in the New Zealand data, everyone actively contributes to small talk, though not all the meeting participants at the pre-meeting phase talked in the Japanese data.

To summarise, silence was evaluated both as normal and as uncomfortable by the Japanese participants. However, there were two conditions when silence was acceptable. Silence (i.e. not talking) could be acceptable when (1) people of higher status or those who are not well known are present; and (2) there are more than 3 people and at least two people are talking. Concerning silence, there were no differences among the comments from Globe, Y&T, and Sakura.

Another prominent feature regarding small talk was participants' *contributions* to talk and the *tone* of talk. In the New Zealand pre-meetings, every participant actively engaged in talk while in the Japanese pre-meetings, some participants talked but others remained silent. With regard to this feature of small talk, all the participants from Globe (I) and Y&T (I)(D) regarded it as positive or unremarkable by using such terms as "active", "ideal", "often occurring", and "normal".

Three participants had positive impressions about this feature.

> Globe (I)-4: I thought it was **good** and full of energy.
> Y&T (I)-1: It's **ideal**.

Other participants from Globe (I) and Y&T (I)(D) considered it to be "normal", "frequent", and "unremarkable".

> Globe (I)-1: It is **seen very often**. Especially at theme meetings where people come from various places, we wait for others by talking about recent interesting and funny things.
> Y&T (I)-2: It's **normal** at the pre-meeting phase.

On the other hand, all the participants from Sakura (D) took a totally different position. They gave negative impressions especially because of the loudness and liveliness of the talk.

> Sakura (D)-3: They are talking cheerfully. They should talk in smaller voices when they are talking about topics unrelated to meetings. How loudly they talk about topics unrelated to the meeting! It's so different. Small talk is done in much smaller voices.
> Sakura (D)-2: Applying to Japan, it is like starting conversation with colleagues at a bar in Japan. It is not businesslike – they are having conversations cheerfully.

Lively and animated conversations sound to them like those occurring at non-business situations, or leisure situations such as at bars.

To summarise concerning the second feature of small talk – being lively and animated – there was a clear distinction between Globe (D) and Y&T (I)(D) on the one hand, and Sakura (D) on the other. The former groups regarded it as positive or at least normal while the latter group described the behaviour as strongly negative.

Turning to a third aspect of small talk, it is important to consider how the participants evaluated features of small talk observed both in the New Zealand and Japanese meeting data. The common features included interwoven small talk with business talk and zero small talk or intense business talk. These results are addressed here.

Instances of *interwoven small talk* with business talk in the New Zealand informal meeting were selected. No participants except one participant from Globe (I) had negative impressions. Though the one participant said it was too casual, other participants used such terms as "normal", "the same", "unremarkable", "casual", "frank", and "not-uncomfortable".

There were comments addressing reasons why interwoven small talk was regarded as unmarked or normal.

> Y&T (I)-2: It's **an informal meeting** between a boss and a subordinate and I had **no uncomfortable feeling**.
>
> Sakura (D)-1: It's **fine** as this is **an informal meeting** between two people.

Most participants referred to informal meetings, *uchiawase* in Japanese, as a condition where interwoven small talk and business talk would be unremarkable. They regard this interwoven talk as unremarkable if it is occurring at an informal meeting between two people.

This tendency corresponds to the analysis result of the New Zealand and Japanese informal meetings. One of the salient, common features of small talk in the informal meetings was its abrupt and sudden appearance. More specifically, in both the informal meeting data, small talk was finely interwoven with business talk, while in the formal meeting data, small talk tended to occur in particular phases of meetings. It can be argued that the comments imply that interwoven small talk may not be accepted at a formal meeting. Whether a meeting was formal or informal could determine the degree of tolerance for relational talk.

Regarding the other common feature – *zero small talk* or intense business talk, in the middle of a formal meeting – it was also regarded as normal or unremarkable by most of the participants.

To summarise, the different features of small talk in the New Zealand data evoked various impressions from positive to negative among the Japanese business people. In terms of the common features found in the New Zealand and Japanese data, overall, they did not create negative impressions.

Humour and laughter

In the analysis of features of humour in the New Zealand and the Japanese formal and informal meetings discussed in Chapter 6, the first salient difference was *who contributes* to the humour. In the New Zealand meetings, all members were free to contribute to the humour, while in the Japanese meeting data, those who are of higher social status or are in charge contributed most of the humour. This difference was also reflected in the types of humour. In the New Zealand data, meeting members cooperatively constructed humour, while in the Japanese data, those who are in charge of the interaction or the meeting, or who are in authority, initiated the humour and other members added to it with humorous utterances and/or responded to it with laughter.

Another salient difference was *when* humour occurs. In the New Zealand data, humour often occurred in situations where there would be tension or anxiety. The data analysis showed that humour served to defuse tension. In the Japanese meeting data, on the other hand, there were very few occurrences of such humour.

In terms of the first feature, collaborative humour, discourse segments were selected where everyone actively contributed to humour and made fun of their boss because he used an unpopular and old-fashioned expression. Though the intended target discourse feature was everyone's active contribution to the humour, the participants also gave comments about subordinates teasing their boss.

The comments were different according to workplace. The participants from Globe (I) had positive impressions toward the discourse.

> Globe (I)-1: There is a **good atmosphere** in the team. Good circumstance where everyone can say their ideas. Open human relationships among them, considering the scene where Jaeson gave a unique response.
> Globe (I)-3: There is a **very good atmosphere**.

The participants from Y&T (I)(D) felt the humour unremarkable, and used such terms as "normal" and "common" in their comments.

> Y&T (I)-4: It **normally** happens in Japan. Close relationships among meeting members.
> Y&T (D)-4: **It's a common scene**. I don't feel uncomfortable about a scene where when a boss is wrong, subordinates make fun of them. I don't have an uncomfortable feeling. It frequently happens in our company.

All the participants from Sakura (D) had negative impressions.

> Sakura (D)-2: It's **not appropriate**.
> Sakura (D)-3: It's **not tolerable**. They should speak more politely.

In sum, collaborative humour and making fun of bosses were evaluated from positive to negative. The evaluations were shared by all workplace members in a given workplace. The participants from Globe (I) had positive impressions; those from Y&T (I)(D) felt it unremarkable, and those from Sakura (D) had negative impressions.

Regarding another salient feature of humour in the New Zealand data, humour occurring where there would be tension or anxiety, two scenes from the New Zealand meeting data were selected. One is where members are discussing a serious topic – the company's rebranding – in a humorous way at a formal meeting. The other is where two meeting members are discussing a sensitive topic – a client's sudden death – in a humorous way at an informal meeting.

Overall, there was a clear line drawn between Sakura (D) and the other two companies, Globe (I) and Y&T (D)(I). Sakura (D) responded to both cases of discourse with strong negative evaluations while most members of the other two companies regarded them as at least understandable or acceptable.

With regard to the discourse where humour occurs when talking about a serious matter, participants from Globe (I) and Y&T (I) had positive impressions.

> Globe (I)-4: I thought this is a **good and positive** team where everyone can say their ideas freely.
>
> Y&T (D)-2: There is a **good and harmonious** atmosphere. They look lively.

People from Sakura (D), on the other hand, gave strongly negative comments.

> Sakura (D)-3: It doesn't seem to me at all that they are discussing a serious matter. …**What a surprise!**

It is interesting to find that Sakura (D)-1 pointed out how to discuss serious matters. He said that discussing a serious matter should not be done frivolously, as follows:

> Sakura (D)-1: If they are brainstorming, it is OK. They are too frivolous, though, if they are discussing a serious matter.

Also in terms of the other discourse where humour occurs when talking about a sensitive matter – the sudden death of a client – the participants from Globe (I) regarded this discourse as understandable from a business point of view, while admitting that talking about a client's death would be inappropriate, as follows:

Globe (I)-2: If I'm asked whether it is appropriate for the situation or not, I feel it is inappropriate because the talk addresses a serious problem, a person's death, but they seem to make it funny. However, from a business point of view, I think this would happen. There are scenes in business where people make a tough situation humorous or funny in order to take it easy.

Globe (I)-4: If this happens in Japan, the mood would be serious and gloomy in such a serious situation. However, in a sense, such cheerfulness would be good for business.

People from Y&T (I)(D) also regarded the discourse as acceptable and understandable. It is interesting to find that more than half the participants referred to the point of view of a person working at an advertising company. This would be because the company in the video clips is in a related industry.

Y&T (D)-1: It's not so serious for a situation where one person died. On the contrary, it seemed to me that they are happy about making **a new advertisement**.

Y&T (I)-2: It is like **an advertising company** because they take a serious situation humorously.

By contrast, participants from Sakura (D) again responded with strongly negative comments.

Sakura (D)-1: **I don't like** it. Business comes before someone's death. How can they laugh in such a serious situation?

Sakura (D)-3: **I totally dislike** it. They should worry about someone's death. I would absolutely not laugh. I would absolutely not laugh. How rude they are!

With regard to humour for defusing tension, the participants' evaluations ranged from negative to positive. There was a clear line with Globe (I) and Y&T (I)(D) on the one hand, and Sakura (D) on the other. People from Sakura (D) expressed strong negative impressions toward this feature of humour.

Another similar discourse segment from the New Zealand informal meeting data was selected, where one participant was complaining about their client to another participant in a humorous way. The participants, mostly regardless of their workplaces, said that humour at an informal meeting is unremarkable or normal. Those comments could be interpreted as implying that it is not acceptable at formal meetings. It could be argued that whether a meeting was formal or informal would be the decisive factor in determining the degree of tolerance of relational talk.

In sum, for the different features of humour in the New Zealand data, the Japanese business people's evaluations ranged from positive to negative.

7.5.2 What influences participants' perceptions

The analysis results of the previous section can be summarised as follows:

1. The Japanese business people did not evaluate the same discourse features in the same way, but each individual did not evaluate them differently.
2. There were clear tendencies (as shown in No. 3-5 below) among the participants' evaluations.
3. For some examples of discourse, participants' evaluations were different according to their workplace.
4. For some discourse segments, there was a clear distinction regarding the participants' comments between Globe and Y&T on the one hand, and Sakura on the other.
5. Toward some discourses features especially similar to the Japanese data, evaluations were generally shared among the participants regardless of the workplace.
6. There was not a clear difference between evaluations of the target discourse features between (I) and (D) groups.

From the analysis results, it is clear that we cannot say that participants' evaluations were totally different nor that they were the same. There were certain tendencies in terms of their evaluations. Their evaluations were shared among a range of members of a particular workplace, among several workplaces, or among all participants. It is clear that workplace expectations or norms influenced people's perceptions. But this does not automatically lead to the conclusion that the implicit or underlying expectations of workplaces alone affected the participants' evaluations.

In the following section, research question No. 2 — what influences their perceptions and evaluations — is addressed by analysing the participants' comments.

Underlying norms and expectations

In terms of what norms or underlying expectations influence people's evaluations, there were several key terms in the participants' comments. The first key terms are terms that indicate the participants' workplace.[8]

Sakura (D)-1: **In our workplace**, it's informal before meetings start and it's formal at meetings. So I don't like the embarrassing atmosphere like in this scene. 【Uncomfortable silence】

In the example above, Sakura (D)-1 refers to "in our workplace", which indicates that his evaluation was based on his workplace expectations. He used "*bokura no syokuba de wa*", which literally means "in our company" and is the only use of this expression in the discussion data. In other examples as shown below, the participants employed "*uchi*", which literally means "inside" in Japanese but refers to a group where a person belongs and indicates their workplace in the comments.

Sakura (D)-3: They are talking cheerfully. They should talk in smaller voices when they are talking about topics unrelated to meetings. How loudly they talk about topics unrelated to a meeting! It's so different. Small talk is done in much smaller voices. **In our workplace (*uchi no baai wa*)**, we are quiet and don't talk at the pre-meeting phase. 【Overlapping】
Y&T (I)-3: I feel uncomfortable about bringing food. It's uncommon **in our workplace (*uchi de wa*)**. 【Casual atmosphere】

Another key term is "in Japan", which indicates nation-level, national cultural norms or underlying expectations.

Globe (I)-3: There are many occurrences of similar scenes **in Japan**.
【Uncomfortable silence】

Globe (I)-3 evaluated the discourse by referring to the term "Japan", which indicates that the national cultural standard influenced her evaluation.

Bilbow (1997a, 1997b) and Spencer-Oatey and Xing (2003, 2004, 2005, 2007) contend that members of the same national group are likely to evaluate the same discourse in the same, or at least similar, ways. This suggests that national cultural norms or underlying expectations are common among those who have the same national background. The following comments support this contention.

Sakura (D)-1: A common scene **in Japan**. 【Zero small talk】
Sakura (D)-2: It's normal **in Japan**. 【Zero small talk】

Both Sakura (D)-1 and Sakura (D)-2 regarded the same scene as normal or common based on their implicit expectations. This indicates that their underlying socio-cultural expectations are the same. The following examples show that people from different workplaces share the same expectations:

> Globe (I)-4: If this happens **in Japan**, the mood would be serious and gloomy in such a serious situation.
> 【Humour for defusing tension (2)】
> Y&T(I)-4: **In the case of the Japanese**, they would show more sympathy. 【Humour for defusing tension (2)】

Both participants regard talking seriously or sympathetically when talking about someone's death as the shared socio-cultural norm.

However, regarding a particular discourse feature, there were more cases where "in Japan" does not refer to the same underlying expectation among people from different workplaces. The following comments are referring to the same discourse feature from the three participants.

> Y&T (I)-2: It's normal at the pre-meeting phase. Similar **to Japan**.
> 【Overlapping】
> Y&T (I)-4: Having small talk. It's normally seen **in Japan**.
> 【Overlapping】
> Sakura (D)-2: Applying **to Japan**, it is like the starting conversation with colleagues at a bar **in Japan**. It is not businesslike — they are having conversations cheerfully. 【Overlapping】

The first two participants from Y&T both regard overlapping, actively occurring conversations at pre-meetings as normal in Japan. However, the third comment from Sakura shows a totally different evaluation to those from Y&T people. Sakura (D)-2 regards the same discourse not as normal pre-meeting talk but as "bar talk" in Japan.

In the following examples, too, the same kind of talk is evaluated differently based on socio-cultural expectations.

> Y&T (I)-4: **It normally happens in Japan**. There are close relationships among meeting members. There are good relationships and they can use humour among them. **It's the same as our company**··· It's fine in my company. 【Collaborative humour】
> Sakura (D)-2: It's not appropriate. **Quite rare in Japan**.
> 【Collaborative humour】

In the above examples, too, the participants' evaluations based on their impressions of Japanese socio-cultural norms are opposite. Y&T (I)-4 considers collaborative humour as normal in Japan, while Sakura (D)-2 regards the same discourse as rare in Japan. It is interesting that the above comment by Y&T (I) explicitly shows he regards the scene as normal in Japan and also at his company.

The analysis results so far suggest that socio-cultural norms are not always the same among the same cultural group members. It is also found that the participants in the same workplace mostly had the same cultural expectations and that those from different workplaces could have different cultural norms. It can be argued that the participants' perceptions of national cultural norms or expectations would be affected or eclipsed by their workplace's implicit norms and expectations. It is reasonable that because all the video clips were from workplace discourse, workplace experience is the most easily accessible for the participants when evaluating discourse, and workplace norms or expectations play a major role in their evaluation and perception.

The following examples show how workplace norms and expectations influence the participants' understanding of their cultural norms.

> Y&T (D)-4: It's a common scene. **I don't feel uncomfortable** about a scene where when a boss is wrong, subordinates make fun of them. I don't have an uncomfortable feeling. **It frequently happens in our company.** 【Collaborative humour】
> Y&T (I)-2: It's **normal** at the pre-meeting phase. **Similar to Japan.**
> 【Overlapping】

As shown in the above examples, when the target discourse feature follows the norms and expectations of the participants' workplace or their national cultural norms – i.e. the participants are familiar with the target discourse feature – they were likely to regard it as positive or unremarkable. When the behaviour is different from norms and expectations of the participants' workplace or their national socio-cultural norms, the participants tended to give negative evaluations.

> Y&T (I)-3: I feel **uncomfortable** about bringing food. **It's uncommon in our workplace** (*uchi de wa*). 【Casual atmosphere】
> Sakura (D)-2: It's **not appropriate** ⋯ Quite rare in Japan
> 【Collaborative humour】

This tendency was also observed in Tannen's (1984, 2005) research, which analysed conversational styles that serve a relational function in dinner time conversations among friends. The conversational styles include such features as tone, pitch, silence, irony and humour, and narratives. Tannen (1984, 2005) found that one's conversational style has a positive effect when used with others who share the style, but a negative effect with those whose styles differ. That is, when one's style is similar to another's conversational style, the participants will have a positive feeling, while when different, they will have a negative feeling.

To summarise so far, it is evident from the analysis results that people's evaluations are mainly influenced by the underlying norms and expectations of their workplace, although we cannot neglect people's national level socio-cultural norms.

International business experiences

There was not a clear difference regarding participants' evaluations between domestic groups and international groups. However, this does not directly indicate that extensive international business experience does not play a role in people's evaluations.

There were several interesting findings from the international group. First, the international group gave comments based on their international business experience.

> Y&T (I)-4: My image of Western companies is that subordinates are obedient to their bosses.⋯ I think that Americans seemed to flatter or to be obedient. 【Zero small talk】
> Y&T (I)-2: I agree with Y&T (I)-4. China is similar. People are obedient to their bosses. They don't disagree directly with their leaders.
> 【Zero small talk】

Y&T (I)-4 has had extensive business experience with Western companies, while Y&T (I)-2 lived in China for seven and a half years. They both refer to their own experiences.

The participants in the international group also referred to cross-cultural differences.

> Globe (I)-3: In the video, they are talking about someone's death in a humorous way. **The Japanese** would talk about it more sympathetically though nobody knows whether they truly sympathise or not. **Foreigners** regard it as more businesslike and more practical when the person who died is a stranger. It's different.
> 【Humour for defusing tension (2)】
> Globe (I)-1: A big difference is seen at lunch meetings. **Foreigners** talk while eating, but **the Japanese** never eat while talking or also while other people are talking. So much food is left. It's a big dif-

ference. 【Casual atmosphere】

Both Globe (I)-3 and Globe (I)-1 regularly have intercultural meetings in English. Globe (I)-3 compares Japanese expectations when talking about one person's death with foreigners. Globe (I)-1 compares Japanese expectations of not eating at meetings and about foreigners' eating at meetings. Though their colleagues include people from various countries including Western and Asian countries, it is interesting that both Globe (I)-1 and Globe (I)-3 differentiate their colleagues as Japanese or foreigners.

As shown in the above example, there were comments where international group participants compared Japanese interactional behaviours to those of people from other countries as shown in the following examples:

> Y&T (I)-1: In Europe, they don't serve food at meetings. Drink is served. I'm afraid that chocolate would be inappropriate at a monthly meeting. **I understand it depends on the country,** though. 【Casual atmosphere】
>
> Globe (I)-3: In our company, when we have something to say to the boss, which means we have a problem, we seldom talk to him/her like telling a story, in our department, I think. On the contrary, I think the boss would ask what you'd like to say or what you want him/her to do. The boss would point these out, I think. So in one to one conversation, we seldom talk like the woman in the video, but **I understand it varies according to one's own workplace cultures.** 【Complaining in a humorous way】

As shown in bold, both participants acknowledge differences according to countries or workplaces. It can be argued that awareness of cultural differences contributes to tolerance of differences. Moreover, the international people's comments showed that they had options as to what is appropriate according to different situations.

> Globe (I)-2: I would also think that it depends on the situation. Personally I really like it. At global meetings, refreshments are always served. But at meetings where members are all Japanese or most members are male, when I brought sweets, they took a negative attitude toward me, thinking of me as unserious, at this company. **It depends on who is attending.** 【Casual atmosphere】
>
> Globe (I)-3: There is a very good atmosphere. After all, in Japan, even though we could ask a person in higher status what he/she said means, it would be very difficult to make fun of them. Here, **it**

> depends on who they are. If a boss is a foreigner, something similar would happen. But if a boss is Japanese, maybe the Japanese way would be followed. 【Collaborative humour】

These participants say that what would be appropriate depends on who attends the meetings. This suggests that their interactional behaviour is likely to change according to meeting participants. However, it is interesting that here again, Globe (I)-3 takes an alternative perspective. She says that appropriate behaviour depends on whether the boss is Japanese or non-Japanese.

These comments show that international business experience may promote awareness and possibly tolerance of cultural differences. However, this may not always be the case. In the following example, the participant evaluates cultural differences based on her own cultural values while simultaneously referring to the difference.

> Globe (I)-1: I've experienced similar situations many times at meeting with American companies. They tactically make the discussion casual after tough discussions. But this kind of situation never happens at meetings with Japanese or Asian companies. Because **they emphasise conversations based on courtesy.**
> 【Humour for defusing tension (1)】

In the above example, the participant is talking about humour for defusing tension, or talking about a serious matter in a humorous way. Acknowledging that American people also adopt this linguistic behaviour, she also notes that Asian people (including Japanese) do not. She demonstrates here that her international experience has led to awareness of cultural differences. However, in the last comment, "[b]ecause they emphasise conversations based on courtesy", it is evident that her evaluation is based on her own standard. Though the reality is that the way of showing courtesy is different between American people and Asian people, her way of evaluation is done only from her (or an Asian) perspective, which might indicate that, despite awareness of intercultural differences, her own socio-cultural underlying norms or expectations still affect her evaluation.

The analysis results indicate that the participants' personal experiences, especially international experiences, also affected their perceptions.

Implications on emic constructs

As has been discussed so far, participants' perceptions about a particular discourse segment were influenced mostly by the underlying norms and expectations of their workplace. However, throughout the group discussions, there were characteristics shared in the participants' comments irrespective of their workplace. Many comments referred to *ba* – field or contexts – of the interaction, including the nature of the settings, situations, participants, and other contextual elements.

Some participants employed the term *ba* in their comments as follows:

> Y&T (I)-1: There are only two people here, aren't there? It's normal to talk to her **to soften the atmosphere of the conversation/"break the ice"** (*ba o nagomasu*). I had a somewhat uncomfortable feeling. 【Uncomfortable silence】
> Sakura (D)-1: Well, it's very delicate, but I think it's too much making fun of the boss. Once or twice would work **to soften the atmosphere of the conversation/"break the ice"** (*ba mo nagomu*), but this is too much. 【Collaborative humour】
> Globe (I)-2: I would also think that it **depends on the situation** (*ba ni yoru*). 【Casual atmosphere】

The comments above imply that the participants evaluate the discourse based on *ba* (the conversational field or the situations) of the interaction. *Ba* is an important factor in evaluating a particular discourse segment.

There were comments where components of *ba*, such as the nature of the setting and who the participants of the interaction are, were referenced. In the following two examples, the participants mention the nature of the setting:

> Sakura (D)-1: It's **fine** as this is **an informal meeting** between two people. 【Interwoven small talk】
> Y&T (I)-4: I think it would depend on **the degree of formality** of a monthly meeting. For example, if people of very high status are coming, chocolate would be going too far.
> 【Casual atmosphere】

Sakura (D)-1 regards interwoven small talk with business talk as acceptable because it is at an informal meeting, while Y&T (I)-4 considers bringing chocolate inappropriate when higher status people are coming, i.e. in such a formal situation. From their comments, the nature of the setting, or the degree of formality, is a factor in evaluating a discourse segment.

Who the other participants are in the interaction also plays an important role in evaluating discourse. There were comments about one's position in relation to hearer.

> Globe (I)-4: In Japan, **when talking with boss**, people would be more se-

rious and conversations would be more formal.
【Interwoven small talk】

Globe (I)-3: After all, in Japan, even though we could **ask a person in higher status** what he/she said means, it would be very difficult to make fun of them. 【Collaborative humour】

A shared underlying expectation is found in the comments that people's linguistic behaviour in Japan varies according to the hearer or one's relationships with the hearer in the interaction.

Y&T (I)-4: If there is **someone outside our company**, maybe I'll just ask a question to the boss. 【Collaborative humour】

Sakura (D)-1: I would not talk if there is someone outside our company. If there is **someone outside our company** and the boss is moderator, I would not talk with feeling out of modesty.
【Zero small talk】

Y&T (I)-4 and Sakura (D)-1 have the shared expectation that if there is someone outside their company in the interaction it influences their behaviour.

The following is a stretch of discourse from a discussion at Sakura. Sakura (D)-3 and Sakura (D)-2 are talking about the scene where meeting members are discussing a serious matter in a humorous tone.

Sakura (D)-3: It doesn't seem to me at all that they are discussing a serious matter. Especially, there is no hierarchy among members. [Pointing to a man in the centre, the CEO, in the video clip.] Not at all between the man in the centre and the other participants. What a surprise!

Sakura (D)-2: That's right. Is the man sitting in centre a CEO? I thought the man sitting to the right side [pointing to Harry] was the CEO! 【Humour for defusing tension (1)】

They point out that the CEO is not talking much while a particular young participant, Harry, actively initiates the humour. They share an implicit expectation that people who are in authority in the interaction should initiate the humour. This implies that where one is standing in relation to other participants in the interaction influences people's discursive behaviour. This is also supported by the following examples:

Sakura (D)-3: People are reluctant to express their ideas in Japan. They would listen to when a boss says his idea, then would express their ideas at the end. People don't express their ideas actively, so a boss asks members their opinion one by one according to seniority. 【Zero small talk】

Sakura (D)-4: By the way, in Japanese meetings, it's difficult to say one's idea. Because the order of who speaks is important in Japanese meetings. 【Humour for defusing tension (1)】

An implicit expectation is that the order of expressing one's idea is decided according to seniority or social rank in the interaction, as shown in the above comments. This also indicates that people's discourse behaviour in Japan should be consistent with one's place in the *ba*.

I introduced the logic of *ba*, or dual mode thinking, as an explanatory emic construct in Chapter 6. Applying this to manifestations of small talk and humour in the Japanese business meetings, I pointed out that *ba* plays an important role in influencing Japanese linguistic behaviour. *Ba* can be paraphrased as the field or contexts of the interaction including participants, the nature of the settings, and the other contextual elements. Speakers in Japan generally perceive where they are standing in *ba* and their linguistic behaviours are the manifestations to index the contextual construct – or the speaker's sense of place – in relation to the other participants, to the nature of the setting, and to the other contextual elements.

The analysis results in this section support the view that an emic construct or communicative norm, the logic of *ba*, influences not only people's choice of linguistic behaviour but also their perceptions. It can be argued that this emic construct functions as an underlying expectation in Japan at the macro level in people's perceptions and interpretations of discourse. Thus, the participants' perceptions and evaluations can be accounted for appropriately using an emic perspective. Incorporating an emic perspective helps in understanding Japanese people's interactional behaviour, not only from a speaker's but also from a hearer's perspective.[9]

7.6 Summary

I address the following research questions based on the data analysis in this chapter.

1. How do Japanese business professionals evaluate the manifestations of small talk and humour in New Zealand business meetings?

The analysis suggests the need for a more complex account of peoples' perceptions of business interaction in a different cultural context from their own than has been reported in previous research in this area (e.g., Bilbow 1997a, 1997b; Spencer-Oatey and Xing 2003). The data analysis indicated that Japanese business professionals did not always have identical evaluations, even though they share the same national background. On the other hand, the participants' evaluations were broadly similar.

There were discernable tendencies among the evaluations. The participants' evaluations tended to be similar if they worked in the same workplace. Moreover, manifestations of small talk and humour in the New Zealand meetings were not necessarily evaluated by the Japanese business professionals in the same or similar way as the New Zealand meeting participants. Regarding the different features of small talk and humour in the meeting data in Japan, the participants' evaluations varied from positive (or at least acceptable) to negative. In most cases, participants from Globe and Y&T were likely to evaluate the discourse as "positive" or "understandable", while Sakura participants tended to take negative stances. Features similar to those in the Japanese meeting data were typically regarded as unremarkable.

2. What influences their perceptions and evaluations?

The analysis results indicate that participants' evaluations and perceptions were mainly affected by the norms and underlying expectations of their workplace culture. However, this does not lead to a conclusion that these norms and underlying expectations alone influenced the participants' evaluations. In the participants' comments key terms were identified indicating that their evaluations were based on the participants' workplace (e.g., "In my workplace ⋯") and their national background (e.g., "In Japan ⋯").

As all the scenes are from workplace discourse, it is reasonable that the underlying expectations or norms of each workplace played a major role in evaluating the target discourse. However, the analysis results showed that national cultural norms also played a role. It can be argued that people's evaluations and perceptions are not made based on a single norm but are constructed complexly based on the various norms and expectations with which the person identifies. The participants are not only members of particular workplaces but also a nationality among other groups, and it is reasonable that expectations from both of these affect their evaluations.

Moreover, international group participants often evaluated the target discourse features based on their own international business experience. Considering participants as "historical agents" (Bourdieu 1991; Sunaoshi 2005) who are "manifestations of their life histories" in the process and outcome of interactions (Sunaoshi 2005: 189), it is reasonable that participants' experiences so far, especially those related to business meetings in this case — as well as the various norms and expectations that pertain — inevitably affect their perceptions.

It is difficult to precisely indentify what is an emic construct or communicative norm in Japan and how it functions in interaction, but the analysis results in this chapter could shed light on this question in some respect. It was suggested that the logic of *ba* influenced participants' perceptions at the macro level. Incorporating an emic perspective helps in understanding Japanese people's linguistic behaviour, not only as speakers but also as hearers, more adequately.

The analysis suggests that the manifestations of Relational Practice in New Zealand business meetings are not necessarily evaluated by Japanese business people in the same way as by New Zealand people. All the discourse features addressed in the perception task functioned in the New Zealand meetings effectively and positively from a relational perspective, while, on the contrary, there were cases where they gave negative impressions to Japanese business people. From the point of view of politeness, Japanese business professionals' perceptions allow us to understand that appropriate behaviour in discourse is constructed discursively among participants.

Notes

1 Some sections of this chapter have appeared in Murata (2012b, 2014b).
2 Two out of nine scenes however show common features of relational talk in New Zealand and Japanese meetings.
3 In simplifying utterances in the scenes, I am greatly indebted to my supervisors and LWP researchers. I deeply appreciate their support.
4 I wish to thank the staff at the School of Linguistics and Applied Language Studies for helping me make these simulation video clips.
5 Sample pages of the questionnaire are provided in Appendix VII.
6 See Appendix VIII and IX.
7 I follow Spencer-Oatey and Xing's (2004, 2005) way of showing comments in interviews. That is, in this study although the comments were originally spoken in Japanese, their English translations by the researcher are shown because the research focus is what they said rather than how they said it. If key words appear in the examples, they are marked in bold by the researcher.
8 In sections from 7.7.1, comments about different video clips appear in mixed order. I add 【video clip's name】 after each comment in order to show to what the comment is referring.
9 The focus here is on Japanese communicative norms and there is no implication that context and relationships are unimportant in New Zealand.

CHAPTER 8

Conclusion

This study has explored Relational Practice, providing a contrastive study of small talk and humour in business meeting discourse, in formal and informal meetings, in New Zealand and Japan. The first phase of the contrastive study was cross-cultural, comparing meetings in New Zealand and Japan, and the second phase of the study involved formal meetings (*kaigi*) and informal meetings (*uchiawase/miitingu*). This study has also investigated how Japanese business people perceive the discourse features of small talk and humour in New Zealand meetings, and what influences their perceptions.

This final chapter of the book summarises the major findings and discusses this study's contributions to academic knowledge. Finally I consider some suggestions for future research.

8.1 Major findings

In Chapter 1, three research questions were posed. The following sections summarise the answers that were revealed by the data analysis.

8.1.1 Formal meetings vs. informal meetings

The first research question focussed on the structural characteristics that signal the organisation of formal and informal meetings. This question was posed as a preliminary step to analysing small talk and humour. A consensus in the existing literature suggests that small talk and humour tend to occur around topic transitional points as well as at the opening and closing phases of meetings (e.g., Holmes & Marra 2002a; Chan 2005). Analysing these Relational Practice strategies in meetings requires attention to both macro and micro level meeting structures. Thus, it was necessary to look at how formal and informal meetings are structured. Chapter 4 addressed this question by analysing the meeting data of this study. The analysis results revealed that formal and informal meetings are structurally different, and furthermore that there are many similar structural characteristics in the same meeting category across the two CofPs, i.e. company N in New Zealand and company J in Japan.

Most noticeably, the structures of the formal meetings in both CofPs were similar at the macro level. As in Chan (2005), the formal meetings consisted of five sections. The openings and closings were routinised and their procedures were generally predetermined. In the main discussion phases, smooth topic transitions were co-constructed between the chairperson and the meeting members with the assistance of transitional markers such as "okay" and "alright" in English, and their counterparts, *hai* and *jaa* in Japanese. Silence also served as a transitional marker across the CofPs. In terms of topic progression, a linear pattern was found across the CofPs. At the micro level, however, differences were found according to each CofP. For example, the openings and closings were more ceremonial at company J.

The informal meetings were similar, in general, when considering the meeting structures across the CofPs. In both cases the section durations were not clearly distinguished. Meeting openings and closings were short and not as ritualised as those of the formal meetings. In the discussion sections, meeting topics and other topics − including humour and small talk − were interwoven. These findings indicate that the management of informal meetings is not pre-determined and routinised but follows a more dynamic process than formal meetings.

These structural features have revealed that the contrastive study of formal and informal meetings is valuable, and that paying attention to the formal/informal dimension is necessary when examining meeting discourse.

8.1.2 Manifestations of small talk and humour

The second research question concerned the manifestations of small talk and humour in New Zealand and Japanese formal and informal meetings. Small talk in the meetings was analysed in Chapter 5 and humour was the focus of Chapter 6.

The comparison of small talk in formal and informal meetings identified a difference in the distribution of small talk across the two CofPs. In formal meetings, corresponding to the findings of Chan (2005), small talk was concentrated in the pre-meeting sections. By contrast, in informal meetings, small talk mostly occurred during the main discussion sections. One reason is that the data suggests that in informal meetings small talk tends to be tolerated more and can occur anywhere, even during the main discussion phases. Another reason is that in informal meetings, small talk is finely interwoven throughout meeting talk.

Comparing small talk in meetings at company N with that found in meetings at company J, the following three differences were observed: the topics of small talk, the relationship between small talk and silence, and the construction of small talk. While the topics of small talk were similar across the two CofPs, in the meetings of company N topics were often triggered by the preceding discussion and developed in new directions. Secondly, small talk was almost obligatory in company N's meetings when no urgent talk was required during the pre-meeting phase. In company J's meetings, on the other hand, silence was tolerated. The analysis results suggest that, from a relational perspective, small talk plays an important role in company N's meetings, while a balance of silence and small talk is valued in company J's meetings. Regarding the contruction of small talk, at company N, small talk is cooperatively constructed by meeting members. At company J, by contrast, some participants talk but others remain silent; members speak with no continuity and new topics seldom develop.

While the manifestations of small talk differed between formal and informal meetings, as well as between the two CofPs, the analysis showed that small talk functions as Relational Practice, serving to create team spirit and build rapport among meeting members across both kinds of meetings and both CofPs. In addition, it was found that small talk is often interwoven with meeting talk and it is difficult to draw a clear dividing line between them.

The results of the contrastive study on humour can be summarised in the following way. Comparing humour in formal and informal meetings, a difference in distribution was found across the two CofPs. In formal meetings, consistent with the previous research (e.g., Holmes & Stubbe 2003; Schnurr 2005), while humour mostly occurred at the boundaries of the interaction, including opening and closing phases, it also occurred in the discussion phases − interwoven with business-related talk. In informal meetings, humour was seen to occur anywhere in the meetings.

Comparing humour at company N's and company J's meetings, four differences in its manifestations were evident: its instigators, the categories, types, and functions of the humour. In the meetings at company N, it appears that any participant was free to contribute, while in those at company J, not everyone was free to make humorous remarks; only particular people could instigate the humour. This difference affected the types of humour. At company N, meeting members equally and jointly constructed humour, and thus cooperatively constructed humour sequences were salient. At company J, by contrast, particular people initiated humour and others responded to it. Thus most of the humour consisted of a single remark. Generally, the instigators of humour at company J were those people who were in authority and/or who are in charge of the interaction, e.g., the chairperson. This difference regarding who instigates humour similarly affected the categories of humour. Among the most prevalent categories of humour in company N's meetings were "mutual teasing" and "fantasy humour", both of which were constructed cooperatively by meeting members. However in meetings at company J, teasing was conducted only by people in authority or in higher status than the target.

While humour helped to build rapport and create team spirit across the two CofPs, it also served a unique function for each CofP. At company N, humorous talk was employed when talking about sensitive or serious matters, and it could help mitigate tension. In meetings at company J, it is likely that through the initiation and responses to humour, various aspects of identities and power-relations were constructed discursively and dynamically. Thus it can be argued that humour creates identity and is a strategy to affirm power.

Across the two kinds of Relational Practice strategies, there are similar results. First, both discursive strategies effectively functioned as Relational Practice across the CofPs and the types of meetings, serving to create team spirit and build rapport among meeting members. While employing small talk and humour facilitates cooperation towards organisational objectives, these discursive strategies tended to occur at peripheral positions during meetings such as topic transitional phases, especially in formal meetings. In informal meetings, however, small talk and humour were more tolerated during the main discussion phases.

Though small talk and humour served as Relational Practice, their manifestations were distinctive in each CofP. This suggests that meeting members are enacting Relational Practice through small talk or humour in ways that meet the underlying expectations of each CofP. The data also showed that small talk and humour was finely integrated into on-going meeting talk, and small talk was often accompanied by humour and laughter. This indicates that any talk, including social talk and work-related talk, is multifunctional and should be analysed at the discourse level.

8.1.3 Perceptions of small talk and humour

The third research question, regarding perceptions toward small talk and humour, was two-fold. The first sub-question was concerned with what perceptions Japanese business professionals have about New Zealanders' use of small talk and humour in formal and informal meetings. The second sub-question was concerned with what influences these perceptions.

In terms of the first sub-question, certain tendencies among the evaluations were observed. Contrary to the previous research findings (e.g., Spencer-Oatey and Xing 2003; Bilbow 1997a), the data showed that Japanese business professionals did not always have identical evaluations despite belonging to the same national cultural group. Their perceptions were mostly similar, however, if they worked in the same workplace. Furthermore, the analysis indicated that manifestations of small talk and humour in the New Zealand meetings were not necessarily evaluated by the Japanese business people in the same or similar way as by the New Zealand meeting participants.

In terms of the second sub-question, the analysis indicated that participants' evaluations and perceptions were mainly affected by the norms and underlying expecations of their workplace culture. Since the target video clips (based on the New Zealand meeting data and used to elicit perceptions) addressed business meetings, i.e. workplace discourse, it is reasonable that the workplace norms or expectations had a notable effect on the evaluations of the target discourse. However, the analysis results showed that national cultural norms also played a role. It can be argued that people's evaluations and perceptions are not made based on a single factor but complexly constructed based on the various norms and expectations with which the person identifies. The participants are not only members of particular workplaces but also a nationality, and it is reasonable that expectations from both of these affect their evaluations.

Moreover, participants from groups with significant international business histories often evaluated the target discourse features based on their own experience. Considering participants as "historical agents" (Bourdieu 1991; Sunaoshi 2005) who are "manifestations of their life histories" in the process and outcome of interactions (Sunaoshi 2005: 189), we should expect that participants' experiences so far, especially those related to business meetings in this case – as well as the various norms and expectations that pertain to these – inevitably affected their perceptions.

8.2 Research contribution

I now turn to consider how this study makes a contribution to academic knowledge in a number of areas.

8.2.1 Contribution to research on meetings and on workplace interaction

In Chapter 1, I indicated two possible areas for further research on meetings. The first relates to types of meetings. Although previous researchers acknowledge that formality is a crucial dimension of meetings, most research has focussed on only formal meetings (Asmuß & Svennevig 2009). Moreover in Japan, although there are different terms to refer to formal and informal meetings respectively, no researcher has undertaken contrastive research on *kaigi* (formal meetings) and *uchiawase/miitingu* (informal meetings).

Thus this study contributes as an empirical, contrastive study between formal and informal meetings. In Chapter 4, the data analysis demonstrated the differences regarding structures between formal and informal meetings across the CofPs. The data in Chapters 5 and 6 also showed that the distribution of small talk and humour is different between formal and informal meetings across the CofPs. Occurrences of small talk and humour were more tolerated in informal meetings than in formal meetings. These findings indicate that a contrastive study in this research is warranted, and the formality dimension is necessary when examining meeting discourse, not only in regard to structure but also from a relational perspective.

The other research area which has been a focus is the relational perspective. Though meetings serve a relational function which helps maintain and strengthen collegiality and rapport among meeting members, most of the previous research on meetings has paid little attention to the relational aspects. This study thus also makes a contribution as an empirical study on meetings from a relational perspective. The data analysis in Chapters 5 and 6 has revealed the following four findings. First, small talk and humour play important relational roles, serving to create team spirit and building rapport among meeting members across the CofPs and kinds of meetings. Second, there are potentially important differences in manifestations according to the CofP. Third, Relational Practice is constructed among meeting members discursively and dynamically. Last, meeting members are enacting Relational Practice through small talk and humour in ways that meet the underlying expectations of each CofP. Thus this study sheds light on the ways of realising relational functions in meetings, and on the importance of the relational aspects of meetings.

In terms of research on workplace interactions, I argued in Chapter 1 that there has been very little research based on authentic interactions in Japanese. The present study is based on authentic meetings in Japan including *kaigi* (formal meetings) and *uchiawase/miitingu* (informal meetings). It is thus a good starting point in workplace discourse study in the Japanese context, and the analysis findings provide valuable insights for future research.

8.2.2 Contribution to politeness research

This study employed politeness theory as the analytic framework. In Chapter 2, politeness theory was reviewed, and the position taken for the study was explained. I selected a neo-Politeness approach, making use of Relational Practice as the analytic framework, which incorporates the concept of a CofP as the contextual focus. The assumptions in analysing authentic interactions for

Relational Practice can be summarised in the following ways: (1) politeness is considered as negotiated in on-going interaction among interactants; (2) a CofP can develop in each workplace or each particular working group if the three crucial criteria of a CofP (ongoing regular interaction, shared objectives of the team or group, and a set of linguistic resources common among group members) are met, and the CofP subsequently plays an important role in people's linguistic behaviours regarding Relational Practice; (3) analysis within the Relational Practice and CofP approach not only focusses on each CofP but also provides the basis for microanalysis across CofPs.

Research on Relational Practice (Holmes & Marra 2004; Holmes & Schnurr 2005) indicates that small talk and humour are exemplary Relational Practice strategies. Consistent with the previous research, in the meeting data, both discursive strategies served positively to create team spirit and build rapport among meeting members across the CofPs and kinds of meetings. Corresponding to one important component of Relational Practice, regardless of their important relational roles, small talk and humour generally tended to occur at peripheral phases such as around topic transitional points in the meeting data.

The data analysis discussed in Chapters 5 and 6 clearly supports these three assumptions. As discussed in the analysis chapters which considered small talk and humour, Relational Practice was constructed among meeting participants in on-going interaction. All three dimensions of a CofP were applicable both to the Japanese and New Zealand business meeting groups, which each constituted a CofP. The data has demonstrated that meeting members are enacting Relational Practice through small talk and humour in ways that meet the underlying expectations of each CofP. Furthermore, analysing the meeting data within the Relational Practice framework has highlighted similarities and differences in manifestation of small talk and humour between the two CofPs.

It was found that Relational Practice is applicable to not only the New Zealand data but also the Japanese data. The analysis results have demonstrated Relational Practice and CofP are useful analysis frameworks in exploring politeness in workplace discourse.

There is another contribution to politeness research. In Chapter 1, I pointed out that hearers' perceptions regarding politeness have not been fully explored empirically. This study can also contribute as an empirical politeness research study from the point of perceptions. The perception data analysis indicated that participants' interpretations are not made automatically and in a straightforward manner, but dynamically according to participants' personal experiences related to the scene, expectations of their own workplace, and national cultural norms. Moreover, while all the discourse features addressed in the perception task functioned in the New Zealand meetings effectively and positively from a relational perspective, there were cases where they gave a negative impression to the Japanese business people.

From the point of view of politeness, these results suggest that both national and workplace cultural expectations influence people's evaluations regarding politeness. They also indicate that appropriate behaviours in discourse are constructed among interactants, with the hearers' evaluation playing an important role in deciding whether or not a Relational Practice strategy functions effectively and appropriately.

As noted in Chapter 2 and discussed in the analysis chapters, Chapters 4, 5, and 6, politeness and culture, i.e. cultural expectations, are deeply interrelated. In the next section, the study's contribution to cross-cultural and inter-cultural research is addressed.

8.2.3 Contribution to cross-cultural and inter-cultural research

In Chapter 2, I took the position that culture is a set of assumptions shared by group members (not limited to national groups) and negotiated among members discursively, not as a static predetermined notion but more dynamically and observably through people's interactions. This position was supported by both the meeting data and the perception data. In the meeting data, we saw that meeting members are enacting Relational Practice through small talk and humour in ways which are consistent with the underlying expectations of each CofP, and that Relational Practice was constructed among meeting members discursively and dynamically. The perception data revealed that not only workplace cultural expectations but also national cultural expectations influenced people's perceptions. Through both the meeting and perception data analyses, this study has shown that people's linguistic behaviours and perceptions regarding Relational Practice are influenced by layers of cultural expectations – i.e. not only by underlying expectations of their workplace or CofP, but also those of the wider society such as the nation in which the CofP resides. These findings will be useful for research on politeness and culture, especially politeness in the workplace.

In terms of conducting cross-cultural research, I took a combined etic-emic approach, considering both global and local constructs. I took Relational Practice as an etic construct in analysing the data. The data analysis has shown that Relational Practice is applicable to the Japanese workplace as well as the New Zealand workplace and could function as an etic construct common to these two national cultural groups. In interpreting the distinctive manifestations which are common in small talk and humour, I have proposed an emic construct, or underlying communicative constraint, for each CofP: "egalitarianism" for company N in New Zealand and the "theory of *ba*" for company J in Japan. The logic of *ba* was applicable to not only the manifestations of small talk and humour but also to their perceptions. The perception data suggests that the logic of *ba* influenced the Japanese participants' perceptions at the macro level. The data indicates that the emic perspective would be useful to interpret the data to better understand cultural differences. It was found from this study that the combined etic-emic approach makes cross cultural study more fruitful and explanatory.

Though this study is cross-cultural, it has implications for inter-cultural research. Bargiela-Chiappini and Harris (2006: 12-13) point out that cross-cultural study is well worth consideration because it "provides insights from within individual cultures that can inform intercultural research projects", and Gudykunst (2000: 314) writes: "Understanding cross-cultural differences in behaviour is a prerequisite for understanding intercultural behaviour."

To the best of my knowledge, this is the first empirical study on workplace interactions involving New Zealand and Japan, although, as noted in Chapter 1, the relationship between these two nations is close and involves many intercultural interactions. As discussed above, this cross-cultural study contributes to our knowledge of intercultural communication. The findings discussed in this study are useful for understanding people's linguistic behaviours from these two countries. The findings in the perception task discussed in Chapter 7 in particular may be helpful in reducing misunderstandings between people from New Zealand and Japan. Therefore, hopefully these findings will benefit not only researchers of workplace interactions but also business people in New Zealand and Japan.

8.3 Future research

Although this study contributes to various research fields (see above), it is important to acknowledge its limitations. First of all, like other explanatory research, this study has narrowed its scope, in this case, to one company from each nation for the meeting data and three business organisations for the perception data. Consequently, the findings based on the limited data can only be carefully generalised. Holmes, Marra, and Schnurr (2008: 193) also emphasise in their research on workplace interactions that "the tendencies identified are based on exploratory research, and further research is needed to confirm or contest [their] tentative generalisations." In their cross-cultural study on meetings in the U.K. and Italy, Bargiela-Chiappini and Harris (1997a: 225) contend that "[r]esearch on a much larger scale, based on an extended typology of meetings from comparable and different organizational contexts is necessary in order to explore feasibility of robust cross-cultural and inter-cultural generic models." Nevertheless, the present study's empirical results have the potential to be a useful starting point for similar future studies.

In addition to the limited data source, another limitation was the setting. Though this study focussed on meetings, there are many other settings in workplace discourse. Moreover, regarding discursive strategies in Relational Practice, there are other possible strategies though this study focussed only on two of them.

There was also another limitation regarding the perception task. Although I take the theoretical position that politeness is dynamically and discursively negotiated among interactants, in the perception task, perceptions from a third party, i.e. people who are not the actual interactants, were examined. It is ideal to explore the perceptions of interactants themselves, but it was impossible to do so in this study because of its cross-cultural nature. The advantages in using third parties is that they are not distracted by knowing the participants and that they can focus on the discourse features; however, the limitation is that their understanding of the contexts is reduced.

Taking these limitations into consideration, I suggest future research. One possible extension of the manifestation analysis of the current study would be to repeat the same procedure in other companies in New Zealand and/or Japan to verify the findings. Formality is a crucial dimension of meetings, and it is important to take this dimension into consideration when collecting meeting data. Another possible extension would be to include companies in other nations since this study addresses only two. As noted in the analysis chapters, most empirical research on workplace discourse is conducted in English speaking societies. More and more research in non-English speaking societies, such as in Asia, is necessary to add a variety of perspectives and make the research more illuminating.

It is difficult to precisely identify what are emic constructs or communicative norms in a CofP and how they function in interaction, but the analysis results in this study could shed light on this question in some respect. Exploring emic constructs is challenging, but it is worth doing in order to better understand cultural differences and for better intercultural communication.

This research focussed on meetings, which are one of the many situations at work. Therefore, other workplace discourse such as office interactions, lunchtime chats, directives given from bosses to subordinates, and so on, could contribute to our understanding of Relational Practice. Moreover, while this study focussed on meetings among members in one CofP, meetings across CofPs, and negotiations among two or more CofPs would be also interesting settings to analyse Relational Practice.

In terms of the analysis of the perception task, one possible option would be to include more organisations in Japan to verify the findings of this study. This study examined Japanese business people's perceptions of New Zealanders' linguistic behaviours; the investigation of New Zealanders' perceptions of Japanese behaviours would be of great interest as well.

As another possible perception study, one could examine interactants' perceptions in intercultural communication. Cultural expectations are not limited to national groups, and especially in workplace interactions, workplace culture influences people's linguistic behaviours. Therefore, (intercultural) interactions among people from different workplaces, i.e. different CofPs, could provide interesting data to examine the interactants' perceptions.

It is evident so far that this research will be valuable to foster better understanding of cultural differences and better intercultural communication. However, this study also has a potential to be applied in an entirely different direction.

As a practical application, since 2008, I have been involved in the Research Centre for the Local Public Human Resources and Policy Development (LORC) at Ryukoku University in Japan.[1] It conducts various research projects that aim to achieve a sustainable local society. In order to realise this, it is important to create a multi-stakeholder partnership in which people from different sectors (local government, businesses, NPOs, and local citizens) gather around the same table to discuss and solve local problems, and to develop *Local Public Human Resources* – a concept that includes those who can work in partnership with people from the different sectors and take active roles in the multi-stakeholder partnership. A development system for Local Public Human Resources is a growing demand in today's local society, and I have been developing educational programmes for Local Public Human Resources with colleagues from the fields of political science, organisational development, and sociology.

The educational programmes which have been developed by the LORC aim to identify ways of effectively facilitating discussions among people from different sectors. In order to examine how effectively people from different sectors, or different CofPs, interact, I have been conducting fieldwork and analysing video-recorded authentic discussions, employing the same methods and frameworks as this study. Integrating the analysis findings of this study, so far I have found that Relational Practice plays important roles to effectively facilitate such discussions and will hopefully contribute to creating the desired multi-stakeholder partnership (Murata 2009d; Murata et al. 2010).

Thus, I hope that this study will contribute to not only better understanding intercultural communication, but also the realisation of a sustainable local society as well.

Notes

1 Details of the LORC are available at the following web site: http://lorc.ryukoku.ac.jp/

Appendix

Appendix I[1]

職場の談話プロジェクト
Language in the Workplace Project at XXX

ご参加いただく皆様へ（研究プロジェクトの説明）
INFORMATION FOR PARTICIPANTS

研究プロジェクトについて

The Language in the Workplace Projectは、ビクトリア大学(ニュージーランド ウエリントン)で1996年から継続して研究が進められているプロジェクトです。(研究代表者　ビクトリア大学教授　Janet Holmes)
(http://www.vuw.ac.nz/lals/research/lwp/index.aspx)

　現在までに、ニュージーランドの政府機関、一般企業、さらに工場や個人事業等から、1500会話(参加協力者450名)を録音させていただきました。そして、職場のさまざまな場面の会話を分析することで、業務を遂行する際の言葉の役割、リーダーシップと言葉、職場の人間関係を円滑に進めるための会話の役割、雑談やユーモアの職場における機能と役割等についての解明を行ってきました。また、研究によって得られた知見は、学術研究分野のみならず、広く社会に貢献するよう努めてきました。グローバル社会となり、異なる言語を母語とする人々によるビジネス交渉の機会が増える中、国際語としての英語の役割や機能を考える際に、実際の職場の会話のデータの分析は、異文化コミュニケーションで起こりうる誤解や衝突を避け、より円滑なコミュニケーションを図るために必要です。すでに、香港の企業とNZ企業における会議の談話構造についての対象研究も行い、この度、日本企業のご協力をお願いすることになりました。

About the project

Researchers from the Language in the Workplace Project (Victoria University of Wellington http://www.vuw.ac.nz/lals/research/lwp/index.aspx) have been studying workplace communication since 1996 under the direction of Professor Janet Holmes. So far, we have collected approximately 1,500 interactions, involving a total of more than 450 people, from office workers in government departments and commercial organisations, from factory workers, and from various small businesses. We have analysed a number of aspects of workplace talk including how people use talk to get things done at work, how people prevent or fix up misunderstandings, and how they use humour and small talk to get on better with their workmates. Because of growing globalisation, there are increased opportunities for business negotiations among people from various language backgrounds. The status of English as a global language means that it is important to explore effective ways of communicating with people from different countries. Research drawing on actual communication data from various workplaces will allow us to identify areas of potential breakdown in intercultural communication. We have already conducted a contrastive research between NZ workplaces and Hong Kong workplaces. We would like you to cooperate with our research project as Japanese participants.

研究プロジェクトの目的

The Language in the Workplace Projectの目標は次の通りです。
1. それぞれの職場での職場の会話の特徴をとらえること。
2. それぞれの組織(職場)においての効果的・円滑なコミュニケーションを行うためのストラテジー(方策)を見出すこと。
3. 録音した会話の分析から得た結果を職場における人材育成・開発に還元すること。
4. 異文化間比較研究を通して国際ビジネスの発展に貢献すること。
　以上の目的を達成するためには、実際に話されている言葉の分析が必要不可欠です。
　録音(録画)の具体的な方法としては、参加者に小型録音機器(例：ICレコーダー)で職場での日常会話の録音をお願いする、あるいはミーティングや会議の録画をお願いするといったものがあげられます。
　録音(録画)資料は、文字化します。文字化の際には、個人名や企業名等は、偽名を使用し、個人が特定できないよう細心の注意を払います。なお、会話を分析する際、その会話の状況等について参加者におうかがいする場合もあります。
　分析が終われば、書面あるいはワークショップやセミナーの開催等で参加いただいた方に、結果のフィードバックをさせて頂きます。

Aims of the project

The aims of the projects are the following:
- To identify distinctive features of workplace talk in different workplaces
- To identify strategies of effective communicators
- To explore the implications of the findings for workplace relationships in order to provide useful input to human resource and professional development programmes
- To explore the implications of the findings in order to contribute to better intercultural business communication

To do this we need to find out how people actually talk to each other as they go about their work. We will ask participants to record some of their everyday conversations and meetings at work. If people are agreeable, we will also video-record some larger meetings.

We will then take the recordings away, transcribe them, and analyse the communication patterns. (We will replace real names with pseudonyms to protect your identity). When we have finished the transcription, we might ask you to comment on particular conversations to facilitate our understanding of what is going on. Afterwards, we will give you a summary of the results, and check whether you or your participating colleagues would like any other sort of feedback, such as a workshop.

個人情報の取り扱いについて

このプロジェクトは、社会科学分野の学術研究の国際倫理基準を遵守し、ビクトリア大学の研究倫理委員会の承認を受けて行われています。研究プロジェクトにご協力いただいた方の個人情報は、個人情報保護法に基づき、重要なものと認識し、その取り扱いについては、細心の注意を払います。

録音(録画)されたデータ、文字化した資料及び関連資料は、Language in the Workplace Projectのデータの一部となりますが、研究及び上で述べた録音に参加いただいた企業におけるフィードバック以外の目的には使用いたしません。研究結果を論文等で公表する際には、必ず匿名性を守ります。学術研究会等で、録音のごく一部を使用する場合にも、個人が特定されることがないよう細心の注意を払います。

また、録音(録画)されたデータ、文字化した資料、及び関連資料は施錠した場所に保管され、研究に関わる研究者以外のいかなる第3者にも提供または開示はいたしません。

なお、この研究への参加・協力は、録音期間(2007年末まで)はいつでも、途中で辞退することができます。

Ethics and confidentiality

The ethical guidelines subscribed to by social scientists internationally will be observed as well as the specific guidelines of Victoria University's Human Ethics Committee.

In terms of personal information, we recognise the importance of The Japanese Personal Information Protection Law. The recordings and other information we collect from you will be incorporated into the LWP corpus and used only for research, publications and presentations based on this research; and evaluation and development of workplace communication in your workplace. We may play short excerpts from the tapes in professional contexts such as seminars, but only if we are sure that no one will recognise you.

All tapes and other information collected as part of this project will be stored securely. No one other than authorised researchers will have access to this information.

All the participants have the freedom to withdraw participation anytime during the data collection, that is, until the end of 2007.

Language in the Workplace Project プロジェクト責任者
ビクトリア大学言語学科教授　ジャネット　ホームズ
Tel: +64-4-463-5614
Email: janet.holmes@vuw.ac.nz

Language in the Workplace Projectプロジェクト
龍谷大学法学部准教授　村田　和代
Tel: 075-642-1111
Email: murata@law.ryukoku.ac.jp
April 2007

Notes
1 The originals of appendices I to VII are written in Japanese only.

Appendix II

フェイスシート (Background information sheet)

次の質問にお答えください。Could you answer the following questions?

1. お名前 (Name)

2. 年齢 (Age)
   20-24   25-29   30-34   35-39   40-44   45-49   50-54   55-59   60-64   65-69
   70-74   75-79   80+

3. 性別 (Sex)   男性(male)   女性(female)

4. 職場名 (your company's name)

5. 役職 (your job title in the company)

6. 職種 (your assigned task at the company)

7. 勤続年数 (the period you have worked for the company)   年   月

8. 最終学歴（大学・大学院の場合は、学部・専攻もご記入ください）(your highest education qualification and your major if you have one)

9. 3ヶ月以上の海外滞在経験がある場合は、その期間と国名をご記入ください。
   (If you have lived in countries outside of Japan for more than three months: the period and the name of the country)

10. 英語学習経験について（中学校・高校の教科以外）
    例）大学でESSクラブに入っていた、英会話学校に1年間通った等
    (English learning experience other than at junior and high schools)
    e.g. I used be a member of ESS club. I have studied English conversation at a

private language school for a year.

11. 英語資格について、取得されている場合はご記入ください。
    例）英検2級、TOEIC600　等
    (English qualification)
    e.g. STEP 2nd grade, TOEIC 600

12. 会議の他の参加者とはどれくらいの頻度で会われますか？（会議以外も含む）
    例）毎日顔をあわす。　週に１度会議でのみ会う。　○○さんとは、毎日会い、××さんとは週に２回、その他のメンバーとは、週に１回程度　等
    具体的にご記入ください。
    (How often do you see the other participants?)
    e.g. I see the other participants every day. I see the other participants once a week at a meeting. I see Mr. A every day and Mr. B and Mr.C twice a week, and the others once a week.

1. XX事務所の方とは？(staff working at XX office)

2. YY事務所の方とは？(staff working at YY office)

3. J社以外の方とは？(staff working outside company J)

Appendix III

承諾書 (Consent form)

私は研究プロジェクトについて理解しました。また、プロジェクトその他についての質問に対し、納得のいく回答を得ました。また、録音期間中いつでも参加を辞退ないしは中止できることも理解しました。私は、録音された会話および、その文字化した資料や、ビデオからの観察データあるいはフェイスシート等で提供した情報は、承認を受けた研究者以外に公開されることがないこと、及び、学術研究以外の目的で使用されることがないことを理解しました。そして提供したデータや情報がThe Language in the Workplace Projectのデータとして将来使用される可能性があることも理解しました。私は、会話の録音及びこれに伴う文字化資料を学術研究の目的で使用することを承認します。

I have understood the aim of this research project. I have had an opportunity to ask questions and have them answered to my satisfaction. I have also understood that I have the freedom to withdraw participation anytime during the data collection, that is, until the end of 2007. I understand that the recordings of my voice and associated transcriptions together with any information including background information I provide will be kept confidential to the approved researchers and will be used for research purposes only. I also understand that these data and information will be incorporated into the LWP corpus and may be used for linguistic research purposes in the future. I understand that my identity will be protected in all current and future use of these data. I give permission for recording of my voice and associated transcription to be used for linguistic research purposes.

日付：date   ご署名: Please print full name

分析結果のフィードバックを郵送、あるいはメールでの送付をご希望の場合は、下記に連絡先をご記入いただければ幸いです。

Write your address or e-mail address if you would like me to send feedback to you by mail or by e-mail.

Appendix IV

職場の談話プロジェクト
ご参加いただく皆様へ（研究プロジェクトの説明）
INFORMATION FOR PARTICIPANTS
Language in the Workplace Project
at [name of workplace]

職場の談話プロジェクト(The Workplace Project at Victoria University of Wellington)では、現在日本とニュージーランド(以下NZ)のビジネスミーティングの比較研究を行っています。既にそれぞれの国の企業のご協力により、会議や打ち合わせの模様を録画(録音)させていただきました。研究の次の段階は印象調査(PerceptionTask)です。これは、日本の方々(business people)にNZのビジネスミーティングのシュミレーションビデオクリップを見ていただき、それについての印象をお答えいただくというもので、小グループのディスカッション形式で行います。調査終了後には、ご協力いただいた方々に調査結果の概要をお知らせさせていただきます。

 Researchers from the Language in the Workplace Project (Victoria University of Wellington http://www.vuw.ac.nz/lals/research/lwp/index.aspx) are conducting a contrastive study between New Zealand and Japanese business meetings. In the first stage of the research we collected recordings of how people actually talk in New Zealand and Japanese workplaces. In this second phase, we would like to gather information about your perceptions of the meeting data we present. This will involve a small group discussion (which will be recorded) where we provide some examples for you to reflect on. At the end of the research we would be happy to provide you with a summary of the results.

研究プロジェクトについて

The Language in the Workplace Projectは、ビクトリア大学(ニュージーランドウエリントン)で1996年から継続して研究が進められているプロジェクトです。(研究代表者　ビクトリア大学教授Janet Holmes)(http://www.vuw.ac.nz/lals/research/lwp/index.aspx)
 現在までに、ニュージーランドの政府機関、一般企業、さらに工場や個人事業等から、1,500会話(参加協力者450名)を録音させていただきました。そして、職場のさまざまな場面の会話を分析することで、業務を遂行する際の言葉の役割、リーダーシップと言葉、職場の人間関係を円滑に進めるための会話の役割、雑談やユーモアの職場における機能と役割等についての解明を行ってきました。また、研究によって得られた知見は、学術研究分野のみならず、広く社会に貢献す

るよう努めてきました。グローバル社会となり、異なる言語を母語とする人々によるビジネス交渉の機会が増える中、国際語としての英語の役割や機能を考える際に、実際の職場の会話のデータの分析は、異文化コミュニケーションで起こりうる誤解や衝突を避け、より円滑なコミュニケーションを図るために必要です。すでに、香港の企業とNZ企業における会議の談話構造についての対象研究も行いました。この度、日本企業のご協力をお願いする運びとなりました。

About Language in the Workplace

The Language in the Workplace research team have been studying workplace communication under the direction of Professor Janet Holmes since 1996. So far, we have collected approximately 1,500 interactions, involving a total of more than 500 people, from office workers in government departments and commercial organisations, from factory workers, and from various small businesses. We have analysed a number of aspects of workplace talk including how people use talk to get things done at work, how people prevent or fix up misunderstandings, and how they use humour and small talk to get on better with their workmates. Because of growing globalisation, there are increased opportunities for business negotiations among people from various language backgrounds. The status of English as a global language means that it is important to explore effective ways of communicating with people from different countries. Research drawing on actual communication data from various workplaces will allow us to identify areas of potential breakdown in intercultural communication. We have already conducted a contrastive research between NZ workplaces and Hong Kong workplaces. We would like you to cooperate with our research project as Japanese participants.

個人情報の取り扱いについて

このプロジェクトは、社会科学分野の学術研究の国際倫理基準を遵守し、ビクトリア大学の研究倫理委員会の承認を受けて行われています。研究プロジェクトにご協力いただいた方の個人情報は、個人情報保護法に基づき、重要なものと認識し、その取り扱いについては、細心の注意を払います。

　記録されたデータ及び関連資料は、Language in the Workplace Projectのデータの一部となりますが、研究及び上で述べた録音に参加いただいた企業におけるフィードバック以外の目的には使用いたしません。研究結果を論文等で公表する際には、必ず匿名性を守ります。学術研究会等で、記録のごく一部を使用する場合にも、個人が特定されることがないよう細心の注意を払います。

　また、記録されたデータ及び関連資料は施錠した場所に保管され、研究に関わる研究者以外のいかなる第3者にも提供または開示はいたしません。

　プロジェクトの趣旨をご理解いただき調査にご協力いただける場合は、承諾書にご署名いただければ幸いです。

Ethics and confidentiality

The ethical guidelines subscribed to by social scientists internationally will be observed as well as the specific guidelines of Victoria University's Human Ethics Committee. In terms of personal information, we recognise the importance of The Japanese Personal Information Protection Law. The recordings and other information we collect from you will be incorporated into the LWP corpus and used only for research, publications and presentations based on this research; and evaluation and development of workplace communication in your workplace. We may play short excerpts from the tapes in professional contexts such as seminars, but only if we are sure that no one will recognise you. All tapes and other information collected as part of this project will be stored securely. No one other than authorised researchers will have access to this information. If you are happy to participate, please fill in the consent form provided.

Language in the Workplace Project
プロジェクト責任者
ビクトリア大学言語学科教授
Janet Holmes ジャネット　ホームズ
Tel: +64-4-463-5614
Email: janet.holmes@vuw.ac.nz z
Director, Language in the Workplace Project
Victoria University of Wellington
School of Linguistics and Applied Language Studies
Professor Janet Holmes
Phone: 04-463-5614
Email: janet.holmes@vuw.ac.nz

Language in the Workplace Project 研究員
龍谷大学法学部准教授　村田　和代
Tel: 075-642-1111
Email: murata@law.ryukoku.ac.jp
Researcher, Language in the Workplace Project
Ryukoku University, Japan
　Associate Professor Kazuyo MURATA
Phone: +81-75-642-1111
Email: murata@law.ryukoku.ac.jp

Appendix V

フェイスシート (**Background information sheet**)

次の質問にお答えください。Could you answer the following questions?

1. お名前 (Name)

2. 年齢 (Age)
   20-24   25-29   30-34   35-39   40-44   45-49   50-54   55-59   60-64   65-69
   70-74   75-79   80+

3. 性別 (Sex)   男性(male)   女性(female)

4. 職場名 (your company's name)

5. 役職 (your job title in the company)

6. 職種 (your assigned task at the company)

7. 勤続年数 (the period you have worked for the company)   年   月

8. 最終学歴（大学・大学院の場合は、学部・専攻もご記入ください）(your highest education qualification and your major if you have one)

9. 英語学習経験について（中学校・高校の教科以外）
   例）大学でESSクラブに入っていた、英会話学校に1年間通った等
   (English learning experience other than at junior and high schools)
   e.g. I used to be a member of ESS club. I have studied English conversation at a private language school for a year.

11. 英語資格について、取得されている場合はご記入ください。
    例）英検2級、TOEIC 600 等 (English qualification) e.g. STEP 2nd grade,

TOEIC 600

12. 3ヶ月以上の海外滞在経験がある場合は、その期間と国名をご記入ください。
    (If you have lived in countries outside of Japan for more than three months: the period and the name of the country)

13. 国際ビジネスの経験について、ご記入ください。(Please write about your intercultural business experience)
    e.g. I have a business trip to the US about once a month and do business there in English. I have a TV meeting with participants from Europe countries once a week and English is used at the meeting. Some of my co-workers in my office are from other countries, such as China, Korea, and Singapore and we communicate among them in English.

Appendix VI

承諾書 (Consent form)

私は研究プロジェクトについて理解しました。また、プロジェクトその他についての質問に対し、納得のいく回答を得ました。また、録音期間中いつでも参加を辞退ないしは中止できることも理解しました。私は、録音された会話および、その文字化した資料や、ビデオからの観察データあるいはフェイスシート等で提供した情報は、承認を受けた研究者以外に公開されることがないこと、及び、学術研究以外の目的で使用されることがないことを理解しました。そして提供したデータや情報がThe Language in the Workplace Projectのデータとして将来使用される可能性があることも理解しました。私は、会話の録音及びこれに伴う文字化資料を学術研究の目的で使用することを承認します。

I have understood the aim of this research project. I have had an opportunity to ask questions and have them answered to my satisfaction. I understand that the recordings of my voice and associated transcriptions together with any information including background information I provide will be kept confidential to the approved researchers and will be used for research purposes only. I also understand that these data and information will be incorporated into the LWP corpus and may be used for linguistic research purposes in the future. I understand that my identity will be protected in all current and future use of these data. I give permission for recording of my voice and associated transcription to be used for linguistic research purposes.

日付：date

ご署名: Please print full name

分析結果のフィードバックを郵送、あるいはEメールでの送付をご希望の場合は、下記に連絡先をご記入いただければ幸いです。
Write your address or e-mail address if you would like me to send feedback to you by mail or by e-mail.

Appendix VII

Sample pages of the perception task questionnaire

Video Clip 1 (left side of two-page spread)
ビデオクリップ 1

状況
月例定例の会議が始まる前のシーンです。会議にはいろいろな部署の長11名が参加します。2名の参加者Evan(finance manager)とVeronica(general administrator)が他の参加者が来るのを待っています。

Situation
This is a scene where a formal meeting is about to start. The meeting is a monthly management meeting. There are 11 participants, most of whom are managers from various departments. Two of the participants, Evan, finance manager, and, Veronica, general administrator, are waiting for other participants coming. They quickly look at some documents.

ビデオを見た第一印象を書いてください。(英語が理解できなくても構いません)
Write your first impression about the video clip. (Don't worry if you don't understand English. Write down just what you felt about the video clip).

Video Clip 1 (right side of two-page spread)

ビデオクリップ　1　もしあなたがこのシーンにいたらどのような印象を持たれますか？1〜4の中から選んでください。また、コメントがあれば自由にお書きください。**Rating sheet**

① ビデオの登場人物たちは「礼儀正しい／ていねい」だと思いますか？　それとも「礼儀正しくない／ていねいでない」と思いますか？ polite / impolite

　　　　1　　　　2　　　　3　　　　4

礼儀正しい／ていねい polite　　　　　礼儀正しくない／ていねいでない impolite

コメント：

② ビデオ全体として、登場人物のふるまいは「ふさわしい」と思いますか？それとも「ふさわしくない」と思いますか？ appropriate / inappropriate

　　　　1　　　　2　　　　3　　　　4

ふさわしい appropriate　　　　ふさわしくない inappropriate

コメント：

③ ビデオ全体として、登場人物のふるまいは「フォーマル」だと思いますか？それとも「インフォーマル（カジュアル）」だと思いますか？ formal/informal(casual)

　　　　1　　　　2　　　　3　　　　4

フォーマル formal　　　　　インフォーマル（カジュアル）informal(casual)

コメント：

④ もしあなたが同席していたら、「心地よい」と感じたでしょうか？　それとも「不愉快」だと感じたでしょうか？ comfortable/uncomfortable

　　　　1　　　　2　　　　3　　　　4

心地よい comfortable　　　　不愉快だ uncomforable

コメント：

⑤　もしあなたが同席していたら、参加者たちのふるまいが好きですか？それとも嫌いですか？ like/dislike

　　　　　　　1　　　　2　　　　3　　　　4
　　　好き like　　　　　　　　　　嫌い dislike

コメント：

⑥　ビデオに見られる会議前のシーンは日本の会議前と同じですか？　それとも違いますか？ same/different

　　　　　　　1　　　　2　　　　3　　　　4
　　　非常に似ている same　　　　　　非常に異なる very different

コメント：

Appendix VIII

Scenarios of the video clips

No.1

This is a scene where a formal meeting is about to start. The meeting is a monthly management meeting. There are 11 participants, most of whom are managers from various departments. Two of the participants, Evan, finance manager, and, Veronica, general administrator, are waiting for other participants coming. They quickly look at some documents.

Evan:	Just you and me.
Veronica:	Yep it'll be a quick meeting, won't it?
Evan:	Be a quick meeting.
Veronica:	Um, can I have your notes?
	(2 second pause) just to really brief them (2 second pause)
Evan:	Yeah. That'll be fine.
	(36 second pause)
Veronica:	How is the financial year end going, will it be easier than last time?
Evan:	Yeah, (2 second pause) it will, um we'll still have an audit though.

No. 2

This is a scene from a formal meeting at an advertising company. The meeting is a monthly management meeting. There are 11 participants, most of whom are managers from various departments. Five of the participants are discussing their company's re-branding. They are renaming the business and changing the colours to bright orange and green. The five participants (left to right) are Jaeson, general manager and chairperson, Sharon, marketing manager, Ben, managing director, Evan, finance manager, and Harry, production manager.

Ben:	So there's gonna be no more red and white signs
Sharon:	/no\
Jaeson:	/correct\
Harry:	Oh

Jaeson:	gone
Sharon:	gone
Harry:	ok, so we're back to plain brown
Sharon:	1/no\1 2/(pause)\2 3/[laughs]\3
Evan:	1/[laughs]\1
Ben	2/[laughs]\2
Jaeson:	3/let's not think that\3
Ben:	There'll be no mistaking them.
Sharon:	They'll be bright colours, orange and green now.
Harry:	That was the whole idea—getting our signs all around the country
Jaeson:	All the way to the South Island?
Evan:	[laughs]
Harry:	In the car park?
Sharon:	Yeah, no they were there already.
All:	[laughter]
Ben:	But if anyone hasn't been upstairs, go up and have a look, because it's starting to really get busy up there.

No. 3

This is a scene where a formal meeting is about to start. The meeting is a monthly management meeting. There are 11 participants, most of whom are managers from various departments. Five of these participants (left to right), Evan, finance manager, Ben, managing director, Harry, production manager, Sharon, marketing manager, and Jaeson, general manager and chairperson, are waiting for other participants coming. There are two conversations at the same time: Evan and Ben are talking, and Harry and Sharon are talking. One conversation is about a projector and the other is about text messages. You may find it especially difficult to understand these conversations, but just try to focus on how people are talking, not what they are saying.

(First conversation)

Evan:	Oh, as I was saying, Wendy brought home a data projector last night from work and got me to set it up at home, because she's got three or four of her staff coming to our place this morning for a meeting, because they're trying to get out of work for an hour or two
Ben:	Yeah

Evan:	Jeez, it was awesome eh. (1 second pause) I projected it on the wall.
Ben:	You watched TV?
Evan:	No, I watched a DVD.
Ben:	Oh yeah was it really good was it?
Evan:	Mind you it was pitch black outside.
Ben:	Yeah
Evan:	Yeah it's just so flexible—you can make the picture this big or you can make it um that big. Project it on any wall you like.

[Ben turns and joins other conversation]

(Second conversation)

Jaeson:	It's just a different language isn't it? My son texted me in this language, and I just texted him back saying "okay."
Sharon:	It's just that t m t m b.
Harry:	It says Kevin. What's it, what to do with Kevin?
Sharon:	I don't know. What does t m b mean?
Harry:	I don't know.
Sharon:	Thumb.
Harry:	(yeah) (2 second pause) or just text number thumb.
Sharon:	Text number thumb. [laughs] (1 second pause) Definitely a text isn't it? Yeah.

[Ben enters]

Ben:	Who is it who's /who sent you a text\ Kevin?
Harry:	/I don't understand\
Ben:	I don't understand half these texts I get. (2 second pause) People abbreviate them (1 second pause)
Sharon:	Mmm (2 second pause)
Harry:	That's why kids can't spell.
Sharon:	It's a new language.

No. 4

This is a scene from an informal meeting of an advertising company. There are 2 participants. Sharon, marketing manager, and Jaeson, general manager, are having a catch-up meeting and talking about a problem a client is having. They have created lots of advertising for this client, and one of the people that has her name and photo in the materials has died suddenly. They realize they need to be sensitive, but are happy since this means they'll get a lot more work for this client.

Sharon:	This morning I had a woman ring me from, Bryant's and, she said that someone has died, someone who's a quite significant figure there.
Jaeson:	Hmm
Sharon:	Yeah and her name is mentioned in a lot of a lot of their advertising, and also her photograph appears in the brochures, and so everything with her name appears or where her photograph is has to be destroyed and remade.
Jaeson:	Cool.
Sharon:	Yeah that's what I thought
Sharon:	but I didn't say it to her.
Jaeson:	Sorry, oh, I mean how sad
Sharon:	So, you know, she but, it's the whole client thing you know, she rung and she said about this person dying and then she just stopped, and obviously was waiting for me to
Jaeson:	Yeah, burst into tears.
Sharon:	Yeah, and I had to tell her, you know, that's terrible, that's
Jaeson:	How can we possibly help?

No. 5

This is a scene from a formal meeting. The meeting is a monthly management meeting. There are 11 participants, most of whom are managers from various departments. Jaeson, a general manager, who is the boss for most of the participants and chairperson, starts the meeting. Just after the meeting starting words, Jaeson mentions that they have a new manager, for I.S. (information systems). The term, I.S., is less popular than I.T. (information technology) and sounds old-fashioned, and everyone is teasing Jaeson by making language jokes. The participants (left to right) are Jaeson, general manager and chairperson, Paul, sales manager, Sharon, marketing manager, Evan, finance manager, Harry, production manager.

Jaeson:	Okay (2 second pause) let's get into it (1 second pause).
	Okay, thanks everyone for coming along.
	I'd just like to welcome our newest member to the management team, Darryl, who's now serving as the, um client manager and,

	um we have a new I.S. manager
Paul:	I.S.?
Jaeson:	I.S. (1 second pause) how's that
Harry:	is that
Paul:	The information system, sounds better than, than info than I.T.
All:	[laughter]
Evan:	[laughs]: Waiting for that one.
All:	[laughter]
Jaeson:	Yeah, it's twenty-first century now, it's called I.S.
Evan:	Oh, okay.
Harry:	I.T. comes after I.S.
Jaeson:	Is it [laughs]
Jaeson:	Okay, so um well, (1 second pause) that's um going well, anyway

No. 6

This is a scene from an informal meeting. There are 2 participants. Jaeson, general manager, and Paul, sales manager, are having a catch-up meeting. They have been talking about a budget issue. Then they mention that their company is going to invite top clients to a popular rugby tournament; they discuss whether their boss (Ben) will sit with them, and how much it will cost. They talk about how happy some of the female clients will be. They also mention that those female clients are planning a vacation to a similar tournament in Hong Kong and Jaeson teases Paul, asking him if he is going. Then again they go back to working on planning their calendar.

Paul:	So, yeah, there's more money in it now.
	Um, also I'm going to get Anna to organise a group for the rugby tournament next year as well,
	So, I spoke to Ben about it and he said "absolutely"
	and I said "well you'll be up in the corporate box, won't you?"
	He said "does that mean I'm not going to be included with your group"
	and I went "oh I didn't think you'd want to be with the little people"
	and he said "I'd rather be with the little people"
Jaeson:	Oh, that's a good idea.
Paul:	Yeah
Jaeson:	And the girls from Anderson Associates, they will love that, right?

	Are those girls still talking about going to the tournament in Hong Kong?
Paul:	They are going.
Jaeson:	They are? Yeah. Are you going to go with them?
Paul:	No, no too much grief.
Jaeson:	Yeah
Paul:	Yeah, um no my wife just said,
	I think she sort of came to the realisation that I was going to be travelling with six women and, she was not really happy about it.
Jaeson:	When you told me you might go, I was thinking jeez mate. There's no way I would be allowed to do that.

No. 7

This is a scene from a formal meeting. The meeting is a monthly management meeting. There are 11 participants, most of whom are managers from various departments, including Jaeson, general manager and chairperson, Evan, finance manager, Sharon, marketing manager, Paul, sales manager, and Ben, managing director. The participants are talking about the budget for a particular project, how they built profit margins into the budget, and how they are able to meet the cost for the budget.

Jaeson:	There's, um like all the, um design component and, um illustration. All that sort of thing that's all invoiced up front.
Evan:	Oh good
Jaeson:	And anything they use which is going to be quite a large portion of it /will be invoiced as\
Sharon:	/it's about fifty percent isn't it\
Jaeson:	Well, yeah. Yeah so
Evan:	Oh, that's good.
Paul:	So just the production costs
Jaeson:	but you're right /and\
Evan:	/yeah\
Jaeson:	We've incorporated um extra margin in there. The balance is full and paid.
Evan:	Fair enough.
Jaeson:	Um the other thing which is really good too, I wanted to mention you guys have done well in controlling the overtime and casuals, um that's virtually been zero for January which is 1/really good\1
Ben:	1/zero\1 for January.

Sharon:	2/not quite\2
Jaeson:	2/I mean\2 not quite zero, but you know, really really low—yeah which is good.

No. 8

This is a scene where a formal meeting is about to start. The meeting is a monthly management meeting. There are 11 participants, most of whom are managers from various departments. The five participants, Paul, sales manager, Jaeson, general manager and chairperson, Veronica, general administrator, Evan, finance manager, and Harry, production manager are waiting for other participants coming. Sharon, marketing manager, enters the meeting bringing chocolate. They talk about who the chocolates are for, and joke about eating them.

Harry:	[goofy voice]. Oh.
Sharon:	No, they're all mine!
Veronica:	No, that's for Sharon, as we're going through the meeting.
Sharon:	[laughs]
Paul:	Good grief.
Sharon:	No, they're not.
	[laughter]
Sharon:	They're from John's team.
Harry:	It's your lucky day, Sharon.
Sharon:	You just behave yourself, all right. They're for everybody.
Harry:	Well, everybody better be quick.
Paul:	Oh, okay, I'm obviously getting the wrong food—all that healthy stuff is no good. I need sweets and fats!
Veronica:	[laughs]

No. 9

This is a scene from an informal meeting. There are 2 participants. Sharon, the marketing manager, and Jaeson, the general manager, are having a catch-up meeting. They are discussing the building company they hired to do some repairs in their main office building. The building company promised to finish the repairs by the day before the meeting, but so far, had only put up scaffolding. Sharon talks about how she's tried to push them to get the job done.

Jaeson:	Well, they've put up some safety cones.
Sharon:	I know, but they put up the cones last Friday. You're not allowed outside that or you might get hit by a train.
Jaeson:	[laughs]
Sharon:	And then we'd have to file an incident report /[laughs]\
Jaeson:	/[laughs]\
Sharon:	Um, but the scaffolding's not up so I emailed Brian AGAIN and I said "look it's two o'clock—there's no sign of any scaffolding."
Jaeson:	Yeah, cos then like it will rain tomorrow and blah blah blah blah blah
Sharon:	He said that they'll get there today, and I said "no, no I want it finished today. It has to be finished today. That was the deal. They were supposed to start this morning, /not\ just get here this afternoon
Jaeson:	/yeah\
Sharon:	and put some metal down
Jaeson:	turn up and drop a whole pile of scaffolding on the ground
Sharon:	They're so naughty so naughty
Jaeson:	yeah

Appendix IX

Casts with pictures

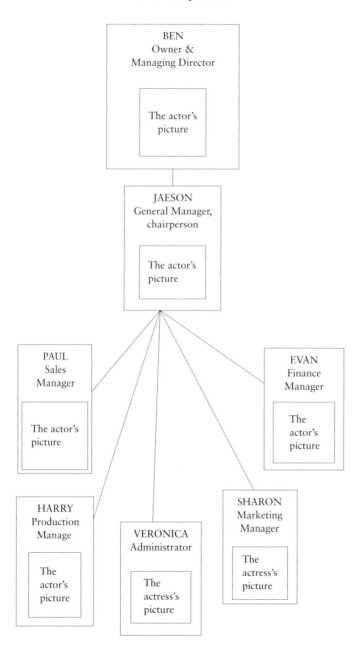

Appendix X

Transcription conventions

NZ data	Japanese data	
yes	はい	Underscore indicates emphatic stress
[laughs]: :	[笑]: :	Paralinguistic features in square brackets, colons indicate start/finish
[laughter]	[笑いが起こる]	general laughter
+	+	Pause of up to one second
++	++	Pause of up to two seconds
(3.0)	(3.0)	Pause of specific number of seconds (above two)
xx/xxxxx\xx	xx/xxxxx\xx	Simultaneous speech
(hello)	(そうですね)	Transcriber's best guess at an unclear utterance
( )	( )	Unintelligible word or phrase
?	?	Rising or question intonation
-	-	Incomplete or cut-off utterance
...	...	Section of transcript omitted
XM/XF	XM/XF	Unidentified Male/Female
[company name]	[会社名]	Name of company/product/client etc.
[*comments*]	[コメント]	Editorial comments italicized in square brackets (including information to assist in understanding the meaning of the English translation in JP data)

All names used in examples are pseudonyms.

References

Abrams, Meiyer H. 1993. *A Glossary of Literary Terms (6th ed.)*. Forth Worth: Harcourt Brace Jovanovich.

Ackroyd, Stephen and Paul Thompson. 1999. Only joking? from subculture to counter-culture in organizational relations. In *Organizational Misbehaviour*, edited by S. Ackroyd and P. Thompson. London/Thousand Oaks: Sage, 99-120.

Albert, Michael. 1985. Assessing cultural change needs. *Training & Development Journal* 39 (5):94-98.

Alberts, Jess K. 1992. An inferential/strategic explanation for the social explanation of teases. *Journal of Language and Social Psychology* 11 (3):153-177.

Antunes, Pedro, Carlos J Costa, and Joao A Pino. 2006. The use of genre analysis in the design of electronic meeting systems. *Information Research (an international electronic journal)* 11 (3): [Available at http://InformationR.net/ir/11-3/paper251.html].

Apte, Mahadev. 1985. *Humor and Laughter. An Anthropological Approach*. Ithaca: Cornell University Press.

Ashkanasy, Neal M., Edwin Trevor-Roberts, and Jeffrey C. Kennedy. 2004. The egalitarian leader: leadership in Australia and New Zealand. In *Leading in High Growth Asia*, edited by D. Tjosvold and K. Leung. Singapore: World Scientific. 231-252.

Asmuß, Birte and Jan Svennevig. 2009. Meeting talk: an introduction. *Journal of Business Communication* 46 (1):3-22.

Bantz, Charles R. 1983. Naturalistic research traditions. In *Communication and Organizations: Advances in Theory, Research, and Methods*, edited by L. L. Putnam and M. E. Pacanowsky. Newbury Park, CA: Sage. 55-71.

Bargiela-Chiappini, Francesca, ed. 2009. *The Handbook of Business Discourse*. Edinburgh: Edinburgh University Press.

Bargiela-Chiappini, Francesca and Sandra Harris. 1996. Interruptive strategies in British and Italian management meetings. *Text* 16 (3):269-297.

———. 1997a. *Managing Language: The Discourse of Corporate Meetings*. Amsterdam: John Benjamins.

———, eds. 1997b. *The Language of Business: An International Perspective*. Edinburgh: Edinburgh University Press.

———. 2006. Politeness at work: issues and challenges. *Journal of Politeness Research* 2 (1):7-33.

Bargiela-Chiappini, Francesca, and Chatherine Nickerson. 1999. Business writing as social action. In *Writing Business: Genres, Media and Discourses* edited by F. Bargiela-Chiappini and C. Nickerson. Harlow: Longman. 1-32.

———. 2002. Business discourse: old debates, new horizons. *IRAL* 40 (4):273-286.

———. 2003. Intercultural business communication: a rich field to studies. *Journal of Intercultural Studies* 24 (1):3-16.

Bargiela-Chiappini, Francesca, Chatherine Nickerson, and Brigitte Planken. 2007. *Business Discourse*. New York: Palgrave Macmillan.

Barke, Andrew. 2010. Manipulating honorifics in the construction of social identities in Japanese television drama. *Journal of Sociolinguistics* 14 (4):456-476.

Barnes, Rebecca. 2007. Formulations and the facilitation of common agreement in meetings talk. *Text & Talk* 27 (3):273-229.

Barretta-Herman, Angeline. 1990. The effective social service staff meeting. In *Business Communication: New Zealand Perspective*, edited by F. Sligo. Palmerston North: Software Technology NZ. 136-146.

Barsoux, Jean-Louis. 1993. *Funny Business: Humour, Management and Business Culture.* London: Cassell.

Basch, Charles E. 1987. Focus group interview: an underutilized research technique for improving theory and practice in health education. *Health Education Quarterly* 14:411-448.

Beck, Leif C., WIlliam L. Trombetta, and Share Scott. 1986. Using focus group sessions before decisions are made. *North Carolina Medical Journal* 47 (2):73-74.

Bell, Nancy D. 2009a. Responses to failed humor. *Journal of Pragmatics* 41 (9):1825-1836.

———. 2009b. Impolite responses to failed humor. In *Humor in Interaction*, edited by N. R. Norrick and D. Chiaro. Amsterdam/Philadelphia: John Benjamins Publishing Company. 143-163.

Bennington, Ashley, Judy Shetler, and Thomas Shaw. 2003. Negotiating order in interorganizational communication: discourse analysis of a meeting of three diverse organizations. *The Journal of Business Communication* 40 (2):118-143.

Berg, Bruce L. 1998. *Qualitative Research Methods for Social Sciences.* Needham Heights, MA: Viacom Company.

Berry, John W. 1969. On cross-cultural comparability. *International Journal of Psychology* 4:119-128.

Bilbow, Grahame. 1995. Requesting strategies in the cross-cultural business meeting. *Pragmatics* 5 (1):45-55.

———. 1997a. Cross-cultural impression management in the multicultural workplace: the special case of Hong Kong. *Journal of Pragmatics* 28:461-487.

———. 1997b. Spoken discourse in the multicultural workplace in Hong Kong: applying a model of discourse as 'impression management'. In *The Languages of Business: An International Perspective*, edited by H. Sandra and F. Bargiela-Chiappin. Edinburgh: Edinburgh University Press.

———. 1998. Look who's talking: an analysis of "chair-talk" in business meetings. *Journal of Business and Technical Communication* 12 (2):157-197.

———. 2002. Commissive speech act use in intercultural business meetings. *IRAL* 40:287-303.

Blau, Peter. 1955. *The Dynamics of Bureaucracy.* Chicago: University of Chicago Press.

Boden, Deirdre. 1994. *The Business of Talk: Organizations in Action.* Cambridge: Polity Press.

Bonisch-Brendnich, Brigitte. 2008. Watching the Kiwis: New Zealanders' rules of social interaction. *Journal of New Zealand Studies* 2008 (6-7):3-15.

Bourdieu, Pierre. 1977. *Outline of a Theory of Practice.* Cambridge: Cambridge University Press.

———. 1988. *Terms of Address: Problems of Patterns and Usage in Various Languages and Cultures.* Berlin: Mouton de Gruyter.

———. 1991. *Language and Symbolic Power.* Cambridge: Polity Press.

Boxer, Diana and Florencia B. Corte's-Conde. 1997. From bonding to nipping to biting: conversational joking and identity display. *Journal of Pragmatics* 27:275-294.

Brown, Penelope and Stephen Levinson. 1987. *Politeness: Some Universals in Language Usage.* Cambridge: Cambridge University Press.

Brown, Reva B. and Dermont Keegan. 1999. Humor in the hotel kitchen. *Humor* 12 (1):47-70.

Cameron, Deborah, Elizabeth Frazer, Penelope Harvey, Ben Rampton, and Kay Richardson, eds. 1992. *Researching Langue: Issues of Power and Method.* London: Arnold.

Candlin, Christopher N. 2000. General editor's preface. In *Small Talk*, edited by J. Coupland. London: Longman. xiii-xx.

Caudron, Shari. 1992. Humor is healthy in the workplace. *Personnel Journal* 71 (6):63-66.
Chan, Angela. 2005. Openings and closings in business meetings in different culture, Unpublished PhD Thesis, Victoria University of Wellington, New Zealand.
Cheepen, Christine. 1988. *The Predictability of Informal Conversation*. London: Pinter Publishers.
———. 2000. Small talk in service dialogues: the conversational aspects of transactional telephone talk. In *Small Talk*, edited by J. Coupland. London: Longman. 288-311.
Chiaro, Delia. 1992. *The Language of Jokes: Analyzing Verbal Play*. London: Routledge.
Cicourel, Aaron V. 1987. The Interpenetration of communicative contexts: examples from medical encounters. *Social Psychology Quarterly* 50 (2):217-226.
Clancy, Patricia M. 1986. The acquisition of communicative style in Japanese. In *Language Socialization across Cultures*, edited by B. B. Schieffelin and E. Ochs. Cambridge: Cambridge University Press. 213-250.
Clouse, Wilburn R. and Spurgeon L. Karen. 1995. Corporate analysis of humor. *Psychology: A Journal of Human Behaviour* 32 (3-4):1-24.
Clyne, Michael. 1994. *Inter-Cultural Communication at Work: Cultural Values in Discourse*. Cambridge: Cambridge University Press.
Coates, Jennifer. 1989. Gossip revisited: language in all-female groups. In *Women in their Speech Communities*, edited by J. Coates and D. Cameron. London: Longman. 94-121.
———. 1996. *Women Talk: Conversation between Women Friends*. Oxford: Blackwell.
Consalvo, Carmine M. 1989. Humor in management: no laughing matter. *Humor* 2 (3):285-297.
Consedine, Bob. 1989. Inequality and the egalitarian myth. In *Culture and Identity in New Zealand*, edited by D. Novitz and B. Willmott. Wellington: Bookprint Consultants. 172-186.
Cook, Haruko M. 1998. Situational meaning of the Japanese social deixis: the mixed use of the *masu* and plain forms. *Journal of Linguistic Anthropology* 8:87-110.
———. 2008. Style shifts in Japanese academic consultations. In *Style Shifting in Japanese*, edited by K. Jones and T. Ono. Amsterdam, The Netherlands: John Benjamins. 9–38.
Cooren, Francois, ed. 2007. *Interacting and organizing: Analyses of a management meeting*. Mahwah, NJ: Lawrence Erlbaum.
Coupland, Justine, ed. 2000a. *Small Talk*. London: Longman.
———. 2000b. Introduction: sociolinguistic perspectives on small talk. In *Small Talk*, edited by J. Coupland. Harlow, England: Pearson Education. 1-25.
Coupland, Justine, Nikolas Coupland, and Robinson Jeffrey. 1992. How are you?: negotiating phatic communion. *Language in Society* 21:207-230.
Coupland, Nikolas and Virpi Ylanne-McEwen. 2000. Talk about the weather: small talk, leisure talk and the travel industry. In *Small Talk*, edited by J. Coupland. London: Longman. 164-182.
Cuff, E.C. and Wes W. Sharrock. 1985. Meetings. In *Handbook of Discourse Analysis (Vol.3)*, edited by Teun A. van Dijk. London: Academic Press. 149-159.
Dannerer, Monika. 2001. Negotiation in business meetings. In *Negotiation and Power in Dialogic Interaction*, edited by E. Weigand and M. Dascal. Amsterdam: John Benjamins. 91-106.
Davis, Alan and Brian H. Kleiner. 1989. The value of humor in effective leadership. *Leadership and Organization Development* 10 (1):i-iii.
Davis, Jessica M., ed. 2006. *Understanding Humor in Japan*. Detroit: Wayne State University press.
De Cillia, Rudolf, Reisigl Martin, and Wodak Ruth. 1999. The discursive construction of na-

tional identities. *Discourse and Society* 10 (2):149-173.

Decker, Wayne H. 1987. Managerial humor and subordinate satisfaction. *Social Behavior and Personality* 15 (2):225-232.

Deetz, Stanley A. and Astrid Kersten. 1983. Critical modes of interpretive research. In *Communication and organizations: Advances in Theory, Research, and Methods*, edited by L. L. Putnam and M. E. Pacanowsky. Newbury Park, CA: Sage. 147-171.

Doi, Takeo. 1971. *Amae no Kozo [The anatomy of Dependence]*. Tokyo: Kobundo.

Drew, Paul and John Heritage, eds. 1992. *Talk at Work: Interaction in Institutional Settings*. Cambridge: Cambridge University Press.

Du-Babcock, Bertha. 1999. Topic management and turn taking in professional communication: first- versus second-language strategies. *Management Communication Quarterly* 12:544-572.

Du-Babcock, Bertha and Richard Babcock. 1997. Communication patterns in multicultural organizational meetings: the influence of language and culture. *Perspectives* 9 (1):1-34.

Duncan, Jack W., Larry R. Smeltzer, and Terry L. Leap. 1990. Humor and work: applications of joking behavior to management. *Journal of Management* 16 (2):255-278.

Durkheim, Emile. 1954. *The Elementary Forms of Religious Life*. (translated from the French by Joseph W. Swain) London: George Allen & Unwin Ltd.

Eckert, Penelope and Sally McConnell-Ginet. 1992. Think practically and look locally: language and gender as community-based practice. *Annual Review of Anthropology* 21:461-490.

———. 1999. New generalizations and explanations in language and gender research. *Language in Society* 28 (2):185-201.

Eelen, Gino. 2001. *A Critique of Politeness Theories*. Manchester: St Jerome.

Eisenberg, Ann. 1986. Teasing: verbal play in two Mexicao homes. In *Language Socialization Across Cultures*, edited by B. Schieffelin and E. Ochs. Cambridge: Cambridge University Press. 182-198.

Emerson, Joan. 1969. Negotiating the serious import of humor. *Sociometry* 32:169-181.

Ervin-Trip, Susan M. and Martin Lampert. 2009. The occasioning of self-disclose humor. In *Humor in Interaction*, edited by N. R. Norrick and D. Chiaro. Amsterdam/Philadelphia: John Benjamins Publishing Company. 165-186.

Feather, Norman T. 1994. Attitudes toward high achievers and reactions to their fall: theory and research concerning tall poppies. *Advances in Experimental Social Psychology* 26: 1-73.

Fisher, Sue. 1982. The decision-making context: how doctors and patients communicate. In *Linguistics and the Professions*, edited by R. J. Di Pietro. Norwood, NJ: Ablex. 51-81.

Fletcher, Joyce K. 1999. *Disappearing Acts: Gender, Power, and Relational Practice at Work*. Cambridge: MIT Press.

Foley, William. 1997. *Anthropological Linguistics*. Oxford: Blackwell.

Ford, Celia. 2010. Questioning in meetings: participation and positioning. In *Why do you ask?*, edited by S. Erlich and A. Freed. Oxford: Oxford University Press. 211-234.

Fraser, Bruce and William Nolan. 1981. The association of deference with linguistic form. In *The Sociolinguistics of Deference & Politeness*, edited by J. Walters. The Hague: Mouton, 93-111. Special issue (27) of the *International Journal of the Sociology of Language*.

Fry, William F. 1992. Humor and chaos. *Humor* 5 (3):219-232.

Geyer, Naomi. 2008. *Discourse and Politeness: Ambivalent Face in Japanese*. London: Continuum.

Giles, Howard, Nikolas Coupland, and John Wiemann. 1991. 'Talk is cheap ...' but 'My word is my bond': beliefs about talk. In *Sociolinguistics Today: International Perspectives*,

edited by K. Bolton and H. Kwok. London: Routledge. 218-243.
Giles, Howard and Peter F. Powesland. 1975. *Speech Style and Social Evaluation*. London: Academic Press.
Glenn, Phillip. 2003. *Laughter in Interaction*. Cambridge: Cambridge University Press.
Goffman, Erving. 1959. *The Presentation of Self in Everyday Life*. Garden City, NY: Doubleday.
———. 1967. *Interaction Ritual: Essays on Face-to-Face Behavior*. Garden City, NY: Anchor Books.
Graham, John L. and Yoshihiro Sano. 1984. *Smart Bargaining : Doing Business with the Japanese* Cambridge, Mass: Ballinger Publishing Company
Grice, Paul H. 1975. Logic and conversation. In *Syntax and Semantics 3: Speech Acts*, edited by P. Cole and J. Morgan. New York: Academic Press. 41-58. Reprinted in Grice 1989: 22-40.
———. 1989. *Studies in the Way of Words*. Cambridge, MA: Harvard University Press.
Grinsted, Annette. 1997. Joking as a strategy in Spanish and Danish negotiations. In *The Language of Business: An International Perspective*, edited by F. Bargiela-Chiappini and S. Harris. Edinburgh: Edinburgh University Press. 159-182.
Gu, Yueguo. 1990. Politeness phenomena in modern Chinese. *Journal of Pragmatics* 14:237-257.
Gudykunst, William B. 2000. Methodological issues in conducting theory-based cross-cultural research. In *Culturally Speaking: Managing Rapport through Talk across Cultures*, edited by H. Spencer-Oatey. London: Continuum. 293-315.
———. 2002. Cross-cultural communication research. In *Handbook of International and Intercultural Communication*, edited by W. B. Gudykunst and B. Moday. Thousand Oaks, CA: Sage. 19-23.
Gunthner, Susanne. 2008. Negotiating rapport in German-Chinese conversation. In *Culturally Speaking: Culture, Communication and Politeness Theory*, edited by H. Spencer-Oatey. London: Continuum. 207-226.
Haakana, Markku. 2002. Laughter in medical interaction: From quantification to analysis, and back. *Journal of Sociolinguistics* 6 (2):207-235.
Hamaguchi, Eshun. 1983. *Kanjin-shugi no shakai Nihon [Japan, Society of Contextual Men]*. Tokyo: Toyo Keizai.
———. 1985. A contextual model of the Japanese: toward a methodological innovation in Japan studies. *Journal of Japanese Studies* 11:289-321.
Hanak, Irmi. 1998. Chairing meetings: turn and topic control in development communication in rural Zanzibar. *Discourse and Society* 9 (1):33-56.
Harris, Sandra. 2007. Politeness and power. In *The Routledge Companion to Sociolinguistics*, edited by C. Llamas, L. Mullany and P. Stockwell. London: Routledge.122-129.
Harris, Sandra and Francesca Bargiela-Chiappini. 1995. Towards a generic structure of meetings in British and Italian managements. *Text* 15 (4):531-560.
———. 1997. The language of business: introduction and overview. In *The Languages of Business*, edited by F. Bargiela-Chiappini and S. Harris. Edinburgh: Edinburgh University Press. 1-18.
Hatch, Mary J. and Stanford B. Ehrlich. 1993. Spontaneous humor as an indicator of paradox and ambiguity in organizations. *Organization Studies* 14 (4):505-526.
Haugh, Michael. 2005a. What does 'face' mean to the Japanese? understanding the import of 'face' in Japanese business interactions. In *Asian Business Discourse(s)*, edited by F. Bargiela-Chiappini and M. Gotti. Bern: Peter Lang. 211-239.
———. 2005b. The importance of "place" in Japanese politeness: implications for cross-cul-

tural and intercultural analyses. *Intercultural Pragmatics* 2 (1):41-68.

———. 2007. Emic conceptualisations of (im)politeness and face in Japanese: implications for the discursive negotiation of second language learner identities. *Journal of Pragmatics* 39:657-680.

Hawkins, Roger. 1993. Regional variation in France. In *French Today: Language in its Social Context*, edited by C. Sanders. Cambridge: Cambridge University Press. 55–84.

Hay, Jennifer. 1994. Jocular abuse patterns in mixed-group interaction. *Wellington Working Papers in Linguistics* 6: 26-55.

———. 1995. Gender and humour: beyond a joke, Unpublished MA Thesis, Victoria University of Wellington, New Zealand.

———. 1996. No laughing matter: gender and humour support strategies. *Wellington Working Papers in Linguistics* 8:1-24.

———. 2001. The pragmatics of humor support. *Humor* 14 (1):55-82.

Hayakawa, Haruko. 2003. "The meaningless laughter": laughter in Japanese communication, Unpublished PhD Thesis, University of Sydney, Australia.

Hill, Beverly, Sachiko Ide, Shoko Ikuta, Akiko Kawasaki, and Tsunao Ogino. 1986. Universals of linguistic politeness: quantitative evidence from Japanese and American English. *Journal of Pragmatics* 10 (3):347-371.

Hisa, Takahiro. 2003. Jyumin shutai no machi zukuri no torikumi to jissen: koryu no ba o kaku to shita kyodo no machi zukuri shisutemu no tenkai [Grappling and practice of creating a community: development of system for developing partnership based on creating a community] *The Annual Bulletin of Osaka Local Public Employees' Training Center*: 15-25.

Holdway, Simon. 1988. Blue jokes: humor in police work. In *Humor in Society: Resistance and Control*, edited by C. Powell and G. E. C. Paton. London: Macmillan. 106-122.

Holmes, Janet. 1995. *Women, Men and Politeness*. Harlow: Longman.

———. 1999a. Women at work: analysing women's talk in New Zealand workplaces. *Australian Review of Applied Linguistics* 22 (2):1-17.

———. 1999b. Special issue. Community of practice in language and gender research. *Language in Society* 28 (2):171-293.

———. 2000a. Doing collegiality and keeping control at work: small talk in government departments. In *Small Talk*, edited by J. Coupland. London: Longman. 32-61.

———. 2000b. Talking English from 9 to 5: challenges for ESL learners at work. *International Journal of Applied Linguistics* 10 (1):125-140.

———. 2000c. Politeness, power and provocation: how humour functions in the workplace. *Discourse Studies* 2 (2):159-185.

———. 2003. Social constructionism. In *International Encyclopedia of Linguistics (2nd ed. Vol. 4)*, edited by W. Frawley. Oxford: Oxford University Press. 88-91.

———. 2005. Politeness and postmodernism - an appropriate approach to the analysis of language and gender? *Journal of Sociolinguistics* 9 (1):108-117.

———. 2006a. *Gendered Talk at Work: Constructing Gender Identity through Workplace Discourse*. New York, Oxford: Blackwell.

———. 2006b. Sharing a laugh: pragmatic aspects of humor and gender in the workplace. *Journal of Pragmatics* 38:26-50.

———. 2012. Politeness in intercultural discourse and communication. To appear in *Handbook of Intercultural Discourse and Communication*, edited by C. B. Paulston, S. F. Kiesling, and E. S. Rangel. Oxford: Blackwell. 205-228.

Holmes, Janet, Angela Joe, Meredith Marra, Jonathan Newton, Nicky Riddiford, and Bernadette Vine. in press. Applying linguistic research to real world problems: the social meaning of talk in workplace interaction. To appear in *Handbook of Communication in Organisations and Professions* (HAL 3) edited by C.r Candlin and S, Sarangi. Berlin and New York: Mouton de Gruyter.

Holmes, Janet and Meredith Marra. 2002a. Having a laugh at work: how humour contributes to workplace culture. *Journal of Pragmatics* 34:1683-1710.

———. 2002b. Over the edge? subversive humor between colleagues and friends. *Humor* 15 (1):65-87.

———. 2004. Relational practice in the workplace: women's talk or gendered discourse? *Language in Society* 33:377-398.

Holmes, Janet, Meredith Marra, and Stephanie Shnurr. 2008. Impoliteness and ethnicity: Māori and Pākehā discourse in New Zealand workplaces. *Journal of Politeness Research* 4 (2):193-219.

Holmes, Janet, Meredith Marra, and Bernadette Vine. 2011. *Leadership, Ethnicity, and Discourse*. Oxford: Oxford University Press.

Holmes, Janet and Miriam Meyerhoff. 1999. The community of practice: theories and methodologies in language and gender research. *Language in Society* 28 (2):173-183.

———. 2003. Different voices, different views: an introduction to current research in language and gender. In *The Handbook of Language and Gender*, edited by J. Holmes and M. Meyerhoff. Oxford: Blackwell. 1-17.

Holmes, Janet and Stephanie Schnurr. 2005. Politeness, humor and gender in the workplace: negotiating norms and identifying contestation. *Journal of Politeness Research* 1:121-149.

Holmes, Janet and Maria Stubbe. 1995. You know, eh and other 'exasperating expressions': an analysis of social and stylistic variation in the use of pragmatic devices in a sample of New Zealand English. *Language and Communication* 15 (1):63-88.

———. 2003. *Power and Politeness in the Workplace. A Sociolinguistic Analysis of Talk at Work*. London: Longman.

Holmes, Janet, Maria Stubbe, and Bernadette Vine. 1999. Constructing professional identity: "doing power" in policy units. In *Discourse in Medical, Mediation and Management Settings*, edited by S. Sarangi and C. Roberts. Berlin, New York: Mouton de Gruyter. 351-385.

Honey, John. 1998. Sociophonology. In *The Handbook of Sociolinguistics*, edited by F. Coulmas. Oxford, UK: Blackwell Publishers. 92-106.

House, Robert J., Paul J. Hanges, Mansour Javidan, Peter Dorfman, and Vipin Gupta. 2004. *Culture, Leadership, and Organizations: The GLOBE Study of 62 Societies*. Thousand Oaks, CA: Sage Publications.

Huisman, Marjan. 2001. Decision-making in meetings as talk-in-interaction. *International Studies of Management and Organisation* 31 (3):69-90.

Ide, Sachiko. 1989. Formal forms and discernment: two neglected aspects of universals of linguistic politeness. *Multilingua* 8 (2-3):223-248.

———. 1992. On the notion of wakimae: toward an integrated framework of linguistic politeness. In *Mosaic of Language: Essays in Honour of Professor Natsuko Okuda*. Tokyo: Mejiro Linguistic Society (MLS). 298-305.

———. 2006. *Wakimae no Goyoron [Pragmatics of Discernment]*. Tokyo: Taishukan Shoten.

———. 2009. Sasutenaburu na chikyu no tame no ibunka komyunikeshon: kojin shugi no ronri to ba no ronri [The pragmatics of individualism and the pragmatics of contextualism: in search of a sustainable global communication]. *Intercultural Communication Review* 7:11-24.

Ide, Sachiko, Beverly Hill, Yukiko M. Carnes, Tsunao Ogino, and Akiko Kawasaki. 1992.

The concept of politeness: an empirical study of American English and Japanese. In *Politeness in Language: Studies in its History, Theory, and Practice*, edited by R. J. Watts, S. Ide and K. Ehlich. Berlin, New York: Mouton de Guyter. 281-297.

Jackson, Brad. 2000. Portraying leadership in New Zealand: from modest recognition to contemplative action. Paper read at The 2nd Conference of the International Association of insight and Action, at Brisbane, Australia.

Jaworski, Adam. 1993. *The Power of Silence: Social and Pragmatic Perspectives*. Newbury Park, CA: Sage.

———. 2000. Silence and small talk. In *Small Talk*, edited by J. Coupland. London: Longman.110-132.

Kangasharju, Helena. 2002. Alignment in disagreement: forming oppositional alliances in committee meetings. *Journal of Pragmatics* 34 (10-11):1447-1471.

Karen, Tracy and Julie M. Naughton. 2000. Institutional identity-work: a better lens. In *Small Talk*, edited by J. Coupland. London: Longman. 62-83.

Kasper, Gabriele. 1990. Linguistic politeness: current research issues. *Journal of Pragmatics* 14:193-218.

Kecskes, Istvan. 2004. Editorial: lexical merging, conceptual blending, and cultural crossing. *Intercultural Pragmatics* 1 (1):1-26.

Kennedy, Jeffrey C. 2007. Leadership and culture in New Zealand. In *Culture and Leadership Across the World: The GLOBE Book of In-Depth Studies of 25 Societies*, edited by J. S. Chhokar, F. C. Brodbeck and R. J. House. Mahwah, NJ: Lawrence Erlbaum Associates. 397-432.

Keyton, Joann. 2005. *Communication & Organizational Culture: A Key to Understanding Work Experiences*. Thousand Oaks, Calif, London: Sage.

Kita, Sotaro. 2009. Introduction to Prof. Shimizu's theory of *BA*, paper presented at the 3rd Tokyo International Workshop on "Emancipatory Pragmatics", Tokyo, Japan, 25-27, March 2009.

Kjaerbeck, Susanne. 1998. The organization of discourse units in Mexican and Danish business negotiations. *Journal of Pragmatics* 30 (3):347-362.

Koester, Almut. 2006. *Investigating Workplace Discourse*. London: Routledge.

Kondo, Aya. 2004. Nihongo kyoiku no tame no bijinesu komyunikeshon kenkyu [Studies for the Japanese language teaching]. *Daini-gengo-sytutoku-kyoiku no Kenkyu Saizensen -2004 nendo ban- [The State of the Art in Second Language Acquisition and Instruction Research -2004 Version-]* 28:123-126.

———. 2005. Bijinesu ni okeru ibunka-kan komyunikeshon: nihongo no kaigi wa hikouritsu ka [Intercultural communication: are Japnese business meetings inefficient?]. In *Ibunka to Komyunikeshon [Crossculture and Communication]*, edited by S. Ide and M. Hiraga. Tokyo: Hituzi Shobo. 40-60.

———. 2007. *Nihonjin to Gaikokujin no bijinesu komyunikeshon ni kansuru jissho kenkyu [A Study on Business Communication between Japanese and Foreiners]*. Tokyo: Hituzi Syobo.

Kotthoff, Helga. 2006. Pragmatics of performance and the analysis of conversational humor. *HUMOR: International Journal of Humor Research* 19 (3):271-304.

Kuiper, Koenraad and Marie Flindall. 2000. Socials rituals, formulaic speech and small talk at the supermarket checkout. In *Small Talk*, edited by J. Coupland. London: Longman. 183-207.

Lakoff, Robin. 1973. The logic of politeness: or minding your P's and Q's. *Chicago Linguistic Society* 9:292-305.

Lambert, Wallace E. 1967. A social psychology of bilingualism. *Journal of Social Issues*

23:91-108. Reprinted in Paulston and Tucker (eds) 2003: 305-321.
Lambert, Wallace E., Richard C. Hodgson, Robert C. Gardner, and Samuel Fillenbaum. 1960. Evaluation reactions to spoken languages. *Journal of Abnormal and Social Psychology* 60 (1):44-51.
Larrue, Janine and Alain Trognon. 1993. Organization of turn-taking and mechanisms for turn-taking repairs in a chaired meeting. *Journal of Pragmatics* 19:177-196.
Lave, Jean and Etienne Wenger. 1991. *Situated Learning: Legitimate Peripheral Participation.* Cambridge: Cambridge University Press.
Laver, John. 1975. Communicative functions of phatic communion. In *The Organization of Behavior in Face-to-Face Interaction*, edited by A. Kendon, R. Harris and M. Key. The Hague, The Netherlands: Mouton publishers. 215-238.
———. 1981. Linguistic routines and politeness in greeting and parting. In *Conversational Routine: Explorations in Standardized Communication Situations and Prepatterned Speech*, edited by F. Coulmas. The Hague, The Netherlands: Mouton publishers. 289-304.
Lebra, Takie S. 1976. *Japanese Patterns of Behavior.* Honolulu University Press of Hawaii.
Leech, Geoffrey N. 1983. *Principles of Pragmatics.* London/New York: Longman.
———. 2007. Politeness: is there an East-West divide? *Journal of Politeness Research* 3:167-206.
Lehtonen, Jaakko and Kari Sajavaara. 1985. The silent Finn. In *Perspectives on Silence*, edited by D. Tannen and M. Saville-Troike. Norwood, NJ: Ablex. 193-201.
Lengua, Liliana J., Mark W. Roosa, Erika, Schupak-Neuberg, Marcia L. Michaels, Carolyn N. Berg, and Louis F. Weschler. 1992. Using focus groups to guide the development of a parenting program for difficult-to-reach, high-risk families. *Family Relations* 41:163-168.
Linde, Charlotte. 1991. What's next?: the social and technological management of meetings. *Pragmatics* 1 (3):297-317.
Linstead, Steve. 1985. Jokers wild: the importance of humour in the maintenance of organisational culture. *Sociological Review* 13 (3):741-767.
Lytra, Vally. 2007. Teasing in contact encounters: frames, participant positions and responses. *Multilingua* 26:381-408.
Malinowski, Bronislaw. 1927. (2nd edition) The problem of meaning in primitive languages. In *The Meaning of Meaning: A Study of the Influence of Language upon Thought and of the Science of Symbolism,* edited by C. K. Ogden and I. A. Richards. London: Kegan Paul, Trench, Trubner & Co. Ltd. 296-336. (Original work published 1923).
Marra, Meredith. 1998. Okay we'll start now I think: the boundaries of meetings, Unpublished MA Paper, Victoria University of Wellington, Wellington, New Zealand.
———. 2003. Decisions in New Zealand business meetings: a sociolinguistic analysis of power at work, Unpublished PhD Thesis, Victoria University of Wellington, New Zealand.
———. 2008a. Meeting talk: aligning the classroom with the workplace. *Communication Journal of New Zealand* 9 (1):63-82.
———. 2008b. Recording and analyzing talk across cultures. In *Culturally Speaking: Culture, Communication and Politeness* (2nd ed), edited by H. Helen Spencer-Oatey. London: Continuum. 304-321.
Marra, Meredith and Janet Holmes. 2004. Workplace narratives and business reports: issues of definition. *Text* 24 (1):59-78.
———. 2007. Humour across cultures: joking in the multicultural workplace. In *Handbook of Intercultural Communication (HAL 7)*, edited by H. Kotthoff and H. Spencer-Oatey. Berlin and New York: Mouton de Gruyter. 153-172.
Marra, Meredith, Stephanie Schnurr, and Janet Holmes. 2006. Effective leadership in New

Zealand workplace: balancing gender and role. In *Speaking Out: The Female Voice in Public Contexts*, edited by J. Baxter. New York: Palgrave Macmillan. 240-260.

Matsumoto, Yoshiko. 1988. Reexamination of the universality of face: politeness phenomena in Japanese. *Journal of Pragmatics* 12:403-426.

———. 1989. Politeness and conversational universals-observations from Japanese. *Multilingua* 8 (2-3):207-221.

Maynard, Senko. 1993. *Discourse Modality: Subjectivity, Emotion, and Voice in the Japanese Language*. Amsterdam: John Benjamins.

McCarthy, Micael. 2000. Mutually captive audiences: small talk and the genre of close-contact service encounters. In *Small Talk*, edited by J. Coupland. London: Longman. 84-109.

McLeod, Alan L. 1969. *Pattern of New Zealand Culture*. NY: Cornell University Press.

Miller, Katherine. 1999. *Organizational Communication: Approaches and Processes*. 2nd ed. Belmont, CA: Wadsworth Publishing.

Miller, Laura. 1995. Two aspects of Japanese and American co-worker interaction: giving instructions and creating rapport *The Journal of Applied Behavioral Science* 31:141-161.

———. 2000. Negative assessments in Japanese-American workplace interaction. In *Culturally Speaking: Managing Rapport through Talk across Cultures*, edited by H. Spencer-Oatey. London: Continuum. 240-254.

Mills, Sara. 2003. *Gender and Politeness*. Cambridge: Cambridge University Press.

———. 2009. Impoliteness in a cultural context. *Journal of Pragmatics* 41 (5):1047 1060.

Milroy, Lesley and Matthew Gordon. 2003. *Sociolinguistics: Method and Interpretation*. Malden: Blackwell.

Mintzberg, Henry. 1973. *The Nature of Managerial Work*. Englewood Cliffs, NJ: Prentice-Hall.

Mizutani, Nobuko. 1993. Kyowa kara taiwa e [From co-construction to dialog]. *Japanese Linguistics* 12 (4):4-10.

Morreall, John. 1983. *Taking Laughter Seriously*. Albany: State University of New York Press.

———. 1991. Humor and work. *Humor* 4 (3-4):359-373.

Mouly, Souchi and Jankret Sankaran. 2000. The tall poppy syndrome in New Zealand: an exploratory investigation. Paper presented at the 2nd Conference of the International Association of Insight and Action, at Brisbane.

Mulkay, Michael. 1988. *On Humour: Its Nature and its Place in Modern Society*. Oxford: Polity Press.

Mullany, Louise. 2004. Gender, politeness and institutional power roles: humour as a tactic to gain compliance in workplace business meetings. *Multilingua* 23:13-37.

———. 2006. "Girls on tour": politeness, small talk, and gender in managerial business meetings. *Journal of Politeness Research* 2:55-77.

———. 2007. *Gendered Discourse in the Professional Workplace*. Hampshire: Palgrave Macmillan.

Mumby, Dennis K, and Cynthia Stohl. 1996. Disciplining organizational communication studies. *Management Communication Quarterly* 10 (1): 50-72.

Murakami, Megumi and Tetsuo Kumatoridani. 1995. Danwa topikku no kessokusei to tenkai kozo [Cohesion in discourse topics and topic development structure]. *Hyogen Kenkyu* 62:101-111.

Murata, Kazuyo. 2005. Ibogowasha gurupu kaiwa ni mirareru "warai" no bunseki: poraitonesu no kanten kara [Laughter in intercultural conversations from a politeness perspective]. *The JASS (Japanese Association of Sociolinguistic Sciences) 15th Conference Journal*: 120-123.

———. 2007. Laughter in Japanese business meetings: a relational perspective. *Wellington Working Papers in Linguistics* 19: 80-93.

———. 2008. Nihongo bijinesu miitingu ni mirareru warai: taijinkankei kinoumen kara no bunseki [Laughter in Japanese business meetings: an analysis from a relational perspective]. *The JASS (Japanese Association of Sociolinguistic Sciences) 21st Conference*: 56-59.

———. 2009a. Laughter for defusing tension: examples from business meetings in Japanese and in English. In *New Frontiers in Artificial Intelligence: JSAI2008 Conference and Workshops Asahikawa, Japan, June 2008 Revised Selected Paper*, edited by H. Hattori, T. Kawamura, M. Yokoo, and T. Ide. Heidelberg: Springer. 294-305.

———. 2009b. Small talk in business meetings in Japanese and in English *Proceedings of the 11th Annual Conference of the Pragmatics Society of Japan* 4:159-166.

———. 2009c. Humor in business meetings in Japanese and in English, Paper presented at 11th International Pragmatics Conference, Melbourne, Australia, 12-17, July 2009.

———. 2009d. Kyodo gata disukasshon ni okeru fashiriteta no yakuwari: gengo no taijin kankei kinomen kara no kosatsu [Roles of facilitators in discussion among people from the different sectors]. *Proceedings of the 23rd Biannual Conference of the Japanese Association of Sociolinguistic Sciences*: 52-55.

———.2012a. Relational practice in meeting discourse in New Zealand and Japan: a cross-cultural study, Unpublished PhD Thesis, Victoria University of Wellington, New Zealand.

———.2012b. An empirical study on politeness from the hearer's perspective: how do Japanese business professionals evaluate humour in New Zealand business meetings? In *Observing Linguistic Phenomena: a Festschrift for Professor Seiji Uchida on the Occasion of His Retirement from Nara Women's University*, edited by A. Yoshimura, A. Suga, and N. Yamamoto. Tokyo: Eihosha. 485-494.

———.2014a. An empirical cross-cultural study of humour in business meetings in New Zealand and Japan. *Journal of Pragmatics* 60: 251–265.

———.2014b. NZ bijinesu miitingu no tokucho ni tuite no insho chosa [Japanese business professionals' perceptions of relational talk in NZ business meetings]. *The Journal of International Business Communication* 73: 35–43.

Murata, Kazuyo, Yoko Otsuka, Ikuyo Morimoto, Teya Ostheider, Mayumi Bono, and Yoshikazu Watanabe. 2010. Sociolinguistics as welfare-linguistics: contributing to a sustainable society [Jizoku kano na shakai no jitsugen ni mukete watashitachi no dekiru koto: werufea ringuistikusu o mezashite]. *The Japanese journal of language in society* 12 (2):59.

Murphy, Mary Ann. 1998. Re-viewing business communication: a response to Carmichael, White-Mills and Rogers, and Krapels and Arnold. *The Journal of Business Communication*: 35 (1):128-137.

Nabeshima, Naoki. 2007. *Shinran's Perspective on Life: Ethic of Interdependence [Shinran no Seimeikan: Engi no Seimeirinrikan]*. Kyoto: Hozokan.

Nakane, Ikuko. 2006. Silence and politeness in intercultural communication in university seminars. *Journal of Pragmatics* 38 (11):1811-1835.

———. 2007. *Silence in Intercultural Communication: Perception and Performance*. Amsterdam/Philadelphia: John Benjamins Publishing Company.

Newton, Jonathan. 2004. Difficult talk in the workplace: an ESOL resource, Paper presented LWP Roundtable, Victoria University of Wellington, New Zealand.

Norrick, Neal R. 1993. *Conversational Joking: Humour in Everyday Talk*. Bloomington, IN: Indiana University Press.

Norrick, Neal R, and Delia Chiaro, eds. 2009. *Humor in Interaction*. Amsterdam/Philadelphia: John Benjamins Publishing Company.

Norrick, Neal R. and Delia Chiaro. 2009. Humor and interaction. In *Humor in Interaction*, edited by N. R. Norrick and D. Chiaro. Amsterdam/Philadelphia: John Benjamins Publishing Company. IX-XVIII.

Norrick, Neal R. and Alice Spitz. 2008. Humor as a resource for mitigating conflict in interaction. *Journal of Pragmatics* 40:1661-1686.

Okamoto, Shigeko. 1999. Situated politeness: coordinating honorific and non-honorific expressions in Japanese conversations. *Pragmatics* 9:51-74.

O'Quin, Karen and Joel Arnoff. 1981. Humor as a technique of social influence. *Social Psychology Quarterly* 44:349-357.

Parsons, Talcott. 1966. *Societies: Evolutionary and Comparative Perspectives*. Englewood Cliffs: Prentice Hall.

———. 1967. *Sociological Theory and Modern Society*. New York: The Free Press.

Paulston, Christina B. and Richard G. Tucker, eds. 2003. *Sociolinguistics: The Essential Readings*. Malden, MA, USA Blackwell.

Peeters, Bert. 2004a. "Thou shalt not be a tall poppy": describing an Australian communicative (and behavioral) norm. *Intercultural Pragmatics* 1 (1):71-92.

———. 2004b. Tall poppies and egalitarianism in Australian discourse: from key word to cultural value. *English World-Wide* 25 (1):1-25.

Pizzini, Franca. 1991. Communication hierarchies in humour: gender differences in the obsterical/gynaecological setting. *Discourse & Society* 2 (4):477-488.

Plester, Barbara A. 2007. Laugh loud: how organisational culture influences workplace humour, Unpublished PhD Thesis, Massey University, New Zealand.

Pogrebin, Mark R. and Eric D. Poole. 1988. Humor in the briefing room: a study of the strategic uses of humor among police. *Journal of Contemporary Ethnography* 17 (2):183-210.

Poncini, Gina. 2002. Investigating discourse at business meetings with multicultural participation. *IRAL* 40 (4):345-373.

———. 2007. *Discursive Strategies in Multicultural Business Meetings*. Bern, Switzerland: Peter Lang.

Priego-Valverde, Beatrice. 2009. Failed humor in conversation. In *Humor in Interaction*, edited by N. R. Norrick and D. Chiaro. Amsterdam/Philadelphia: John Benjamins Publishing Company. 165-183.

Provine, Robert R. 1993. Laughter punctuates speech: linguistic, social and gender contexts of laughter. *Ethology* 95:291-298.

———. 2000. *Laughter: A Scientific Investigation*. New York: Viking.

Regan, Sandra L. 2000. Sociable talk in women's health care contexts: two forms of non-medical talk. In *Small Talk*, edited by J. Coupland. London: Longman. 269-287.

Rodrigues, Suzana and David Collinson. 1995. 'Having fun?' humour as resistance in Brazil. *Organization Studies* 16 (5):739-768.

Rogers, Priscilla S. 2001. Convergence and commonality challenge business communication research. *The Journal of Business Communication* 38 (1):14-23.

Rosenberg, Lisa. 1998. A qualitative investigation of the use of humor by emergency personnel as a strategy for coping with stress. *Journal of Emergency Nursing* 17:197-202.

Ross, Bob. 1992. *That's a Good One! Corporate Leadership with Humor*. San Marcos, CA: Avant Books.

Sacks, Harvey. 1989. An analysis of the course of a joke's telling in conversation. In *Explorations in the Ethnography of Speaking*, edited by R. Bauman and J. Sherzer. Cambridge: Cambrdige Universtiy Press. 337-353.

Saunders, Christine. 1986. Opening and closing. In *A Handbook of Communication Skills*, edited by O. Hargie. London & Sydney: Croom Helm. 175-200.

Saville-Troike, Muriel. 1985. The place of silence in an integrated theory of communication. In *Perspectives on Silence*, edited by D. Tannen and M. Saville-Troike. Norwood, NJ: Ablex. 3-18.
Schegloff, Emanuel A. and Harvey Sacks. 1973. Opening up closings. *Semiotica* 8:289-327.
Schiffrin, Deborah. 1994. *Approaches to Discourse*. Cambridge, MA: Blackwell.
Schneider, Klaus P. 1988. *Small Talk: Analysing Phatic Discourse*. Marburg: Hitzeroth.
Schnurr, Stephanie. 2005. Leadership and humour. An analysis of workplace discourse, Unpublished PhD Thesis, Victoria University of Wellington, New Zealand.
———. 2009a. Constructing leader identities through teasing at work. *Journal of Pragmatics* 41:1125-1138.
———. 2009b. *Leadership Discourse at Work: Interactions of Humour, Gender and Workplace Culture*. Basingstoke, Hampshire: Palgrave Macmillan.
Schnurr, Stephanie and Angela Chan. 2009. Politeness and leadership discourse in New Zealand and Hong Kong: a cross-cultural case study of workplace talk. *Journal of Politeness Research* 5 (2):131-157.
Schnurr, Stephanie and Janet Holmes. 2009. Using humor to do masculinity at work. In *Humor in Interaction*, edited by N. R. Norrick and D. Chiaro. Amsterdam/Philadelphia: John Benjamins Publishing Company. 101-123.
Schnurr, Stephanie, Meredith Marra, and Janet Holmes. 2007. Being (im)polite in New Zealand workplaces: Māori and Pākehā leaders. *Journal of Pragmatics* 39:712-729.
———. 2008. Impoliteness as a means of contesting power relations in the workplace. In *Impoliteness in language: Studies on its interplay with power in theory and practice*, edited by D. Bousfield and M. Locher. Berlin: Walter de Guyter. 211-230.
Schwartzman, Helen. 1989. *The Meeting: Gatherings in Organizations and Communities*. New York: Plenum Press.
Shimizu, Hiroshi. 1996. *Seimeichi toshiteno ba no ronri [The logic of ba as the knowledge of life]*. Tokyo: Chuuoo-kooron sha.
———. 2003. *Ba no shiso [The logic of ba]*. Tokyo: University of Tokyo Press.
Sifianou, Maria. 1997. Silence and politeness. In *Silence: Interdisciplinary Perspectives*, edited by A. Jaworski. Berlin: Mouton de Gruyter. 63-84.
Silva, Maria. 1994. The analysis of verbal interaction: a meeting. In *Reflections on Language Learning*, edited by L. Barbara and M. Scott. Clevedon, England: Multilingual Matters. 195-203.
Sollitt-Morris, Lynnette. 1996. Language, gender and power relationships: the enactment of repressive discourse in staff meetings of two subject departments in a New Zealand secondary school, Unpublished PhD Thesis, Victoria University of Wellington, New Zealand.
Spencer-Oatey, Helen, ed. 2000a. *Culturally Speaking: Managing Rapport through Talk across Cultures*. London: Continuum.
———. 2000b. Introduction: language, culture and rapport management. In *Culturally Speaking: Managing Rapport through Talk across Cultures*, edited by H. Spencer-Oatey. London: Continuum. 1-8.
———. 2000c. Rapport management: a framework for analysis. In *Culturally Speaking: Managing Rapport through Talk across Cultures*, edited by H. Spencer-Oatey. London: Continuum. 11-46.
———. 2002. Managing rapport in talk: using rapport sensitive incidents to explore the motivational concerns underlying the management of relations. *Journal of Pragmatics* 34 529-545.
———, ed. 2008a. *Culturally Speaking: Culture, Communication and Politeness Theory*. 2nd ed. London: Continuum.

———. 2008b. Face, (Im)Politeness and Rapport. In *Culturally Speaking: Culture, Communication and Politeness Theory*, edited by H. Spencer-Oatey. London: Continuum. 11-47.
Spencer-Oatey, Helen and Jianyu Xing. 2000. A problematic Chinese business visit to Britain: issues of face. In *Culturally Speaking: Managing Rapport through Talk across Cultures*, edited by H. Spencer-Oatey. London: Continuum. 272-288.
———. 2003. Managing rapport in intercultural business interactions: a comparison of two Chinese-British welcome meetings. *Journal of Intercultural Studies* 24 (1):33-46.
———. 2004. Rapport management problems in Chinese-British business interactions: a case study. In *Multilingual Communication*, edited by J. House and J. Rehbein. Amsterdam: J. Benjamins. 197-221.
———. 2005. Managing talk and non-talk in intercultural interactions: insights from two Chinese-British business meetings. *Multilingua* 24:55-74.
———. 2007. The impact of culture on interpreter behaviour. In *Handbook of Intercultural Communication*, edited by H. Kotthoff and H. Spencer-Oatey. Berlin: Mouton de Gruyter. 219-236.
———. 2008. Issues of face in Chinese business visit to Britain. In *Culturally Speaking: Culture, Communication and Politeness Theory*, edited by H. Spencer-Oatey. London: Continuum. 258-273.
Stewart, David W. and Prem M. Shamdasani. 1990. *Focus Groups: Theory and Practice*. Newbury Park, CA: Sage.
Sunaoshi, Yukako. 2005. Historical context and intercultural communication: interactions between Japanese and American factory workers in the American South. *Language in Society* 34 (2):185-217.
Sussman, Steve, Dee Burton, Clyde W. Dent, Alan W. Stacy, and Brian R. Flay. 1991. Use of focus groups in developing an adolescent tobacco use cessation program: collective norm effects. *Journal of Applied Social psychology* 21 (21):1772-1782.
Takano, Shoji. 2005. Re-examining linguistic power: strategic uses of directives by professional Japanese women in positions of authority and leadership. *Journal of Pragmatics* 37 (5):633-666.
Takekuro, Makiko. 2006. Conversational jokes in Japanese and English. In *Understanding Humor in Japan*, edited by J. M. Davis. Detroit: Wayne State University Press. 85-98.
Tanaka, Noriko, Helen Spencer-Oatey, and Ellen Cray. 2008. Apologies in Japanese and English. In *Culturally Speaking: Culture, Communication and Politeness Theory*, edited by H. Spencer-Oatey. London: Continuum. 73-94.
Tannen, Deborah. 1984. *Conversational Style: Analyzing Talk among Friends*. Norwood, NJ: Ablex Press.
———. 1985. Cross-cultural communication. In *Handbook of discourse analysis*, edited by T. A. v. Dijk. London: Academic Press. Vol. 4: 203-215.
———. 1994a. *Gender and Discourse*. Oxford: Oxford University Press.
———. 1994b. *Talking from 9 to 5*. New York: Avon Books.
———. 2005. *Conversational Style: Analyzing Talk among Friends*. Revised ed. Oxford: Oxford University Press.
Terkourafi, Marina. 2005. Beyond the micro-level in politeness research. *Journal of Politeness Research*. 1 (2):237-262.
Tracy, Karen and Nikolas Coupland. 1990. Multiple goals in discourse: an overview of issues. In *Multiple Goals in Discourse*, edited by K. Tracy and N. Coupland. Clevedon: Multilngual Matters. 1-13.
Tracy, Karen and Aaron Dimock. 2004. Meetings: discursive sites for building and fragmenting community. In *Communication Yearbook 28*, edited by P. Kalbfleisch. Tousand Oaks,

CA: Sage. 127-165.

Tracy, Karen and Julie M Naughton. 2000. Institutional identity-work: a better lens In *Small Talk*, edited by J. Coupland. London: Longman. 62-83.

Tracy, Sarah J., Karen K. Myers, and Clifton W. Scott. 2006. Cracking jokes and crafting selves: sensemaking and identity management among human service workers. *Communication Monographs* 73(3):283-308.

Trevor-Roberts, Edwin, Neal M. Ashkanasy, and Jeffrey C. Kennedy. 2003. The egalitarian Leader: leadership in Australia and New Zealand. In *Leading in High Growth Asia: Managing Relationship for Teamwork and Change*, edited by D. Tjosvold and K. Leung. Singapore: World Scientific Publishing. 231-252.

Triandis, Harry C. 1994. *Culture and Social Behavior*. New York: McGraw Hill.

Usami, Mayumi. 2002. *Discourse Politeness in Japanese Conversation : Some Implications for a Universal Theory of Politeness*. Tokyo: Hituzi Shobo.

Vine, Bernadette. 2004. *Getting Things Done at Work: The Discourse of Power in Workplace Interaction*. Amsterdam: John Benjamins.

Vine, Bernadette, Susan Kell, Meredith Marra, and Janet Holmes. 2009. Boundary-marking humor: institutional, gender and ethnic demarcation in the workplace. In *Humor in Interaction*, edited by N. R. Norrick and D. Chiaro. Amsterdam/Philadelphia: John Benjamins Publishing Company. 125-139.

Watts, Richard J. 2003. *Politeness*. Cambridge: Cambridge University Press.

Watts, Richard J., Sachiko Ide, and Konrad Ehlich. 1992. Introduction. In *Politeness in Language: Studies in its History, Theory, and Practice*, edited by R. J. Watts, S. Ide and K. Ehlich. Berlin, New York: Mouton de Gruyter. 1-17.

Wenger, Etienne. 1998. *Communities of Practice*. Cambridge: Cambridge University Press.

Westwood, Robert and Carl Rhodes, eds. 2007. *Humour, Work and Organization,*. London: Routledge.

White, Christine and Ena Howse. 1993. Managing humor: when is it funny - and when is it not? *Nursing Management* 24 (4):80-86.

Yamada, Haru. 1990. Topic management and turn distribution in business meetings. *Text* 10 (3):271-295.

———. 1992. *American and Japanese Business Discourse: A Comparison of Interactional Styles*. Norwood, NJ: Ablex.

———. 1994. Talk-distancing in Japanese meetings *Journal of Asian Pacific Communication* 5 (1-2):19-36.

———. 1997a. *Different Games, Different Rules : Why Americans and Japanese Misunderstand Each Other* New York, Oxford University Press.

———. 1997b. Organisation in American and Japanese meetings: task versus relationship. In *The Languages of Business*, edited by F. Bargiela-Chiappini and S. Harris. Edinburgh: Edinburgh University Press. 117-135.

Yamazaki, Hideo. 2002. Atarashii nihonteki keiei o tsukuru CMC jo no netto waku soshiki [Transformed resurrection of Japanese company-power depends on informal networked organization on computer-mediated communication environment]. *The Annual Bulletin of Knowledge Management Society of Japan* 4:1-16.

Yeung, Lorrita. 2000. The question of Chinese indirectness: a comparison of Chinese and English participative decision-making discourse. *Multilingua* 19 (3):221-264.

———. 2003. Management discourse in Australian banking contexts: in search of an Australian model of participation as compared with that of Hong Kong Chinese. *Journal of International Studies* 24 (1):47-63.

Yukl, Gary. 1989. Managerial leadership: a review of theory and research. *Journal of Man-*

agement 15 (2):251-289.

Zajdman, Anat. 1995. Humorous face-threatening acts: humor as strategy. *Journal of Pragmatics* 23:325-339.

Index

A
advocacy research   49
agenda   53

B
ba   165, 212
banter   127
Brown and Levinson (B&L)   11

C
classic approach   86
closing   62
co-construction   108
collegiality   60, 93, 128
combined etic-emic approach   33
communicative norms   34
community of practice(CofP)   18
company J   47, 65
company N   46, 64
conversation analysis   38
cross-cultural   4
cross-cultural study   30
culture   30

D
daialect   138
discernment   27, 165
discourse feature   178
discourse markers   61
discourse politeness   28
discursive approach   88

E
egalitarianism   163
emic   16, 32
emic constructs   34, 198
emic perspective   161

ethnographic observation   38
etic   16, 32
extended focus group interview   48, 175

F
face   11
face threatening acts   12
fantasy humour   160
first-order politeness   17
focus group interview   175
formal meetings   54

G
group-oriented   164

H
habitus   15
historical agent   202, 209
humour   126

I
identity face   13
identity work   130
(im)politeness   17
impression management   172
incongruity theory   123
informal meetings   54
instigator   133
inter-cultural research   212
interactional sociolinguistics   38
international experience   198

J
joint enterprise   46

K
kaigi 54

L
Language in the Workplace Project 1
laughter 131
Local Public Human Resources 215
logic of *ba* 165
LORC 215

M
macro level 60
macro structure 61
main discussion 61
matched-guise technique 170
meeting structure 60
micro level 60
micro structures 63
modified B&L approach 12
multi-stakeholder partnership 215
multifunctional 93, 108
mutual engagement 46
mutual teasing 159

N
negative face 11
negative politeness 12
negotiative approach 86
neo-politeness approach 20
nontask-sounding talk 95

O
opening 62
organisational chart 45

P
Parosonian perspective 31
perception data 48
phatic communion 86
phatic talk 88
polite behaviour 17

politeness1 16
politeness2 16
politic behaviour 17
polyphonically 121
positive face 11
positive politeness 12
post-meeting 62
post-modern approach 15
power 93
pre-meeting 62

Q
quality face 13

R
rapport 14
relational talk 88
relief theory 123

S
second-order politeness 17
shared repertoire 46
silence 80
small talk 91
social practice 18
sociality rights 14
socio-cultural factor 130
socio-cultural norm 194
solidarity 108
speech-level shift 28
superiority theory 123

T
tachiba 29
target participant 46, 47
team spirit 60
tease, teasing 127
tension release 130
theory of *ba* 212
topic shift 58
topic structure 57

topic transitional point 60
traditional approach 10
transactional talk 88
transitional marker 80

U
uchi 29
uchiawase/miitingu 54

V
video-based perception task 173
volition 28

W
wakimae 27
workplace culture 202
workplace discourse 6

村田和代（むらた かずよ）

略歴

奈良県出身。
2001年奈良女子大学大学院
人間文化研究科博士課程単位取得退学。
2011年ニュージーランド国立ヴィクトリア大学大学院言語学科 Ph.D.（言語学）。
龍谷大学法学部講師、准教授を経て、
龍谷大学政策学部教授。

Kazuyo Murata is professor of the Faculty of Policy Science at Ryukoku University, Kyoto, Japan. She received her Ph.D. in Linguistics from Victoria University of Wellington, New Zealand, in 2011.

主な著書・論文

- 『ポライトネスと英語教育—
  言語使用における対人関係の機能』
  （ひつじ書房、2006、共著、
  大学英語教育者学会賞
  〈学術出版部門〉受賞）
- 『語用論』
  （朝倉書店、2012、執筆者として参加）
- 『英語談話表現辞典』
  （三省堂、2009、執筆者として参加）
- 「まちづくり系ワークショップ・
  ファシリテーターに見られる
  言語的ふるまいの特徴とその効果—
  ビジネスミーティング司会者との
  比較を通して」『社会言語科学』
  第16巻 第1号（2013）

Hituzi Language Studies No.1
Relational Practice
in Meeting Discourse
in New Zealand and Japan

発行	2015年2月18日 初版1刷
定価	6000円＋税
著者	©村田和代
発行者	松本功
ブックデザイン	白井敬尚形成事務所
印刷所	三美印刷株式会社
製本所	小泉製本株式会社
発行所	株式会社 ひつじ書房

〒112-0011 東京都文京区
千石2-1-2 大和ビル2F
Tel: 03-5319-4916
Fax: 03-5319-4917
郵便振替 00120-8-142852
toiawase@hituzi.co.jp
http://www.hituzi.co.jp/
ISBN978-4-89476-739-3

造本には充分注意しておりますが、
落丁・乱丁などがございましたら、
小社かお買上げ書店にて
おとりかえいたします。
ご意見、ご感想など、小社まで
お寄せ下されば幸いです。